WALKING IN THE
CAIRNGORMS

About the Author

Ronald Turnbull (seen here at the Shelter Stone) is based in southern Scotland, with a particular interest in long backpacking trips through the Highlands. He first slept under the Shelter Stone above Loch Avon in June 1988, and was impressed not only by the situation and the view but by the way it snowed on him overnight. However, his connection with the Cairngorms goes back further. He only exists because the ice of Loch Avon, crossed during a thaw by a direct ancestor, did not collapse.

He writes frequently for the main UK walking magazines; his previous book for Cicerone, *The Book of the Bivvy*, won the Outdoor Writers' Guild Award for best outdoor book 2002. He has completed the 42-peak Bob Graham Round in the Lake District, and also likes hot, rocky, Spanish-speaking bits of Europe. For this book he has particularly enjoyed the rambles through Badenoch and Rothiemurchus Forest, and revisiting all four of the Lochans Uaine.

WALKING IN THE CAIRNGORMS

by Ronald Turnbull

CICERONE

2 POLICE SQUARE, MILNTHORPE, CUMBRIA LA7 7PY
www.cicerone.co.uk

© Ronald Turnbull 2005
ISBN 1 85284 452 3
First published 2005

Sketch maps and photographs: Ronald Turnbull

British Library Cataloguing-in-Publication Data. A catalogue record for this book
is available from the British Library.

ois Ordnance This product includes mapping data licensed from Ordnance
Survey° Survey® with the permission of the Controller of Her Majesty's
Stationery Office. © Crown copyright 2002. All rights reserved. Licence number
PU100012932

Front cover: Ascending from Loch Avon to Ben Macdui by the Avon Slabs
(Route 34)

CONTENTS

Acknowledgements

Thank you to the rangers of Rothiemurchus, Glenmore, Cairngorm, Glenlivet, Mar Lodge, Invercauld and Balmoral estates. In between helpfully answering my emails they find time to repair the paths, look after the hills, and supervise the resurgence of the capercaillie. Particular credit goes to the National Trust for Scotland for painstakingly removing Landrover tracks from Mar Lodge Estate.

Thanks to the Ordnance Survey and Harveys for supplying up-to-date mapping; and to the Scottish Parliament and Scottish National Heritage for the new access law and code.

This book is dedicated to the hill folk of my family: to Thomas, for posing on crag tops all the way across; to Barbara and Matt for reassurance (and on Pygmy Ridge a rope as well) on many of the scrambles; and to my father, not just for ancestral word-of-mouth Gaelic, but for suggesting the best route here, number 34.

From afar the Cairngorms appear gently rounded. Close up, you find the Corrie of Lochnagar (Route 100)

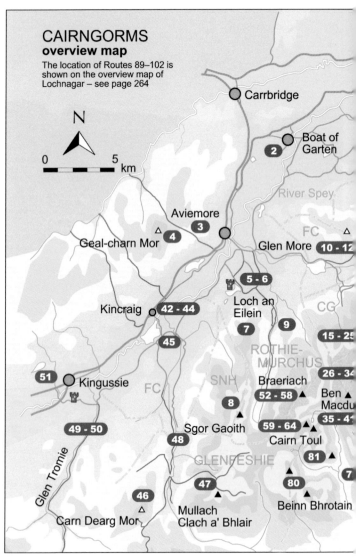

CAIRNGORMS
overview map
The location of Routes 89–102 is
shown on the overview map of
Lochnagar – see page 264

N

0   5
km

Carrbridge

Boat of
Garten
2

River Spey

Aviemore
3

Geal-charn Mor △ **4**

FC

△

Glen More **10 - 12**

5 - 6

Loch an
Eilein

7   **9**

CG

Kincraig ○ **42 - 44**

45

ROTHIE-
MURCHUS

15 - 25

51 ○ Kingussie

FC

SNH

Braeriach
52 - 58 ▲

26 - 34

Ben ▲
Macdu

49 - 50

8
▲
Sgor Gaoith

59 - 64 ▲▲
Cairn Toul

35 - 4

Glen Tromie

48

GLENFESHIE

81 ▲

7

46
△
Carn Dearg Mor

47
▲
Mullach
Clach a' Bhlair

80
▲
Beinn Bhrotain

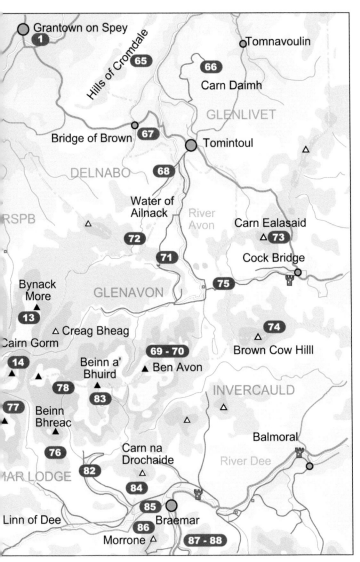

Map key

– – – –	route
– – – –	variants, and adjacent routes
	on overview maps, estate boundaries (see Appendix II: Access)
▨▨▨▨▨	A-road
▬▬▬▬	minor road
▬▬▬	unsurfaced track
∼∼∼	stream
∼∼∼	river
⌒⌒	lake
⬚	crag
1	route number
1	variant number
P	parking (typically at walk start)
● ○	town/village
🚲	bike drop-off point, on walks that can be started on bike
▫	building
⌂	bothy
▲	Munro
△	other summit of interest: on overview maps, the Corbetts

	castle
	ground above 1150m / 3500ft
	ground above 900m / 3000ft
	ground above 750m / 2500ft
	ground above 600m / 2000ft
	ground above 450m / 1500ft
	ground above 300m / 1000ft
	ground above 150m / 500ft

Contour intervals chosen to feature the Munro and Corbett levels at 3000ft and 2500ft. There is no ground below 150m in the area.

Route symbols on OS maps

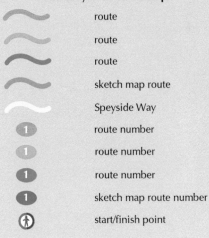

	route
	route
	route
	sketch map route
	Speyside Way
1	route number
1	route number
1	route number
1	sketch map route number
⊛	start/finish point

For OS symbols key see OS maps

Waterfall above Lochan Uaine of Derry Cairngorm (Route 77)

INTRODUCTION

CAIRNGORMS: THE HIGHS AND THE LOWS

The Cairngorms are Britain's biggest hills, above the 900m mark for 30km (if you discount a couple of glacier-gouged gaps). Here are 18 Munros (3000-footers, as listed by Sir Hugh Munro in 1891) linked by a high granite plateau that's unique in these islands.

With so many fine mountains, it may seem odd that I should be writing a book just as much about the low places of this high ground.

The first time I walked eastwards out of Kincraig and along the River Spey, I wasn't expecting to enjoy it. I was tired, I had very sore feet, I was carrying 15kg, and I'd just spent five days coming across the tops of some of the finest mountains in western Scotland.

But my bad feet – and even the wonders of the high-level west – were knocked out by the beauty of the birch trees. The path switch-backed above the river, sometimes just glimpsing it between the branches, sometimes looking across its wide brightness to miles and miles of forest and the dun-coloured hump of Braeriach.

When the following dawn brought the sound of birches beating in a gale, I abandoned my plateau ambitions. Instead I walked for a morning through the pine and juniper of Rothiemurchus. Between the wet tree trunks, lochans

Across Rothiemurchus Forest to Cairn Lochan and the Lairig Ghru

Cairn Toul, Britain's fourth-highest hill, with Corrour bothy and the River Dee

were thrashed white by the wind; the grey-black cones of Eilrig and Lurcher's Crag came and went through the moving boughs; the miles of forest crashed and sighed like the sea.

At lunchtime I emerged through the cattle-thieves' pass of Ryvoan, beside the green lochan. The weather was still not right for the heights, and this was confirmed when a man came down off Bynack More, bashed against a boulder by the wind and with a broken rib. So I went up to the mid-level, the 750m mark. This is where the heather gets shorter, and granite gravel shows between the stems; and where, from behind the hump of a moor, the great slabbed crags around Loch Avon start to appear.

Creag Mhor is seldom walked on: at 895m it's too low to be counted by the Munro-bagging fraternity. Accordingly, Creag Mhor is pathless, bleak as the ice left it 10,000 years ago. Even so, the going is easy, over low tundra vegetation of crowberry and bearberry, cropped by the ptarmigan and swooped over by the lonely piping plover. On the bare rock top I leant into the wind, gazing into the fastness hollow of Loch Avon. Then I descended to Fords of Avon, where the lowly iron shelter stood under a centimetre or two of fresh, wet snow.

Low-level is lovely, and not just on a nasty day. Mid-level is unwalked but very walkable. And yet, as you wander that ancient pinewood or along the banks of the Dee or the Spey, beyond the branches are the snow-topped shapes of Braeriach and Beinn a' Bhuird. As you emerge from the juniper and birch onto one of those mid-height hills, above are the really high ones, grey and purple, topped off with a row of granite pimples. Pinewoods are fine;

16

mighty rivers make great walks; but above all those great walks is the Great Moss. Up there you wander a bleak landscape of stones with a gently winding stream, a clump of moss campion showing pink among the pebbles. It's a land that comes from 10,000 years ago, and from somewhere else altogether – up in the Arctic. Then all of a sudden a top edge of crag rises behind some boulders; and you're high above the Lairig Ghru, looking into a steep-sided scene of wet granite slabs, black peat, and a silver river.

To reach the heart of the Cairngorms you need high ambitions, and pretty strong legs. At the centre of everything lies Loch Avon, its waters level with many of England's mountaintops; but above it, the slopes rise in boulder and bare rock for another 400m. Great chunks have cracked off the crags to lie around the loch shore, and between the rocks are patches of bright bilberry, and little grassy places for the tent.

Low Cairngorms give some of Scotland's loveliest walking. Mid-height hills ask more, and offer in return a level of adventure. And the high Cairngorms can call on all your strength and skill. High or low, Caledonian forest or sub-arctic plateau, the Gorms are British mountain country as grand as it gets.

WALKING CONDITIONS

For **low-level walking**, Speyside has the best network in Scotland, and it's

Heath spotted orchid, Craigellachie Hill (Route 3)

Low-level walking, Rothiemurchus. The very best walks combine forest with open fell (Route 9)

improving all the time. Two years before I wrote this book neither the Allt Mor trail (Route 10) nor the Badenoch Way (Route 42) existed. These paths are sandy and well drained, and sheltered by the pines. Some are waymarked and signposted, some not; it's a good idea to carry a compass and keep a general idea of which way is the road and which way is vast and pathless wilderness.

The **mid-level hills** are more demanding. Apart from one or two favourites such as Meall a' Bhuachaille and Morrone, they are little visited, so there will usually be no path. The hillsides here have heather that's knee-high, or else a wood of pines and juniper. Adventuring through this wilder ground is rewarding in itself; but then you emerge to the deliciously easy

walking across their tops, where nature and the weather ensure low vegetation. On a crisp, clear day of sparkling sunshine, you'll want at some point to get your head above the treetops – that's the day for one of these mid-height hills. And when 100kph winds lash the plateau and the cloud's down – that's also the day for the mid-height, where the weather will be bearable, just about, and for the afternoon you can drop into the shelter of the pines.

The **mountains** of 900m and upwards offer, oddly, easier going than the mid-height. Across the plateau there's no plant life to twine around your ankles; there are boulderfields, but mostly you're on moss, gravel, or patches of old snow. Or else you're on a path; popular ways lead to all the Munro summits. The high ground may

Looking to Loch Morlich from Cadha Mor (Route 7).
Mid-height hills offer wide horizons, ease underfoot, and solitude.

High plateau, and the centre of the Cairngorms: Loch Avon (seen from Route 34)

be comparatively easy, but it is also serious. On the Braeriach plateau you're several hours' walk from any shelter, and that walk may have to find its way down between crags. The weather, when it's bad, is some of the worst in Europe: Cairn Gorm summit has 150kph winds in any month. With those winds can come cloud and (also in any month) snow, to slow you down and cover the onward path.

From Aviemore station the Cairngorms appear gently rounded and almost flat. Getting to know them means getting onto more and more of the rock. A day on foot through forest, lochside, heather and gravel is embellished still further by an interlude with hands on granite. Much of the **scrambling** potential of the area remains unrecorded; I've included some of the easier ones, and there's a round-up and explanation of grading in Appendix VI.

WHEN TO GO

April is still winter on the summits, but low-level routes already offer good walking then and in May. The leaves are breaking and birds are at their noisiest. Low-level routes are also excellent in October as the birch leaves turn gold. But again, they're just as special under winter's snow.

May and June are enjoyable at all altitudes. July and August can be hot and humid, with less rewarding views and midges infesting the forest. Cairngorm midges may be less frightful than those of the Western Highlands, but can still be pretty grim – the trick is to keep moving, and when you stop, stop high.

Midges hang on to about the first Saturday of September. September and October often bring clear air and lovely autumn colours. In between times there'll be gales. Over most of the

19

WEATHER AND SNOW CONDITIONS

The most useful and accurate internet forecast is at Mountain Weather Information Systems **www.mwis.org.uk**. There's a telephone forecast, webcam and snow report from Cairngorm Mountain on **01479 861261 www.cairngormmountain.com**.

The Scottish Avalanche Information Service issues forecasts of snow conditions and avalanche risk daily December–Easter at **www.sais. gov.uk/latest_forecast**; they have previously also had a free phone line.

Cairn Gorm summit's weather: weather readings from Cairn Gorm summit are at **www.phy.hw.ac.uk**.

The weather station on Cairn Gorm summit frequently records winds approaching 200kph

National Park there are no access restrictions during stag stalking, and even where there are, helpful phone lines are available. So with a little care and consultation, you can have hill days here during the stalking season more readily than elsewhere in Scotland (see Appendix II).

Winter is a time of short days and often foul weather. Snow usually lies on the high tops from December to April, with patches in the corries obstructing some routes as late as June. While snow can fall in summer, it usually stays soft and melts quite quickly. Winter blizzards can last for days on end, forming cornices along cliff tops and sliding in avalanches off the slopes below. Well-equipped walkers skilled in navigation and with ice axe love the winter most of all, for the beautiful bleakness of the plateau, the frosted rocks, the 100km views through the winter-chilled air.

When the weather isn't foul, low-level walks can be very rewarding in winter conditions (and even better on cross-country skis).

SAFETY IN THE MOUNTAINS

The high Cairngorms are Britain's most serious mountain range. Safety in the mountains is best learnt from companions, experience, and perhaps a paid instructor; such instruction is outside the scope of this book. For those experienced in smaller hills, you'll need some extra fitness and endurance, and the level of map expertise that enables you to get away safely when the headwind that's cutting you off from your descent route is also going to shred your map should you attempt to unfold it.

The international mountain distress signal is some sign (shout, whistle, torch flash or other) repeated six times over a minute, followed by a minute's silence before repeating the signal. The reply is a sign repeated three times over a minute, followed by a minute's silence.

To signal for help from a helicopter, raise both arms above the head and then drop them down sideways, repeatedly. If you're not in trouble, don't shout or whistle on the hills, and don't wave to passing helicopters.

To call out the rescue, phone 999 from a landline. From a mobile, phone the international emergency number 112: this will connect you via any available network. Reception is patchy in the Cairngorms: the signal is likely to be better on the plateau, but in extreme weather it may be safer not to go up there to find out. Once connected to the emergency operator, ask for Grampian police.

Given the unreliable phone coverage, it is wise to leave word of your proposed route with some responsible person (and, of course, tell that person when you've safely returned). Youth hostels have specific forms for this, as do many independent hostels and B&Bs. You can also leave your intended route with the Cairngorm ranger at Coire Cas (and you should certainly do this if intending to leave a car there overnight).

Rescue teams are close to being overwhelmed by trivial call-outs from mobile phones. Being lost or tired is not sufficient reason for calling the rescue service, and neither, in normal summer weather, is being benighted.

There is no charge for mountain rescue in Scotland – teams are voluntary, financed by donations from the public, with a grant from the Scottish Executive and helicopters from the Royal Air Force and Royal Navy rescue services. You can make donations at youth hostels, TICs and many pubs.

MAPS

The mapping used on the low-level and mid-level walks in this book is from the Ordnance Survey's

I reckon we're in Coire Bhrochain...

Landranger series at 1:50 000. These are the best maps for grasping how the various walks intertwine and relate. For high mountain walks, too, these maps were for about 40 years the only ones available, and are perfectly satisfactory. The northern Cairngorms are on sheet 36 (Grantown & Aviemore), the southern on sheet 43 (Braemar & Blair Atholl) – these two sheets have a large overlap so that Cairn Toul and Ben Macdui are on both maps. For Lochnagar you need sheet 44 (Ballater & Glen Clova).

For detailed exploration of crags and corries and pathless boulder slopes, you will be helped by the extra contour detail at 1:25 000 scale. Harveys Superwalker maps score very highly here. They are beautifully clear and legible, mark paths where they actually exist on the ground, and do not disintegrate when damp. However, their coverage is incomplete. The sheet Cairn Gorm only extends from the Great Moss to the Lairig an Lui, excluding in the east Ben Avon and Beinn a' Bhuird, and in the west Glen Feshie. Similarly, their sheet Lochnagar doesn't go far enough north to cover approaches from Deeside.

Also at 1:25 000 is the Explorer series of the Ordnance Survey. All the relevant sheets are double-sided. Number 403 (Cairn Gorm & Aviemore) covers the western Cairngorms to Linn of Dee and the Lairig an Lui; 404 (Braemar, Tomintoul & Glen Avon) covers Beinn a' Bhuird and Ben Avon. The Lochnagar sheet is 388. The maps

have excellent coverage of the area, including the approach routes. They are not well designed: contour detail and paths are hard to read, especially in poor light under trees, or through wet spectacles. The OS paths also mark theoretical (but non-existent) rights of way, as well as 150-year-old stalkers' routes, long fallen into disuse. They do, however, name many individual rock buttresses and gullies, which is very useful if you're a climber in the mist.

When you need a map to supplement this book, I'd suggest the Landranger series for its completeness and clarity. For intricate mountain explorations, the Harvey maps are a very valuable add-on.

Magnetic deviation in the Cairngorms is about 4° West: to convert a map bearing to a compass one, add 4. GPS receivers should be set to the British National Grid (known variously as British Grid, Ord Srvy GB, BNG, or OSGB GRB36).

HOW TO USE THIS BOOK

A glance ahead into the book will show two different sorts of mapping. The mountain walks are illustrated with sketch maps. The **low-level** and **mid-level** routes have 1:50,000 mapping; this scale is large enough for the maps to be used on the actual walk.

However, two of the low-level walks are illustrated with sketch maps only. These are the very long Routes 10 and 42/43. By way of compensation, the two sketch maps for these routes

'Good winter weather' means 50kph winds, sub-zero temperatures, and spindrift blowing waist-high across the plateau. Climbers prepare for a roped descent of the Goat Path (Route 22)

show all the low-level walks in Glen More and Badenoch. There are at least 12 ways to walk from Glenmore village to Kingussie, and readers are encouraged to use these two sketch maps, and the cross-references in the margins, to link the various routes.

The sketch maps used for the **mountain walks** are, quite intentionally, inadequate for route-finding on the actual mountaintop. Full-sized walkers' maps are needed (and are given in the box at the start of the route description) so that you can see not just the route you're walking, but also the bad-weather escape routes which may take you into a different glen altogether.

Each of the **Munros** (3000ft/914m mountains) has its well-worn 'standard route'. That will be the quickest and most convenient – and fairly straightforward – route, but usually not the

most interesting. I have pointed out those routes in the preambles, and they are listed in several guidebooks including Steve Kew's *Walking the Munros Vol 2* (Cicerone, 2004). However, I've concentrated on what I consider to be the most rewarding routes for each hill. These may also be a little bit more demanding, as they seek out the steeper scenery and avoid the flat Landrover track.

But for the five finest hills I have left the choice to you. **Macdui**, **Cairn Gorm**, **Braeriach**, **Cairn Toul** and **Lochnagar** these are hills you will want to ascend lots of times by many different routes. For each I have given a 'summit summary', with the standard route and the adventure around the back, the rocky scramble and the long, long walk in from somewhere else altogether.

Many of the mountain routes start off along one of the low- or mid-level

24

The **difficulty ratings** are on a rough scale of 1 to 5:

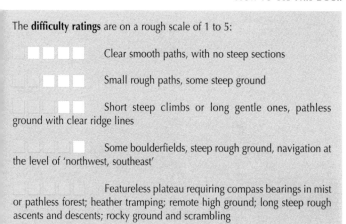

Clear smooth paths, with no steep sections

Small rough paths, some steep ground

Short steep climbs or long gentle ones, pathless ground with clear ridge lines

Some boulderfields, steep rough ground, navigation at the level of 'northwest, southeast'

Featureless plateau requiring compass bearings in mist or pathless forest; heather tramping; remote high ground; long steep rough ascents and descents; rocky ground and scrambling

ones. Accordingly, the starts of high-level routes are marked (in green) on the 1:50,000 mapping of the lower ones.

The icons at the start of each walk should, I hope, be fairly self-explanatory. First is an icon indicating the **type** of walk (low level, mid-level or mountain) – see box, right. This is followed by ratings of its **length** and its **difficulty** (see box above). (There are no difficulty ratings on scrambles: instead, refer to the scrambling grade in the box at the start of the route description.)

The **length ratings** correspond with the approximate times given in the box at the start of the walk: one blob is up to 4 hours; two blobs up to 6 hours; and the full five blobs are for walks of over 10 hours – those could also be enjoyed over two days using a tent or bothy. The approximate times are based on 1 hour for 4 horizontal

The type of walk is indicated as follows:

Low level

Forest and riverside walks, below 600m

Mid-level

Moorland and foothills, below 900m

Mountain

Mountain walks above 900m

Carn a' Mhaim from Glen Luibeg on a wet autumn afternoon (Route 36)

km or for 400m of height gained, with extra time added where the ground is particularly steep or rough. They'll be about right, including brief snack stops, for a moderately paced party. (Note: There are no length ratings in the Summit Summaries as these routes are uphill only.)

Many of the routes can be approached by mountain bike along the estate tracks. While this may lose you a riverside or forest footpath, it gains quite a lot of time. Where appropriate, cycle ways have been detailed and a little bike symbol appears on the map.

Where a bus or train can be used to link the two ends of a linear route, or to go up one route and come down another, this is noted in the routes concerned. Other public transport information is in Appendix VII. The heading 'Food on Route' mentions snack stops (if any) occurring within a route: there will often also be cafes or pubs at or near the finish point.

PART 1

AVIEMORE AND THE SPEY

Those who like their Cairngorms quick and convenient will always enter by Aviemore. Aviemore is easy to get to, with trains and coaches from south and north. It's easy to get out of, whether on footpaths into the forest or on the excellent Cairngorm Link bus that runs up and down to the high car parks. And it's easy to stay in as well, with shops for food and outdoor gear, with hostels both SYHA and independent, bars, cafes and chip shops.

Unfortunately, Aviemore is rather unattractive. It's a 1960s concrete dream, reproducing all the ugliness of a purpose-built ski resort in Switzerland. Never mind. Walks in the birchwoods of Craigellachie start at the village centre, and give views to the big hills you may have in mind for the following days. A couple of miles away is the lovely Loch an Eilein. The River Spey flows through, and downstream are Boat of Garten and the handsome planned town of Grantown: I've given a walk in each in case you prefer to stay in attractive surroundings albeit further from the action.

Creag Dhubh (Route 7) seen from Loch an Eilein

SPEYSIDE

1 Grantown and Spey

Length

■ □ □ □ □

Difficulty

■ □ □ □ □

Start/finish	Grantown-on-Spey NJ035280
Distance	12km/7.5 miles
Ascent	70m/200ft
Approx time	3hr
Max altitude	210m
Terrain	Tracks and paths

A planned town, a military bridge, an interesting glacio-fluvial feature, and a tree for hanging people on: but the real point of this walk is the great Spey and the pinewood. Grantown dates from the 17th century, and was built by James Grant. The little museum at the walk start provides the history, and also has a stuffed wildcat.

Start at the car park beside Grantown's small museum. From the bottom of the car park turn left in South Street, and at once right into Golf Course Road. It becomes a tarred track across the golf course, with the clubhouse (CH on the map) on the left. At green buildings, the track bends left along the forest edge and in a few yards a gate on the right leads into the forest.

Take the wide path ahead, soon with the Red Trail and Spey Way markers joining from the right. Keep on the main track, following the red and Spey waymarks to bear left at two junctions, then right at a third. With a stream and a new fence on the left, the Red Trail turns away to right; but take the main track and Spey Way which continue ahead through a gateway, to emerge from the forest.

At a track junction, bear right through a strange chained stile. The path beyond reaches a track, runs alongside it briefly, then exits onto it. Cromdale Bridge and church are just ahead, and worth a visit, with a signboard at the church explaining the small battle that took place in 1690 on the Heughs of Cromdale opposite.

Return across Cromdale Bridge and back into the track, following it through a gate and across a small bridge. It runs alongside the Spey, and after 2km re-enters the forest at a balconied fishers' hut. It passes under gloomy trees, then runs back out to the river, and becomes a green path that rises up the riverbank to a house, **Craigroy**.

Join the exit track from this house, out through a gate. Take the track ahead for 300m, as it bends away from the river, then back left to the river again. As the track again bends away right, keep ahead on a small path. It follows the top of river banking, then drops left to the riverside and joins a new track.

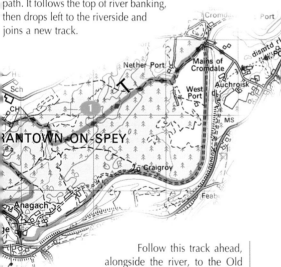

Follow this track ahead, alongside the river, to the Old Bridge of Spey (built by Major Caulfield as part of the military road system). Steps lead up to the bridge end. Turn right, away from the

The Spey below Grantown

Short cut Follow the Spey Way on along the road and right, up the military track, into Grantown.

bridge, through **Anagach** settlement. ◀ Immediately after the last house, turn right up a narrow path into the woods, past a collapsed bench, to a path just above. Here turn right, on combined Red/Blue Trail. The path runs along the top of a stony ridge – an esker – within the forest. After 500m, fork left with a red-blue waymark, and in another 50m at a path T-junction, turn left following the blue pole.

ESKERS

An esker is the bed of a river that once ran under an ice sheet. These glacial features, being totally enclosed within the ice, can run along the sides of valleys, uphill as well as down, and vanish at the point at which they returned into the body of the glacier.

In 200m the Green Trail joins from the left. Keep ahead – now Green/Blue – to pass either side of a tree in mid-path. This was the hanging tree where the bodies of executed criminals were placed on display. At the next junction, where Blue departs to the right, keep ahead on the Green Trail.

At a five-way junction, keep ahead northwest, on what – if it were a roundabout – would be second exit. You soon pass a reassuring green waymarker. Keep northwest across paths to emerge between two posts onto a track at the golf course edge. About 50m left is a car park, small and often full, with a trail map signboard. Here turn up right on tarmac, going straight across a junction near the fire station, to arrive along the edge of the Square onto Grantown's elegant main street. Turn right, past the Square, looking out for a small passageway just past the Grant Arms Hotel. It leads down into the museum car park.

2 Spey at Boat of Garten

Start/finish	Boat of Garten NH946191
Distance	10km/6 miles
Ascent	100m/300ft
Approx time	2.5hr
Max altitude	265m
Terrain	Paths and tracks

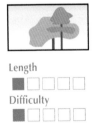

Length
■ □ □ □ □

Difficulty
■ □ □ □ □

Rather like the previous route, this is a walk of pinewood and the River Spey. I walked them in one day and enjoyed them both. This one, in case you like your big river in small doses, has a short-cut variant that's a mere 5km/3 miles.

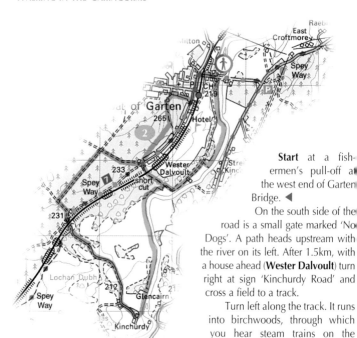

► **Start** at a fish-
ermen's pull-off at
the west end of Garten
Bridge. ◄

On the south side of the
road is a small gate marked 'No
Dogs'. A path heads upstream with
the river on its left. After 1.5km, with
a house ahead (**Wester Dalvoult**) turn
right at sign 'Kinchurdy Road' and
cross a field to a track.

Turn left along the track. It runs
into birchwoods, through which
you hear steam trains on the
Speyside Railway. At a bend, a
signpost has 'Kinchurdy Road' ahead. ◄
However, bend round left on the unsignposted main
track, to pass through a gate and rejoin the riverside. The track runs green along field edges, to meet a
broad gravel track just before the fishermen's hut
at **Kinchurdy**.

Turn right, away from the hut and river, to pass
through a farmyard. There is a loch on the left as the track
continues away from the river. The **Spey Way** joins from
the left, and the track runs under the railway to a junction.

Ignoring all signposted directions, take a rough track
half-right, past a barrier and into pinewoods. At a
signpost, turn right ('Woodland Walks') on a straight
track. After 1km, at a three-way signpost, turn right for
Kinchurdy Road. Just before reaching the end of this

Boat of Garten was,
before this bridge,
an important ferry
over the Spey.

Shorter version Take
this path through
birches to cross the
railway and pass the
end of Kinchurdy
Road. In 30m turn
right at a signpost
'Creag Bheag'.

The Spey at Boat of Garten

tarred village road, turn left at a sign 'Creag Bheag' (**the short cut rejoins here**).

The track shrinks soon to a path among the trees, with the backs of houses 50m away on the right. The path climbs slightly to the top of the small crag Craig Bheag (Craig Bheag actually means small crag, and is known locally as the Craigie).

Keep ahead, signposted 'Woodland Walks', but at the next signpost bear left for Fairy Hill. In 200m is another signpost. Ahead is 'The Village', but first turn left to the 265m rock summit of Fairy Hill. It has cairn and bench, and once they've cut down a few trees will have a view. Return to the signpost and this time take the path for the village. It runs downhill past a bench, then past a court for floodlit netball. At a final signpost, turn right and then fork right to stay just inside the trees, emerging onto Kinchurdy Road. Turn left to the Boat Hotel and the road down to Garten Bridge.

AVIEMORE

3 Craigellachie Birches

Length

■ □ □ □ □

Difficulty

■ ■ ■ ■ □

Start/finish	Aviemore Tourist Information Centre NH894119
Distance	5km/3 miles
Ascent	280m/900ft
Approx time	2hr
Max altitude	490m
Terrain	The full route has a steep descent between crags, but there are easier alternatives.

The full route is a figure-of-eight, with a short section (contouring northwards through the birches) getting done twice over.

Start at the TIC, heading out of the village and turning right, towards the youth hostel. Pass to the right of the hostel, onto a signed wide path through woods, to a tunnel under the A9.

A signboard indicates the two trails, red and green – both very short. Follow the arrows, ignoring a fork right after a few metres towards the lower lochan. In 400m, bear left (red/green arrows) onto a smaller path, ascending quite steeply. At a waymark arrow turn sharp back left (Green: the Red Trail short-cuts ahead) to zigzag up to a level with views out through the trees across the top of Aviemore. The path contours northwards to meet a track. ◀

Geal-charn
824
Mòr

Very short, short cut
Turn right here and skip down five paragraphs.

Turn left here, following the track up for 150m to its end at a covered reservoir. A small path continues uphill through heather under birches. With crag above, the path slants up to the right, into the small col defined by **Creag**

A spare hour in Aviemore? Take a walk through the birchwoods at the back of the town. Two spare hours? Extend that walk to a viewpoint that reveals the whole of the northern Cairngorms, spread out ready for your next few days of walking. An extra half hour after that? Go on upwards, to the summit of Craigellachie, an even finer viewpoint that also takes in the lochs along the upper Spey.

But if your name should be Grant, only the third of these options is open. Craigellachie is the home hill of Clan Grant, and 'On, Craigellachie!' your battle cry; clearly you have to climb it all the way.

Birch pool,
Craigellachie Reserve

nan Gabhar (Gower – crag of goats). The small path continues uphill, bending left (southwest) with a small stream to its right. At the stream top the path turns left to a first viewpoint overlooking Aviemore and Strathspey.

The path continues south for 100m along the crag rim, then turns uphill, southwest, to pass a cairn and reach the larger one at NH881124, the summit of **Craigellachie**.

The continuing path from this point divides confusingly; the correct line is steep while incorrect ones arrive above crags. If you don't have both the time and the mental toughness for coping with getting lost, it's better to return by the ascent route. Time in hand and mentally tough? Then continue on the now very small path south to a second cairn (Point 490m, with grand views up the Spey). Continue southeast, now with a dead fence on the right, to another cairn. After a steep little drop the path divides – keep on southeast on the right fork, crossing a knoll and a wet area beyond to a final cairn (NH885117) overlooking the Spey Bridge.

This is the edge of the summit plateau, and the steeper descent starts. The small path leads southeast, down an ill-defined spur with small crags and heather. The path bends gradually to the left, contouring northwards above the treeline then slanting down northeast among the first knee-high birches to reach a rock knoll (NH888119) above the Hilton tower.

Continue down the spur crest, gently at first then very steeply towards the upper lochan. The path peters out in grassy birchwoods, but keep ahead for a few steps to find the Green Trail just above its divergence from the Red on its upward zigzags. Repeat the contouring section of the Green Trail to meet the track, but this time turn right, downhill, following a green arrow (**the short cut took this right turn first time around**).

Head down the track until the slope levels, where turn right (arrow) to the upper lochan. The path passes to left of it along its shore, then crosses its outflow at a huge stepping stone. Here the Red Trail rejoins from the right. The path heads down slightly left, pitched, for 150m to a path T-junction. Here arrow markers indicate a turn right to rejoin the outward route, following the path ahead to the reserve's entrance and the tunnel under the A9.

4 Geal-charn Mor

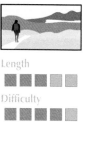

Start/finish	Aviemore NH894119
Distance	18km/11.5 miles
Ascent	700m/2400ft
Approx time	6.25hr
Max altitude	824m
Terrain	Tracks, grassy hillsides, but 1km of rough wet moorland

Length

Difficulty

Some pleasant woodland and upland, but also a long mile of rough and soggy moorland, so this is really a route for those who need to bag the Corbett. An approach from the top of Route 3 (Craigellachie) has roughly the same amount of nasty ground, and might be more interesting.

5min detour About 200m further out along the main street, a street on the right is signed for the Dalfaber Ring Cairn, a minor monument.

Start from anywhere in Aviemore: there's informal parking on an empty lot alongside the Information Centre car park. Head north through the village. Immediately before the school, a path on the left is signed 'Aviemore Orbital'. ◄ Waymarks lead alongside playing fields, bear left to cross Aviemore Burn, then bend right close to the A9. The path runs through a beautiful but noisy wood of heather under birch. Emerge onto lanes, alongside the A9, to a high culvert with a lane running through it.

Turn left through this, under the A9. As the lane becomes track, walk round one locked gate, and climb over a second into pinewoods. Now three side-tracks are on the left in quick succession. Take the third, green and little used, and head up with a burn nearby on the right, to fork at 380m altitude. Here fork left, to ford **Milton Burn** – known locally as Beaver Creek, these particular Beavers being small people in paramilitary uniforms – and go up to left of it to a gate and ladder stile (NH880145).

The rough track continues to the top of the forest as marked, but the path on the left on OS maps doesn't exist. So keep along the track, northwest inside a tree strip, to its end at a gate in a new deer fence (NH869151). Cross the ladder stile and turn left over soggy moorland, for a nasty kilometre alongside the fence. Once on the north spur of **Carn Dearg Mor**, you'll find short walkable heather on the spur crest, all the way up to the summit. Carn Dearg Mor's cairn is not its highest point but has the best view down onto Aviemore.

Head down northwest, following metal poles of a dead fence. In the col, slant out right towards stony ground for shallower heather. Cross the hump 696m, and head southwest across moorland, with some peaty hags passed on their right. A track crosses ahead, with a cairn at its highest point. ◄ From here a little peak-baggers' path heads up smooth terrain to a knee-high cairn at the top of the first rise. A gentle plateau walk leads to the summit of **Geal-charn Mor** (the larger white stonepile).

Short detour Another cairn 100m north has a memorial to a head keeper.

Return to the knee-high cairn, then head down east, to join the track. (Don't lose too much height as you slant down, as the going gets heavy below 650m.) The track runs down the side of wooded **An Gleannan** (the little glen). In birches, fork left (sign 'Right of Way') on a track that's now patchily tarred, and runs out to a farm lane. Cross the bridge on the right and turn left into a track beside the stream, to the A9's bridge. You can pass under this very busy road on river-bed stones to reach the B9152 beyond. Turn left on the grass verge for the last 2km into Aviemore.

LOCH AN EILEIN

5 Around Loch an Eilein

Start/finish	Loch an Eilein NH897085
Distance	5km/3 miles
Ascent	None
Approx time	1.25hr
Max altitude	270m
Terrain	Good paths

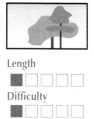

Length

Difficulty

As far as low-level walkers are concerned, Loch an Eilein is the one place that has it all. Forests of both birch and pine rise towards the bare stony summits. The lochan gleams between the reddish trunks, or froths under storm winds, or lies blank under winter's ice. The lochan's island has its castle, once besieged by Hanoverian soldiers, later a nesting place for ospreys.

Wildcats, capercaillie, and perhaps the faery folk wander below the branches, as once did cattle thieves. Locals used to leave a cow tied to a tree trunk overnight, in the hope that thieves would take it and leave the rest.

The walk around the loch is today very popular (even with people who already have all the cattle they require). You may prefer to visit at dawn, or late in the evening, or on a really rainy day. The following Route 6 (Ord Ban) adds in a small but steep hill for even better views.

Start at Rothiemurchus Estate's car park. From its end, a built path leads to the Nature Centre hut (soft drinks and

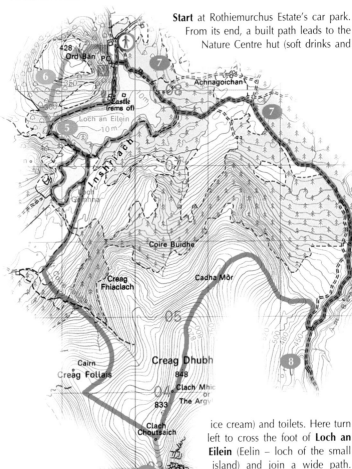

ice cream) and toilets. Here turn left to cross the foot of **Loch an Eilein** (Eelin – loch of the small island) and join a wide path. Turn right, around the loch, ignoring side-paths on the left that lead towards the Lairig Ghru. The path runs along the east and then the south side of the loch. About 100m after a concrete footbridge over a small stream, the path bends

right to a junction. On the right now is a wooden foot-bridge with a view along **Loch Gamhna**.

You can fork right, across the footbridge, for the shorter circuit of just Loch an Eilein. However, even with the extra 1.5km around Loch Gamhna this delicious walk is shorter than you probably want. So fork left on a smaller path, and in 400m fork right to stay close to Loch Gamhna. The path gets a bit boggy as it passes around the head of the loch, then runs back along the west side to a path T-junction.

The footbridge between the lochs is 100m right. Turn left, away from it, and follow the path to the west corner of Loch an Eilein. Here turn right onto a wider track (or short-cut right at a bench just before). You can stay on this track (beware of mountain bikes) or look out for a smaller path on the right between track and loch. After a gate, a new house is on the left; here head down right, to the shore, for the castle view. Continue on the main track, forking left to the Nature Centre hut.

Loch an Eilein with its island castle: the focal point of Speyside's low-level walking

6 Ord Ban

Length
■□□□□

Difficulty
■■■□□

Start/finish	Loch an Eilein NH897085
Distance	7km/4 miles
Ascent	180m/600ft
Approx time	2hr
Max altitude	428m
Terrain	Steep little path, then pathless but straightforward descent
Map	See map for Route 3 (Loch an Eilein)

You can make the walk round Loch an Eilein even better by adding in this craggy little hill. Its bare heathery summit is a superb viewpoint not only down on the loch but also of the mountains and Speyside.

Start at Rothiemurchus Estate's car park, and take the path from its end to the Nature Centre hut. Just before the buildings a ladder stile on the right crosses a deer fence. Head back alongside the fence for 50m, until opposite the car park. Now a small path zigzags up the steep side of Ord Ban. The path gets clearer higher up, slanting up to the left to avoid craggy ground directly above.

Emerging from the trees, the path scrambles across a small slab to the heathery crest, and turns right for 100m to the summit of **Ord Ban** (white hammer), with its white cylinder trig and erratic boulder.

A heather path heads down southwest with Speyside views to reach a plantation fence. Here it heads down, left of the fence, into woods, becoming indistinct as it reaches a crossing deer fence with a gate and a stile (NH887078).

Cross the awkward slatted stile and turn left alongside the fence for 200m, then slant down through the wood,

which has juniper underbrush and is damp in places. Soon the waters of the loch are twinkling between the pine trunks and you reach the wide lochside path.

Turn right along the path, now reversing Route 5 (Loch an Eilein) around the loch. Turn left around the loch head, and after 400m look out for the small path on the right to go around Loch Gamhna, or else continue to the footbridge between the lochs 100m further on.

Continue on the wide path along the southern and then eastern side of Loch an Eilein, with glimpses of the castle island. At the loch foot turn left across a footbridge to the Nature Centre hut.

Ord Ban at dawn across Inshriach Forest

Viewpoint About 400m left is the viewpoint spot for looking at the castle.

7 Argyll Stone

Start/finish	Loch an Eilein NH896085
Distance	15.5km/ 9.5 miles
Ascent	600m/2000ft
Approx time	5.5hr
Max altitude	848m
Terrain	Steep little path up through forest, rough grassland, pathless but easy ground for descent

Length
■ ■ ■ ■ ■

Difficulty
■ ■ ■ ■ ■

This is the typical mid-level walk. Creag Dhubh offers pathless but pleasant going on dwarf heather and gravel, with superb views. But to get to it you'll spend a couple of hours in the forest, first on the flat and then on an almost forgotten path and some fairly rough hillside. To finish, there's another quiet hour among the trees.

The Argyll Stone is one of the more striking tors, as well as being the most westerly and lowest in altitude. A party of Campbells on the way to the Battle of Glenlivet in 1594 is said to have gained a last glimpse of Argyll from this spot.

The Argyll Stone, westernmost and lowest of the Cairngorm tors

Start at Loch an Eilein car park. From the back of the car park, take the path to the Nature Centre hut and head anticlockwise round Loch an Eilein to the footbridge between it and Loch Gamhna. Across this, turn right alongside **Loch Gamhna** for 400m, then fork left on a path through scrubby trees. After 1.2km the path fords the **Allt Coire Follais**. About 150m later the path bends right; here turn off on a small but clear path up to the left

(if you reach the Inshriach bothy, you've overshot this turn-off by 400m).

The small, rough path heads up through the forest, soon running close to the stream on its left. At the top of the trees, there is a stream junction, and in crossing the side-stream the path finally peters out. Head up on mixed grass and heather between the two streams, southeast, until level with the top of the trees on the opposite (north) side of Allt Coire Follais; then turn south up onto the level spur of **Creag Follais**. This is dwarf heather and very pleasant going. Head up southeast to arrive at **Clach Choutsaich**, a split boulder tor, highest of a line of such tors on the southern ridge.

Head up northwards, then horizontally northeast to the cairn at Point 833 and the **Argyll Stone** tor just beyond it on the western slope. Keep on north, past the small cairn on the actual 848m summit of **Creag Dhubh**, to a final cairn at the northern tip of the plateau (NH906047). Now turn northeast down a long spur **Cadha Mor**, bending gradually right, southeast, to the lowest knoll of the ridge at 620m. It's rather rougher for the last few metres down to the track.

Keep on downhill to the lower track, as it's prettier. (However, during the next couple of years there'll be diggers on this lower track renewing the leaky water pipe out of Loch Einich.) On either track, turn left, down the valley.

The upper and lower tracks rejoin, ford a stream, and after 1.8km reach Lochan Deo. Bear left for 100m and turn left on a cycle path running west, to reach after 1km the path round Loch an Eilein. Here turn right, signed 'Aviemore', and follow the main path around the loch to the walk start.

PART 2

GLEN MORE

With the national training centre at Glenmore Lodge, Glen More is in a sense the mountaineering mid-point of Scotland. It's not the centre of the Cairngorms: that's hill-circled Loch Avon. However, it is the convenient access point to the Cairngorm plateau, and to the great forest of Rothiemurchus with its miles of low-level walks and bike rides.

With its campsite, shop and youth hostel, its car parks at 600m altitude, it is tempting to pretend there isn't any other way in to the Cairngorms. Indeed, Glen More makes the mountains slightly too convenient. The Northern Corries are a roadside ice-climbing crag just above the car park. Ben Macdui becomes almost easy, Loch Avon almost accessible, and the ski area makes Cairn Gorm not only small but also sordid.

So avoid the two ski corries, and don't let the ski car parks trick you into omitting all forest from your hillwalks. And then Glen More becomes, as its name implies, the glen that's just great.

Loch Morlich under February rain (seen from Route 11)

COYLUMBRIDGE

8 Gleann Einich and the Sgorans

Start/finish	Whitewell NH916087
Distance	27km/17 miles
Ascent	1000m/3400ft
Approx time	9.25hr
Bike approach	To track junction under Cadha Mor NH924048 (saves 2hr)
Max altitude	1118m
Terrain	Track, rough climb on almost-forgotten path, smooth grassy ridges
Map	OS Explorer 403 Cairn Gorm; Landranger 36 Grantown

Sgor Gaoith is often reached by an up-and-down from the car park at Achlean on the Glen Feshie side of the hill. However, it's just the high point of a ridge known as the Sgorans, running for 7km above Gleann Einich, superbly cragged on its eastern side and ending at the Argyll Stone. This route approaches along majestic Gleann Einich below those eastern crags, finds a witty way onto the ridge by an almost-vanished stalkers' path, and comes back along the full length of the ridge.

Start at Whitewell, where there is no formal parking, but space on the verge for a couple of cars north of the turning area. Alternatively, start at Loch an Eilein.

From **Whitewell**, take a small, rough path east for 300m, and turn right on a track to reach Lochan Deo: here keep ahead through a gate, southwards. (From **Loch an Eilein**, head round the loch clockwise for 1.2km to a cycle path on the left signed for Gleann Einich. Follow this for 1.2km to Lochan Deo, and turn right.)

Note Fords of Beanaidh Bheag and at the foot of Loch Einich make this one a bad choice after heavy or prolonged rainfall.

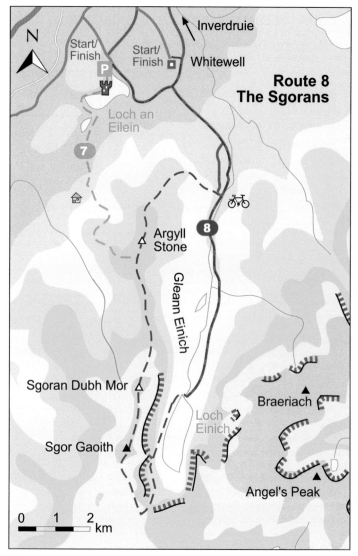

After 2km the track fords a stream and divides. Both go into Gleann Einich – pronounced 'Ennich' – but the lower one, closer to the river, is the more attractive. After 2km the tracks rejoin, with Gleann Einich's final pines just above and an idyllic riverbank campsite sheltered by a heather bank. Here cyclists must hide their vehicles in the heather. The track heads on upstream, after 1km crossing a bridge.

In another 1.5km comes the ford of **Beanaidh Bheag**. ▶ An island 100m upstream can offer a dry-foot crossing.

Continue up the track with **Loch Mhic Ghillie-choil** unseen on the right. At the valley head, pass a path turn-off left, ▶ keeping on the track for another 400m to its end at the foot of **Loch Einich** (from Whitewell 3hr, from Loch an Eilein 3.25hr). The fact that water is extracted for the taps of Carrbridge, 20km away on the Spey, is scarcely apparent.

Cross the loch foot, getting wet feet, and continue along the beach to the northwest corner. Now a small path runs along the shoreline. Two thirds of the way up the loch, under the final corrie of the line of crags, the path slants uphill. It is visible from afar, less so from near – a few discreet marker cairns help here, but periodically get knocked down by people who apparently want this historic path line to disappear back into the wilderness. Follow the old path line up to the **Allt Fuaran Diotach**. The path doesn't cross, but zigzags up to right of the stream to reach the rim of the vestigial corrie.

The sloping floor of this corrie is grass and peat hags. Slant up this sloping corrie floor to the left, to pass below a rocky stony spur (A'Chailleach) into the left-hand, southern section of the corrie, named as Corrie Odhar nan Each. The grassy southern flank of A'Chailleach offers a possible exit onto the ridge above, but there's a better way.

Above you now, the southern wall of Coire nan Each is formed of a succession of chunky ribs and grass. This is bounded on the right by a stream, and 200m right of this is a smaller stream with a tiny gorge section. The face to right of this smaller stream is grassy below, with a line

Here the small path to Braeriach's northern corries, **Route 54**, forks off left.

Route 55, for Coire Dhondail, heads up that path.

*The Sgorans at sunset,
from Lurcher's Crag*

of broken ground, and then grassy above. Look carefully at the grass below, and also at the grass above, and see the zigzags of a forgotten stalkers' path.

The floor of Coire Odhar nan Each has a small outcrop with a flatter grassy top, NN905974. Slant up the corrie floor onto this flatter top, where you'll find the green line of this old path. Follow it ahead (contouring south), then up its first zigzags. To overcome the broken ground it slants up left, to beside the small stream. Here there are 2m on rock, but easy and not exposed, to reach the stream. Now the path turns back right, above the band of broken ground, zigzagging up steep grass with a feeling of exposure due to the craggier ground below.

When the path reaches the plateau, head up right for 20m to join a clear path running towards Sgor Gaoith. This very pleasant path follows the brink of the east-facing crags above Coire Odhar nan Each and Coire na Caillich, before slanting up to the main ridge crest for a sudden view over to the Spey valley. Just ahead is the summit platform of **Sgor Gaoith** (windy crag-hill) perched above the eastern crags, with only a small cairn.

A path continues north along the ridge, dipping across a grassy col and then rising to the much larger cairn on the top of **Sgoran Dubh Mor**. The path continues down northwards to cross a col, with crags down on the right. The next short rise is stony and pathless, but the path reforms through the following col to pass between the two lowest tors of Clach Choutsaich.

If you started from Whitewell, you now complete the walk on Route 7 (**Argyll Stone**) to rejoin the outward route at the bike drop-off point.

Those aiming for Loch an Eilein could do the same. Alternatively, reverse that same Route 7. Turn northwest, down short heather to the shoulder just before Creag Follais. Descend northeast, on rough heather and grass, to Allt Coire Follais. Keep left of this, to find a small path that descends about 20m to left of the stream. At the slope foot turn right on a much wider path, keep ahead alongside Loch Gamhna to cross the bridge between it and **Loch an Eilein**, and pass around the west and north sides of that loch to the car park.

9 Creag a' Chalamain and the Cat Notch

Start/finish	Loch Morlich foot NH958096
Distance	16km/10 miles
Ascent	550m/1800ft
Approx time	5.25hr
Max altitude	787m
Terrain	Tracks, paths, bare hilltops

Length

Difficulty

Eag a' Chait is the Cat Notch – but is more associated with deer, as the Celtic early inhabitants of the forest used it as an ambush point at the end of a deer drive. But today the beast you'll see will be the reindeer, as the Glenmore herd roams here. Bulls may be aggressive during the rut in September and October.

Before the deer hunters, the Cat Notch was a channel for water flowing off the Lairig Ghru glacier, and geographers will note that the river valley flowing out of it eastwards is much too big for the tiny stream it now holds.

Start at the car park on the lake shore. Turn right through the car park, then left on the track over the loch's outflow. A gate leads onto a smooth track under overhanging pines. After 300m, ignore the small track for Glenmore forking off left; in another 400m, a small path under branches on the left lets you visit **Lochan nan Geadas**.

Return to the track. After another 1km, fork right on a wide path signed for Piccadilly and the Lairig Ghru. After 1km the path dips and zigzags to reach Piccadilly path junction.

The path to the left is small but well surfaced, signed Lairig Ghru. After 1km it emerges from the trees high above **Allt Druidh** (Drooey – the 'stream of getting wet'!). In another 2km it joins a stream, passes through a minor col and drops a few metres to cross another stream. Turn uphill here, on grassy patches to left (north) of the stream. As the slope eases, keep ahead to join a small

Silver Hill and Carn a' Chalamain, with Cairn Lochan behind

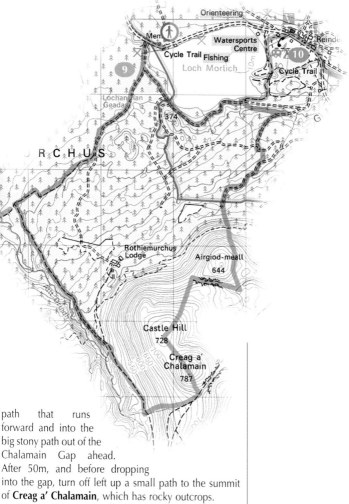

path that runs
forward and into the
big stony path out of the
Chalamain Gap ahead.
After 50m, and before dropping
into the gap, turn off left up a small path to the summit
of **Creag a' Chalamain**, which has rocky outcrops.

Head northwest on short heather and tundra moss,
through a wide col and up the slight rise to the cairn on
Castle Hill. Head down northeast, passing a tiny pool

and heading for the left-hand (west) end of the incised gap Eag a' Chait – the Cat Notch. With a deer fence ahead, turn right into the notch, finding a small path.

The gap is craggy-sided and boulder-floored, the Chalamain Gap in miniature. From the end of the notch, there runs out the valley of the former meltwater river, and the small path follows this valley floor. ◄ Just after emerging from the Eag a' Chait the former river valley turns right, with the deer fence visible above on the left. Go straight up the heathery bank to the deer fence, where a stile will be found (NH968064, 150m east of a fence bend).

The path would eventually join up with the big path running into the Chalamain Gap from the Sugar Bowl car park, **Route 52**.

Cross the stile, with a sign warning of the reindeer. A small path runs through the reindeer enclosure, north, passing to left of **Lochan Dubh a' Chadha**, then down north around the flank of **Airgiod-meall** (silver hill or money hill). The path bends left, northwest, as it drops into trees. It goes under low-voltage power lines and passes a small hut to reach a deer fence. A stile leads to the beginning of a forest road (NH966076).

Follow the forest road downhill. After 1km, pass a large lone pine on the right, and in another 50m a tree gap runs north. (**Beware**: an earlier tree gap also runs north. If you miss the gap, just continue on the track to the next junction and turn left.) Follow the tree gap for 200m to arrive at another track and turn left.

In 150m comes a track junction. Turn right, north, and in 800m look out for the Red Trail path turning off on the left. It leads down to a track that runs beside **Loch Morlich**. Follow this track around the loch to the start point.

LOCH MORLICH

10 Down Cairn Gorm

Start/finish	Coire Cas NH988061
Distance	20km/12.5 miles
Ascent	None
Approx time	5hr
Max altitude	620m
Terrain	Good paths and tracks
Map	Harveys Cairn Gorm, OS Explorer 403 Cairn Gorm, or OS Landranger 36 Grantown; see also route maps 9, 7 and 3
Public transport	Bus 31 'Cairngorm Link' Aviemore to Coire Cas via Glenmore village, roughly hourly from 8am; phone Rapsons 01479 811211
Food on route	Cafes at Glenmore village and the nearby FC information centre; snacks at Loch an Eilein's Nature Centre hut

Length

Difficulty

This walk is covered, in various bits, elsewhere in the book. But it's so natural and so nice that I've regrouped it under its own route number.

Climbing Britain's sixth-highest mountain, entirely downhill? What could be more simple, and more satisfying? The walk starts at 620m in, when I did it, a fearsome thunderstorm. But it finds shelter by the Allt Mor, and soon after that it's under the trees, so can be allowed its 'low-level' icon. It starts at the fairly ugly Coire Cas car park, and from there it just goes downhill. Coire Cas means 'corrie of steepness, or difficulty', so named even before the formation of the White Lady ski run's fearsome moguls.

Just below the main car park is an equally large dirt-surfaced one used by hillwalkers. **Start** near its end,

55

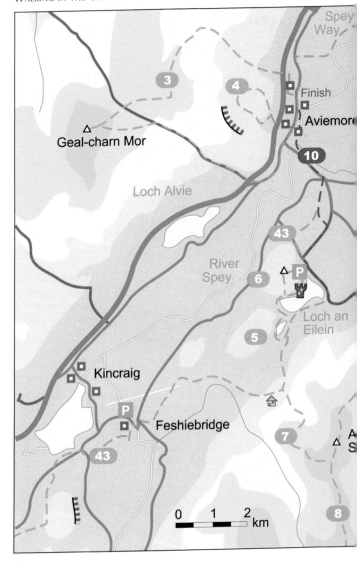

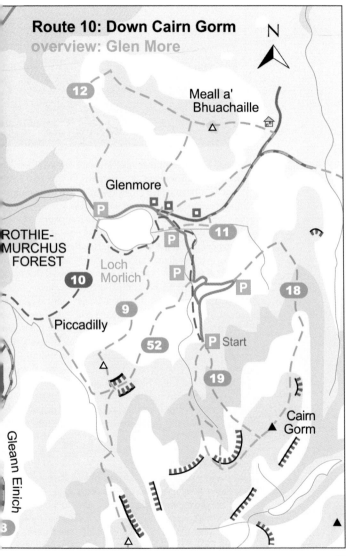

Route 10: Down Cairn Gorm

overview: Glen More

N

Meall a'
Bhuachaille

Glenmore

ROTHIE-
MURCHUS
FOREST

Loch
Morlich

10

12

11

9

52

18

Piccadilly

P Start

19

Gleann Einich

Cairn
Gorm

*Looking across Glen
More from the slopes
of Cairn Gorm*

*Looking across Glen
More from the slopes
of Cairn Gorm*

where a broad new path runs downhill, signed as the Allt
Mor Trail to Glenmore. It runs down to right of the Allt
Mor (big stream), then drops to join it. At a junction by a
long footbridge keep ahead, into woods.

The path crosses the Coire Cas road, back into the
woods, with a stepped wooden section, then reaches
another long footbridge. Cross this to the corner of a car
park, and turn right, staying alongside Allt Mor. Where
the trail bends left, take a smaller path ahead that leads
in a few metres to the roadside at Heron's Field.

Turn right across the road bridge, and follow the
main road and then a lane above it to pass a memorial
stone to Norwegian commandos and reach the youth
hostel. The hostel was the base for the Norwegians, and
an accidental bullet hole in one of the front windows has
been carefully preserved. A little further on and across
the main road is the Glenmore Cafe.

Go down behind the cafe and along the right-hand
edge of the campsite onto a Brown Trail to **Loch Morlich**.
Turn left along its shore, then left again to cross a footbridge of Allt Mor. Take the path south, away from the
river, then bending right onto the Red Trail, to regain the
loch shore and join a track.

After 1.5km keep ahead on a smaller track, still close
to the loch. In 500m it runs into a wider track. Turn sharp
left (southwest) on this, and after 1.2km turn off right on
a wide cycleway path signed for Piccadilly and the Lairig
Ghru. After 1.5km of lovely walking under pines, you
reach Piccadilly path junction (NH937075).

Keep ahead, signed for Aviemore, to cross the Cairngorm Club footbridge and reach Lochan Deo (left of the path; the name could mean 'lochan of the breath of life'). Immediately after the loch, keep ahead (signed 'Aviemore') for a few steps, then turn right on a track that bends left to reach Achnagoichan. Turn right in front of the house, and at once left into a small path (signed 'footpath') between the house and the forest. After 1km it emerges beside **Loch an Eilein**.

Walk round the lochan, clockwise if time allows, to the road end at the entrance to Rothiemurchus Estate's car park (NH897086). ▶ Take a rough track forking right (northeast) marked as for estate vehicles only. After 1km this passes through the scattered houses at Croft. Fork left into a driveway, and pass to right of a garage onto a small path heading north. This goes straight across a wider path, and in another 50m joins another wide path. Follow this ahead to the road triangle at Inverdruie.

Turn left, then right, to meet the main Glenmore road opposite the Rothiemurchus Visitor Centre. Turn left along the pavement for 800m, then keep ahead on a cycle path with a footpath in woods on its left. A bridge crosses the Spey into **Aviemore**, where you turn right along the riverside and take any bridge under the railway to reach the village centre.

Route 43 (Insh to Aviemore) takes an alternative route from here via the Lily Lochan just to the north.

11 Lochan Uaine

Start/finish	Heron's Field NH981094
Distance	8km/5 miles
Ascent	130m/450ft
Approx time	2hr
Max altitude	420m
Terrain	Tracks, wide paths, a small steep path

Length
■□□□□

Difficulty
■■□□□

59

An Lochan Uaine – the Green Lochan – is one of half a dozen so named in the Cairngorms. This particular one is where the faery folk wash their green clothing after a sweaty day in the forest being mischievous or vicious. As well as this sinister but magical spot, the walk visits ancient forest and the shores of Loch Morlich.

Start at the car park beside the bridge over Allt Mor (more parking 500m south, and in Glenmore village). A wide path leads upstream, left of the river. Little signboards describe various items of natural history alongside the path. After 600m, turn left on a less wide path, away from the river. A

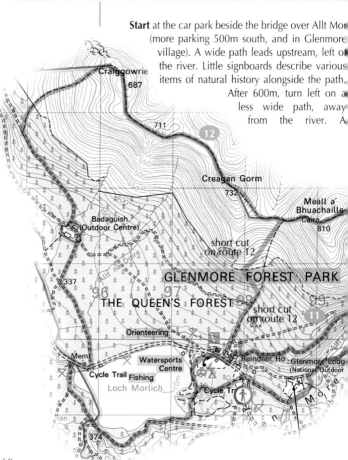

couple more nature indicators confirm that you're on the right track.

With a stile and gate into Glenmore Lodge firing range ahead, the path bends right, then curves back left (northeast) to meet a wide track just east of the lodge's main entrance. Turn right, away from the lodge. Ignore a branch track on the right just after a bridge, and follow the main track northeast to the foot of **Lochan Uaine**. ▶

This route will continue by a path on the left, but first take the stepped path down on the right to the shore of the loch. Then take the small path opposite the loch steps. It heads back down-valley, but soon slants up the valley's northern slope. The path is narrow and steep, but well built. After 800m it arrives at the end of a forest road.

Follow the forest road ahead, across a clear-felled area with views to the big hills. The track enters pines, then bends left to become a lane down into Glenmore village. Opposite the Reindeer Centre and just above the main road turn right, passing the memorial stone to Norwegian commandos and the Forestry Commission shop and cafe, then join the main road for 200m to the village shop and Glenmore Cafe opposite.

Enter the campsite behind the cafe, and follow its right edge to a wide path, with brown-marked waymarker, into the forest. This soon reaches the shore of **Loch Morlich**. Turn left along the beach to the point where the Allt Mor flows into the loch, and follow the riverside path upstream to the road at Heron's Field.

Routes 12 (Meall a' Bhuachaille), **13** (Bynack More), **14** (Beinn Mheadhoin), **15** and **16** (to Cairn Gorm) all continue ahead up this track.

61

12 Meall a' Bhuachaille

Length

Difficulty

Start/finish	Heron's Field NH981094
Distance	19km/12 miles
Ascent	750m/2500ft
Approx time	6.5hr
Max altitude	810m
Terrain	Paths, occasionally boggy, and with one fairly steep climb

Unusually for a mid-level walk, this is on paths all the way. Once up the steep climb onto Meall a' Bhuachaille it's a gentle and pleasant ridge walk high above Loch Morlich.

Meall a' Bhuachaille

Start as Route 11 (Lochan Uaine), following it to **Lochan Uaine**. Keep ahead on the main track to the left of the lochan, past a sign 'End of Waymarking'.

When the track forks, keep left, with the gable of **Ryvoan Bothy** seen ahead. At the bothy turn left, uphill,

on a steep path, through heather with regenerating rowan. Once above the break of the slope the bothy is out of sight, and the path gets peaty. Where it divides, either is OK, but the right-hand one has better views and firmer footing. They rejoin to the large shelter cairn on **Meall a' Bhuachaille** (the hump-hill of the shepherd).

For the first steps down west there's no path, but it restarts at a small cairn. The ridge levels briefly at 650m, ▶ then drops another 30m to a col before the gentle climb up **Creagan Gorm**. The good path continues over a third, unnamed, hill passing a notable erratic boulder, then the ridge drops briefly and bends right, north, to the cairn on **Craiggowrie**.

Continue northwest for 200m to a final low knoll whose cairn is decorated with fence posts. Now the path turns sharp left, down southwest (towards a radio mast), gently peaty among heather. At the forest edge (NH951132) stands a red waymark pole marking the path down through the forest to join a forest road. Turn left, down to the junction before **Badaguish**. Here turn left through the adventure playground for grown-ups.

Leaving Badaguish the track becomes tarred. Ignore a track on the left signed Glenmore. After 1km, at an X-junction, bear left onto a wide smooth track. It runs to meet road beside Loch Morlich.

Cross into the lakeside car park. Turn right, through the car park, and then left on the track over the outflow of Loch Morlich and through a gate. After 300m, the small track for Glenmore forks off left. Follow this, soon following the loch shore, for 2km, then turn left on a path with a red waymark post.

This path runs with **Loch Morlich** on its left, then bends left to a junction. Keep ahead, then at once fork left (white waymark). At the Allt Mor turn right to cross a footbridge.

For **Heron's Field**, simply follow the path upstream. For **Glenmore village**, turn upstream but at once turn back left on a path that leads to the caravan and camp-site. Cross this to a footbridge on the left, beyond which is Glenmore Cafe and shop.

Escape route to Glenmore village, easily missed, forks off down left here towards the forest top.

63

13 Creag Mhor and Bynack More

Start/finish	Heron's Field NH981094
Distance	31km/19 miles
Ascent	1200m/4000ft
Approx time	11hr
Bike approach	To Bynack Stable (saves 2hr)
Max altitude	1090m
Terrain	Paths and some rough hillside
Map	Harveys Cairn Gorm; OS Landranger 36 Grantown or Explorer 403 Cairn Gorm

Length

Difficulty

Away from the busy paths and car parks above Loch Morlich, this route takes you round the corner by Ryvoan. Here is Bynack More, not quite as big as Cairn Gorm and a lot less visited. Here is Creag Mhor, only a Corbett but still all granite with a tor for a top. And here is the true heart of the Cairngorm country, the crag-ringed and remote Loch Avon.

This route is seriously wild, in places pathless, and at its further end romantically remote. It's the antidote to the funicular railway route up Cairn Gorm.

To combine Bynack More via the Saddle with Cairn Gorm see **Route 15**.

Start as Route 11 (Lochan Uaine). Pass to left of the loch to the fork before Ryvoan, and turn right, away from the bothy, signed (ambitiously) for Braemar. This is the Lairig an Lui, one of the old drove roads right through the range (Gaelic spelling Laoigh – pass of the calves – so called as it's easier, though longer, than the other drove road, the Lairig Ghru). After another 2km, the track ends at **Bynack Stable**. (**Note** Bynack Stable blew down in January 2005.)

Just behind Bynack Stable is a footbridge, and then the path forks. Bear left, southeast, up the shoulder of

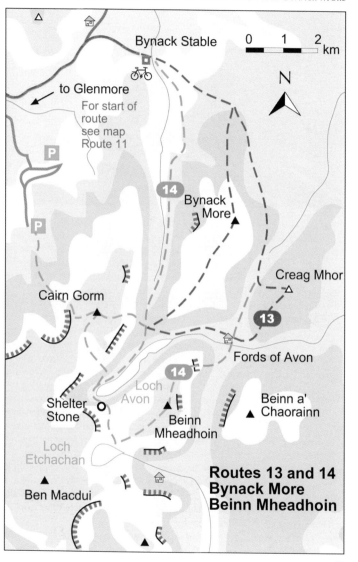

Bynack Stable

0 1 2 km

N

to Glenmore

For start of
route
see map
Route 11

P

P

14

Bynack
More

Creag Mhor

Cairn Gorm

13

Fords of Avon

14

Loch
Avon

Shelter
Stone

Beinn a'
Chaorainn

Beinn
Mheadhoin

Loch
Etchachan

**Routes 13 and 14
Bynack More
Beinn Mheadhoin**

Ben Macdui

On the North Ridge of Bynack More

Option To omit this first hill, just keep on down the valley south to Fords of Avon.

Escape route: From this wide col, a straightforward escape route drops due north into Strath Nethy for Bynack Stable. The path is rough and then very boggy, but sheltered.

Bynack More. The rough stony path reaches almost 800m, then forks again – the right fork, up the north ridge of Bynack More, will be the return route. So take the left one, continuing southeast. The path dips and crosses a stream, then climbs briefly. It bends south to dip again into the pass west of Creag Mhor. ◀

Head up the rough and pathless slope ahead (southeast), onto Creag Mhor's gravelly summit plateau. Despite its lowness, **Creag Mhor** (Krek Vore – large crag) is a true Cairngorm, and so has various granite tors, one of which forms the actual top (4.5hr). Creag Mhor's rough but easy southwest ridge runs down to **Fords of Avon** with its metal box shelter surrounded by stones.

A poorly defined path heads up to right of the stream, to the foot of **Loch Avon**. A large pink boulder gives shelter from windblown spray off the loch. From here a path of peat and large boulders slants up to the right, to reach the Saddle. ◀

From the Saddle the gentle ridge leads easily up to the right (northeast) to A'Choinneach – on the way up it is possible to get entangled in an area of massive granite blocks with deep rifts, but if encountered this is easily avoided on the right.

Continue northeast across a wide col, and join the ridge of Bynack More beside the Little Barns of Bynack.

(The true Barns of Bynack are out of sight down to the east.) The Barns of Bynack offer even less comfort than Bynack Stable, being simple granite towers. From the Little Barns turn up left, north, to the summit of **Bynack More**.

A sharp spur leads down northwards. At the 800m contour the descent slope eases off, and after another 1km northwards the path of the outward journey is met again. Turn left and drop northwest to **Bynack Stable**.

14 Beinn Mheadhoin

Start/finish	Heron's Field car park NH981094
Distance	36km/22.5 miles
Ascent	1000m/3400ft
Approx time	11.5hr
Bike approach	To Bynack Stable (saves 2hr)
Max altitude	1182m
Terrain	Tracks and paths, heathery slope, boulderfields, summit tor
Map	Harveys Cairn Gorm, OS Landranger 36 Grantown or Explorer 403 Cairn Gorm; shares sketch map with Route 13
Scrambling	130m (optional) Grade 1

Start as Route 11 (Lochan Uaine) and keep ahead at Lochan Uaine past the sign 'End of Waymarking'. When the track forks after 500m, keep right past the pine-girt Lochan a' Gharbh-choire to reach Bynack Stable after 2km. Cross the footbridge, and take the wide, rough path ahead up the slope of Bynack More. The path slants up southeast onto the broad north ridge of **Bynack More**, crosses it slantwise, and descends slightly across a dip. Now it bends slightly to the right, heading south through

Note After prolonged or heavy rain the Fords of Avon, and consequently this route, will not be passable.

Beinn Mheadhoin (Vane – middle hill) is, appropriately, the hill in the middle of the Cairngorms. Its summit boulderfield is dotted with granite tors, the Barns of Beinn Mheadhoin; its flanks drop into Loch Avon, Loch Etchachan, and the Lairig an Lui; a ring of even bigger hills protects it from the eye of the valley-dweller. No single hill, not even Macdui, is a finer, remoter, or more serious proposition than Beinn Mheadhoin.

Its standard approach is a long bike ride up Glen Derry, and a rather short walk via Coire Etchachan, with a return the same way. That is an unworthy approach to this august summit: only a really long walk does it justice. So instead I offer an approach from Loch Morlich, and an ascent of the almost untrodden northeast ridge. There's a scramble option on the way up, apt practice for the clamber onto the summit tor. Those last few moves are easy enough (unless iced) but still make this the mainland's second-least-accessible peak.

On the return you'll visit the Shelter Stone and Loch Avon – the finest and fiercest country in the Cairngorms – and be offered an option to cross Cairn Gorm itself as a second course.

the col between Bynack More (right) and **Creag Mhor** (left). It descends the valley of Allt Dearg (Jerrack: red stream) keeping left of the stream, to reach the stone-surrounded tin box of **Fords of Avon** shelter (4.5hr).

Here is a clear path junction. Cross the River Avon immediately beyond the shelter, and follow the path for 100m or so before stopping to assess your route up the northeast end of Beinn Mheadhoin. A band of crag crosses the slope above at 900m. A very small seasonal stream passes down through this, forming a little black gully rather left of centre, with a grassy gap alongside (NJ033027).

Cross the floor of the Lairig, north of the three lochans; this is not boggy (though Harveys think it is). Head up the not-too-heathery slope, with a grassy streak down the lower line of the seasonal stream. Keep on up through the crag gap, at first on bouldery grass to right of the stream, then cross it (deer paths) onto the grass slope on its left (south) side. Head up onto level ridge immediately above.

The direct continuation up the ridge is blocked by a slabby crag with overhangs – so take care with route-finding in mist. Cross the level plateau section westwards, to pass to the right of the crags onto the gentle northeast ridge. From here you can walk straight up the ridge to the summit of **Beinn Mheadhoin**, keeping right of the crag and bypassing tors.

Fords of Avon shelter below Cairn Gorm

SCRAMBLING OPTION (GRADE 1)

Alternatively, a few steps to the left, you can scramble the right-hand edge of the crags, starting up a smooth but very gentle slab (walk up, no hands), then directly up shelves and ledges, slanting to the left for more difficult (but still easy) ground. Above the crag is a fine little tor; scramble over that as well.

Continue up the ridge to the clump of tors at the summit of Beinn Mheadhoin. The biggest is the true summit. It is easily scrambled, up its near, northern, end, but vertical on the other three sides.

From Beinn Mheadhoin ▶ head southwest, on a faint path, over bouldery plateau past tors to the final tor (1163m). A worn-out path descends southwest to just

Option Alternatively, descend ferocious boulders to Stacan Dubha, a rocky Munro top with superb views along Loch Avon.

69

Beinn Mheadhoin, the mainland's second-least accessible summit (equal with Ben Avon)

above **Loch Etchachan**, where you turn right on a better path through a wide damp col.

The path drops towards Loch Avon, becoming rather eroded as it steepens. Keep left at forks to reach the **Shelter Stone**, very large with a cairn on top. Cross boulders north, to quickly pick up a path that crosses Garbh Uisge on boulders at a small island. Turn right on the rocky path to the head of **Loch Avon** (7.25hr so far) and along its north side.

EXTENSION FOR THE AMBITIONS

The ambitious could continue over Cairn Gorm. Just after the head of Loch Avon, fork up left on a path that slants round to the stream below Coire Raibert, joining Route 17. Descend by the ski area or even by Fiacaill Ridge for a splendid day of 31km/19 miles and 1450m/4800ft of ascent.

Follow the very rough path along the north shore of Loch Avon, crossing the Coire Raibert stream after 500m, and after another 500m forking left on a rough (and initially inconspicuous) path that slants up very gradually at first, then steepening to the Saddle.

Ahead, the small path drops into Strath Nethy. This is delightful, albeit rather rough and bouldery, in a small stony ravine with a stream leaping alongside. At the valley floor the path becomes a peat bog wallow, along the right-hand side of the valley, for the last 3km to **Bynack Stable**. Here you rejoin the outward route.

SUMMARY SUMMARY

CAIRN GORM

Gaelic	Cairn: stone-pile-type hill; gorm: blue or green
Altitude	1245m/4084ft, Scotland's 6th highest
First recorded ascent	In years after 1747 one James McIntyre raised the standard that he'd carried at Culloden on Cairn Gorm summit every 19 August, the date that Prince Charlie raised his at Glenfinnan
Maps	All routes are covered on each of OS Landranger 36 Grantown; OS Explorer 403 Cairn Gorm; Harveys Cairn Gorm
Transport	The frequent Cairngorm Link bus connects the northern car parks with Glenmore village and Aviemore. Note also the good Allt Mor Trail (Route 10) linking the northern car parks with Glenmore village. The funicular is not a walkers' link in summer, as there is no access out of the top station building.

Cairn Gorm is thought of as the hill that's been lost to hillwalkers in favour of skiers and rail travellers. It's true that the high car parks make Cairn Gorm smaller than it really deserves to be, that two of the northern corries aren't fit to be visited, and that the summit is usually a populous place.

However, Cairn Gorm is a lot bigger than its ski area. For an easy ascent, take the long and lovely Route 18 by the northern ridge. For a difficult and atmospheric one, use the Goat Path of Coire an t-Sneachda. The Fiacaill Ridge is a superb rocky scramble, one of the walkers' rock routes of Scotland; Pygmy Ridge is a delicious little climb. And then there are ways in around the back, by the shores of Loch Avon, that make Cairn Gorm every bit as big as it really is.

In all this, just avoid Route 19 under the clanking of the chairlifts. It's given here as a descent route for the weary or stormbound, or else, of course, on skis.

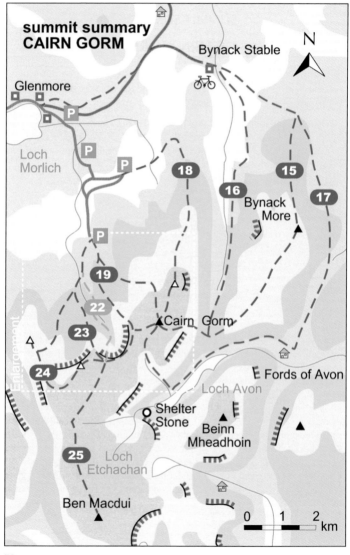

summit summary
CAIRN GORM

Bynack Stable

N

Glenmore

Loch
Morlich

18

16

15

17

Bynack
More

19

22

23

Cairn Gorm

Fords of Avon

24

Loch Avon

Shelter
Stone

Beinn
Mheadhoin

25

Loch
Etchachan

Ben Macdui

0   1   2
km

CAIRN GORM ROUTES

15 Bynack More and the Saddle

16 Strath Nethy and the Saddle

17 Lairig an Lui, Loch Avon, Coire Raibert

18 Lochan na Beinne and Cnap Coire na Spreidhe

19 Coire Cas (descent)

20 Coire an t-Sneachda: Headwall (scramble Grade 1)

21 Coire an t-Sneachda: Pygmy Ridge (scramble Grade 3)

22 Coire an t-Sneachda: Goat Path

23 Fiacaill Ridge of Coire an t-Sneachda (scramble Grade 1)

24 Lurcher's Crag

25 Plateau route from Macdui

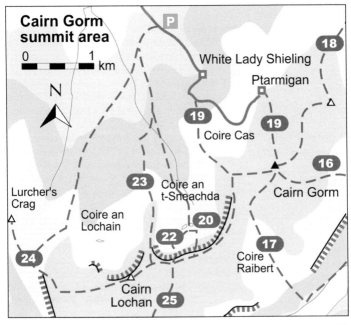

15 Bynack More and the Saddle

Start	Glenmore village NH980094
Distance up	16.5km/10 miles
Ascent	1300m/4300ft
Approx time up	7.25hr
Terrain	Path, stony ridges and plateau

Difficult
■ ■ ■ ■

This long route in around the back bags you a bonus Munro and gives not an inkling of the ski development. The going is fairly easy, but in cloud the navigation gets complicated.

Start at Heron's Field (or any other Glenmore parking place). Head upstream left of the river, and after 600m turn left on a smaller track. Do not enter Glenmore Lodge Firing Range (gate and stile ahead) but take the path continuing on the right. At a wide forest road turn right, passing **Lochan Uaine** in the jaws of the Pass of Ryvoan. After another 400m at a track junction turn right, signed 'Braemar'.

Route 16 turns off upstream.

In 2km the small hut at **Bynack Stable** offered basic shelter, but blew down in 2005. Cross the footbridge ◄ and take the path ahead slanting up onto the shoulder of Bynack More. At the path's highest point ◄ leave it and head directly uphill, south. The final climb starts at a granite tor at the 900m contour. The ascent above this is steep at first, then along a very pleasant ridge with rocky lumps to the summit of **Bynack More**.

Route 17 (Coire Raibert) keeps ahead here.

From the summit head down southwards to three notable tors on the main ridgeline (the Little Barns of Bynack: the true Barns of Bynack are out of sight down on the left). Turn down right, southwest, to cross a wide col and climb onto A'Choinneach. It's an undistinguished flat summit but for the Loch Avon view.

Head south for 300m almost level, then down south-west to **the Saddle**. ▶ Climb the slope opposite, steeply at first to a small granite outcrop which is easily bypassed on the left (south) side. Above that, go straight up a featureless slope to **Cairn Gorm** summit with its weather station and cairn.

Route 16 (Strath Nethy) rejoins.

16 Strath Nethy and the Saddle

Start	Glenmore village NH980094
Distance up	14.5km/9 miles
Ascent	900m/3000ft
Approx time up	6hr
Terrain	Path, very boggy in Strath Nethy; stony slope and plateau

This is the shortest way to gain Cairn Gorm on the ski-free side. The trek up Strath Nethy is unpleasantly peaty, but you do get the Avon-head view from the Saddle. The route is very useful in reverse, as the sheltered escape from Loch Avon: it is described in this direction in Route 14 (Beinn Mheadhoin).

Start as Route 15 (Bynack More) and follow it to **Bynack Stable**. Across the footbridge turn right, and head up-valley on a path that's boggy for the first 3km. As the valley steepens, it gets much nicer, with the path running up a stony ravine, left of the stream, to the Saddle. Here Route 15 is rejoined.

17 Lairig an Lui,
Loch Avon, Coire Raibert

Difficulty

Start	Glenmore village NH980094
Ascent	1100m/3600ft
Distance up	20.5km/13 miles
Approx time up	7.75hr
Terrain	Paths, sometimes sketchy, wet or steep

Taking in Loch Avon is probably the loveliest, but certainly the longest, way to reach Cairn Gorm.

Follow Route 15 to **Bynack Stable**. Once across the footbridge keep ahead, on a path that slants southeast across the northern spur of Bynack More. Still southeast, it drops slightly across shallow Coire Odhar. In the corrie floor the path turns south, climbing a little and dropping to the col point of the pass between **Bynack More** (right) and **Creag Mhor** (left). It descends the valley of Allt Dearg, keeping left of the stream, to reach the stone-surrounded tin box of **Fords of Avon** shelter (4.5hr).

Turn right, on a small rough path, keeping right of the river, to suddenly reach the outflow of **Loch Avon**. A rough path leads along the loch's right (northern) shoreline. After 2km, turn uphill on a path in the notch of the Coire Raibert burn.

The path goes up right of the stream, with the variants close to (or even in) the stream bed being rocky and slightly scrambly, and more comfortable than the gravelly and eroded variants on the right. The stream and path emerge into the wide shallow Coire Raibert. The path continues right of the stream to about the 1050m

*Cairn Gorm is even better from the back:
the Coire Raibert path
above Loch Avon*

contour. Then just strike up stony ground northwards to
Cairn Gorm top.

18 Lochan na Beinne and Cnap Coire na Spreidhe

Start	Sugar Bowl car park NH986074 or Coire na Ciste NH998074
Distance	7.5km/ 4.75 miles
Ascent	800m/2600ft
Approx time up	3.75hr
Terrain	Small paths, stony ridge and plateau

An easy and enjoyable ridge walk, with fine views across the corries as well as eastwards. The upper parts are a bit tricky in mist.

Start at Sugar Bowl car park if planning to descend to Coire Cas, as you can then complete the loop via the fine Allt Mor Trail. Walk east up the road, keeping ahead against the one-way system to the car park at **Coire na Ciste**.

From the far end of the Ciste car park, pass below the foot of a chairlift to a footbridge. Here the main path heads up Coire Laoigh, but turn off left, downstream, then along the top of a moraine hump. Cross the stream at the hump's end, go up the following hump, and cross the outflow of **Lochan na Beinne**.

The path continues up through heather to the left edge of a former experimental plantation (now mostly felled) and up into the ridge gap above. Turn back right (south) to follow the rocky and heathery ridge crest on a small path.

The ridge levels at a small knoll at 1000m. Keep on south across the plateau to a 3m-high tor, an important waypoint in mist. Turn southwest across a wide col and up grassy slopes, turning south again to find (if you can) the cairn of **Cnap Coire na Spreidhe** (Krap Corrie na Sprayah: Hillock of the Livestock Corrie) on its small outcrop. A stony grassy slope rises southwest to **Cairn Gorm** summit.

19 Coire Cas (descent)

Start	Cairn Gorm summit
Finish	Coire Cas car park NH989060
Distance down	3km/2 miles
Descent	600m/2000ft
Approx time down	1.25hr (on skis, 12 min)
Terrain	Paths

Rather than go up Cairn Gorm through the ski area I'd prefer to not go up at all. However, this is the safe escape route from the summit, especially in blizzards. To that end, the only cairns you'll see leading from the summit are the ones marking this descent, all others having been removed.

The descent from Cairn Gorm to the top of the Fiacaill a' Choire Chais is pathless and – in mist – perplexing

Descent From the summit, a line of closely spaced cairns leads down north to the funicular top station at the top of the ski area. Walkers can enter the top station to use the facilities (including the Ptarmigan restaurant), but not to buy a ticket down in the train. From here a track for emergency vehicles runs down to the car park, or there's a path down the right-hand, east, rim of the ski area.

In clear conditions, an equally speedy and slightly nicer way off is to head down west to the cairn (NH99890400) at the top of **Fiacaill a' Choire Chais**. In mist this descent needs careful route-finding as it's pathless. From the cairn a path leads northwest down the ridge.

20 Coire an t-Sneachda: Headwall

Difficulty	Scramble Grade 1
Start	Coire Cas car park NH989060
Distance	5.5km/ 3.5 miles
Ascent	700m/2300ft
Approx time up	3hr
Terrain	Steep grass and easy rocks
Scrambling	100m

In contrast to the Fiacaill Ridge (Route 23), this is a wild-country scramble. Judgement is required to choose between grass and rock, and to find the best route among the crags. The actual rock work is easy; the grass, if you go on that, rather harder. The interest lies not in the scrambling as such but in the situations, in the middle of much harder ground.

Start from the Coire Cas car park. From the end of the lower car park: take a footpath across a footbridge and slant up below a ski tow. From the end of the upper car

park: take a footpath across a higher footbridge, ignore a path up left, and contour across the foot of the ski tow. In a few more steps the paths join.

Keep ahead, west, signed 'Northern Corries'. The well-built path slants round the foot of the ridge Fiacaill a' Choire Chais. Ignore two well-built branch paths forking right, ▶ and follow the main path uphill to stepping stones over Allt Coire an t-Sneachda.

The path runs up 100m to the right of the stream, past temporary markers, to end abruptly at the corrie floor boulderfield of Coire an t-Sneachda. Head slightly left, along the right shore of the back right lochan. Turn left around the lochan to the stretcher box between the two back lochans NH993032. ▶

Immediately above is the area of scrappy rock between Aladdin's Mirror and Central Gully, with the broad Aladdin's Buttress further to the left. Go uphill from the stretcher box, slanting very slightly left, into the gully called Aladdin's Mirror (not 'Aladdin's Gully' which is to the left, east, of Aladdin's Buttress).

The gully slants back to the right. It contains grass and rock, with the best line using the

Looking down into Coire an t-Sneachda. The headwall is immediately beyond the walker; the Fiacaill Ridge forms the right skyline

Route 24 (Lurcher's Crag) takes the first of these side-paths; **Route 23** (Fiacaill Ridge) the second.

Route 22 (Goat Path) turns back right here.

81

clean bare rock of a small dry watercourse. At its top the gully steepens and becomes grassy: here contour out right, onto the ridge alongside, and scramble up gentle rock. After 20m the gully and ridge both end at the foot of an area of steep grass halfway up the corrie headwall.

For **Pygmy Ridge**, a scramble Grade 3, see **Route 21**.

Slant slightly right up this steep grass, on traces of path. Above is a line of crag. The right-hand end of this is Pygmy Ridge, ◄ and the path-traces lead to the foot of the climb.

> To the right of Pygmy Ridge is a minor gully that could be called 'Pygmy Gully'. Cross this onto the gentle rock rib beyond, formed between Pygmy Gully and Great Gully on the right. Scramble the gentle rock rib to its top, where the two gullies kiss and almost merge. Fork right into the grassier Great Gully – rather steep – but after 5m head back left onto the new rib formed as the two gullies diverge. Scramble gentle rock to the plateau.

Turn left to follow the corrie rim east uphill, then north downhill. From the Coire Raibert col, a path slants right to pass below the big cairn at the head of Fiacaill a' Choire Chais. The final slope of **Cairn Gorm** is pathless.

21 Coire an t-Sneachda: Pygmy Ridge

Difficulty	Scramble Grade 3
Approach	Route 20
Scrambling	100m

Pygmy Ridge is, as a scramble, perhaps a little serious, with its steep and exposed opening pitch. As a first taste of roped climbing (climbers' grade Moderate) it is a delight, with large reassuring holds, plenty of protection, and getting ever easier as it unfolds. A 30m rope will let the first pitch go right up to the comfortable niche stance.

Use **Route 20** for the approach. At the right-hand edge of the upper crag, Pygmy Ridge has a flat front 3m wide, and trodden ground at its foot.

25m. Climb straight up the steep front, on excellent holds. After 7m, head from right to left up a small chimney formed behind a flake. Continue straight up the front to a small stance on the right, 20m up the pitch. Slant up left 5m to a large niche stance.

25m. Leave the niche on the left to avoid some loose rock on the otherwise attractive right-hand line. Continue on the crest on the right, or open grooves on the left which are easier and less exposed, to a selection of stances.

25m. Scrambling, or rather harder climbing at the right edge of the ridge front, leads to a levelling in the ridge.

25m. Cross two little pinnacles, and walk to the final tower. Climb this from the right, starting just above the grassland above Pygmy Gully. Stance just below the tower top.

20m. Scramble the crest to the plateau.

Continue to the summit as Route 20 above.

22 Coire an t-Sneachda: Goat Path

Difficulty
▪ ▪ ▪ ▪ ▪

Start	Coire Cas car park NH989060
Distance	5.5km/3.5 miles
Ascent	700m/2300ft
Approx time up	3hr
Terrain	Boulderfield and steep little path

Coire an t-Sneachda (Corrie an Treyach: corrie of the snows), floored with boulder and open water and backed with crag, is one of the finest of Scottish corries. The Goat Path, a rock-climbers' descent route, zigzags up between the crags for a sudden arrival at the plateau. It's the quick and cheerful way up Cairn Gorm.

Contented climber above Coire an t-Sneachda: Fiacaill Ridge overhead

Start as Route 20 (Coire an t-Sneachda Headwall) to the mountain rescue stretcher box.

Now the small Goat Path slants up to the right, southwest, passing up along the base of a slabby crag. It crosses a small stream then zigzags directly up. In places

it's eroded down to bare rock, which forms comfortable steps. At the top it arrives at the plateau just below a large cairn on flat slabs (NH992028). This cairn marks the important col at the head of Coire Domhain.

Turn left to follow the corrie rim east uphill, then north downhill. From the Coire Raibert col, a path slants right to pass below the big cairn at the head of Fiacaill a' Choire Chais. The final slope of **Cairn Gorm** is pathless.

23 Fiacaill Ridge
of Coire an t-Sneachda

Difficulty	Scramble Grade 1
Start	Coire Cas car park NH989060
Distance	6.5km/4 miles
Ascent	800m/2600ft
Approx time up	4hr
Terrain	Path, bouldery ridge, and blocky granite scrambling
Scrambling	200m

'Fiacaill Ridge' means this fine scramble, officially 'Fiacaill Coire an t-Sneachda', on the west side of that corrie. It must not be confused with 'Fiacaill a' Choire Chais', on the east side of Coire an t-Sneachda, which is an easy walk or ski run down into the ski area. Fiacaill means 'tooth'.

The Fiacaill Coire an t-Sneachda is a fine scramble on clean, rough granite, with impressive drops into its corrie. The main lines are well marked with crampon scratches. However, most difficulties can be avoided. The approach over boulders is a little tiresome.

Start as Route 20, and take the second of the branch paths on the right, which starts as a row of flat-topped boulders. As the path crosses the base of the Fiacaill Ridge at 770m, leave it, and head up the crest on boulders and a sketchy path that soon fades.

At 1100m the ridge levels off to a rocky section that can be walked over. After the next level, stony section come three little rocky towers. They can be crested or passed on the right a metre or two below. Behind them is an excitingly narrow section leading to the base of the final tower.

This tower can be taken directly by its crest, or by an open chimney just to the right (west). If

Fiacaill Ridge: in summer conditions a straightforward scramble (Grade 1)

that seems too challenging, a path on the right leads into a short V-chimney that's not exposed, above which you can continue below and to right of the rocks or, better, traverse back left on shelves and ledges to regain the crest at the top of the steep section.

From the top of the steep section, an easier but still exciting crest leads up to arrive suddenly on the plateau.

Turn right, along the rim of Coire an Lochain, if you want to visit **Cairn Lochan**; otherwise descend left along the crag tops to the cairn in the col at the head of Coire Domhain. Here you rejoin Route 22.

24 Lurcher's Crag

Start	Coire Cas car park NH989060
Distance	9.5km/6 miles
Ascent	900m/2900ft
Approx time up	4hr
Terrain	Path, gentle stony ridge, and stony plateau

This route gives a glimpse into the Lairig Ghru, particularly impressive in blowing cloud, and a walk along the whole of the northern rim. I've used it as a sunset descent route, as the lower slopes and paths are easy enough to be done in half-light.

Start as Route 20, and take the first of the branch paths on the right. It runs level until it crosses **Allt Coire an t-Sneachda** 500m later. Again ignore a left fork, but stay on the main path, still southwest but now climbing slightly as it crosses the wide wet moor below Coire an Lochain, then heads up the broad stony spur that forms that corrie's western rim.

At the 1000m level, contour round to the right onto the level area at the top of Lurcher's Gully, and head up to the right to visit the small stony point of **Lurcher's Crag**. The Gaelic Creag an Leth-choin means, literally, 'crag of the half-dog'. The dog was a deerhound that fell to its death from the western crags.

From the summit head south to the brink of the Lairig Ghru for the tremendous views over the edge. Then cross the level ground southeast, and continue up in the same direction to the levelling at the top of the ascent spur. From here ascend gently east, moving to the slope's left edge for the views into Coire an Lochain, and following this crag rim to the plateau top of Cairn Lochan.

Follow the crag edge on the left, with an improving path, down past the top of the Fiacaill Ridge to the col at the head of Coire Domhain with its cairn on flat slabs. Here you rejoin Route 22.

25 Plateau route from Macdui

Difficulty

Start	Ben Macdui summit NN989989
Distance	6.5km/4 miles
Ascent	200m/700ft
Approx time	2hr (plus getting up Macdui)
Terrain	Featureless plateau, stony then on wide path

Head north on no clear path for 400m into the first col, then skirt the left flank of Macdui's North Top with a path gradually forming. After 1.5km is a path fork just before the small **Lochan Buidhe**: the lochan itself may be frozen

This, the archetypal Cairngorm plateau-wander, is an easy stroll in summer; more difficult in the mist or if fresh snow obscures the path; and in winter blizzards a serious question of survival. Route-finding is harder in this northward direction.

and invisible under snow. Bear right, passing just left of the lochan on a clear path that contours northeast across the head of the very shallow valley of Feith Buidhe and then along the flank of the equally shallow Coire Domhain. Feith Buidhe (Fay Bui) means Yellow Bog, though the valley is actually fairly firm.

A cairn on flat slabs (NH992028) marks the sudden arrival at the plateau rim, in the col east of Cairn Lochan and at the head of Coire Domhain, with the Goat Path continuing down directly ahead. Turn right, joining Route 22 (Goat Path, upward direction) around the plateau rim to **Cairn Gorm** summit.

Use any of **Routes 35–40** (Summit Summary Macdui) or **31, 34** (Shelter Stone Summary) to reach Macdui's summit with its large trig-topped cairn.

On Ben Macdui's North Top, looking back across the plateau towards Cairn Gorm

SHELTER STONE SUMMARY

Gaelic	Clach Dhion (Clach Yun)
Altitude	750m/2500ft
First visit	The 17 armed clansmen were already in residence in the 1790s (see below)
Maps	OS Landranger 36 Grantown, plus 43 Braemar for routes from the south; all routes are covered on OS Explorer 403 Cairn Gorm and Harveys Cairn Gorm

SHELTER STONE ROUTES

26 Strath Nethy and the Saddle

27 Lairig an Lui, Loch Avon

28 To Coire Cas or Cairn Gorm by Coire Raibert

29 From Coire Cas by Coire Domhain

30 From Linn of Dee by Loch Etchachan

31 To Ben Macdui by Loch Etchachan

32 To Carn Etchachan by Pinnacle Gully (scramble Grade 1)

33 Forefinger Pinnacle (scramble Grade 3)

34 To Ben Macdui by Avon Slabs (scramble Grade 1 or 2)

see also

14 To Glenmore by the Saddle and Strath Nethy

The Shelter Stone is a long way from civilisation, and even further now you can't use mechanical aid to the top of the ski runs on Cairn Gorm. Far from anywhere, it is correspondingly close to the hearts of hillwalkers. A 1500-ton boulder fallen from the crags of Carn Etchachan, it has beneath it space for 17 armed clansmen – or about five walkers with all their gear.

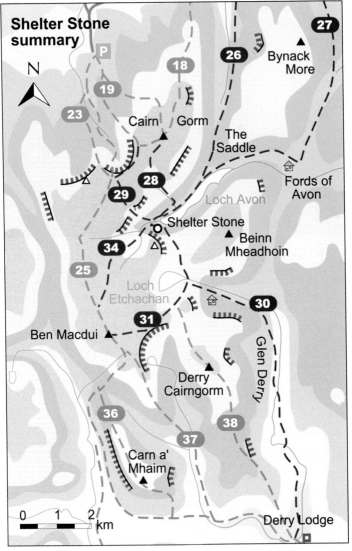

Loch Avon, with the Shelter Stone Crag at its head (seen from approach route 27)

Its main disadvantages are darkness and dirt – the floor is composed of orange plastic sheeting, earth, old tea bags, and worse. Its main advantage is 'location location location'. On summer weekends, or winter ones with good snow conditions, it fills up, and various nearby stones have inferior shelters beneath them. Most midges are discouraged by the chilly darkness.

In summer at least, the stone is fairly easy to find. It's the lowest-down of the large boulders in the group; it has a cairn on top; and the paths lead to its door. For GPS users, it's at NJ00190159. All routes in are strenuous and interesting; after heavy rain, those from the north may involve a long detour at the head of Loch Avon to cross the combined streams of Feith Buidhe and Garbh Uisge. The routes out include the area's finest scramble.

26 Strath Nethy and the Saddle

Start	Glenmore village NH980094
Distance	15.5km/9.5 miles
Ascent	500m/1700ft
Approx time	5hr
Terrain	Rough paths

The shortest low-level route, and one with many changes of scenery along the way.

Start at Heron's Field (or any other Glenmore parking place) and follow Route 16 to **the Saddle**. Slant down right (southwest) on a rough path that continues along the northern shore of Loch Avon. Cross the Garbh Uisge at a clump of islands (NJ002017) to the **Shelter Stone**.

27 Lairig an Lui, Loch Avon

Start	Glenmore village NH980094
Distance	19km/12 miles
Ascent	600m/2000ft
Approx time	6.25hr
Terrain	Rough paths

A rather longer route than by Strath Nethy, but on a better path.

Start as Route 17, by **Bynack Stable**, to **Fords of Avon** refuge.

Turn right on a path to right of the River Avon to the foot of Loch Avon. Continue along the north shore, or cross the River Avon (provided it's not in spate) to take the even rougher path along the south shore. Both paths lead to the **Shelter Stone** at the loch head.

28 To Coire Cas or Cairn Gorm by Coire Raibert

Difficulty
■ ■ ■ □ ■

Start	Shelter Stone NJ001015
Finish	Coire Cas car park NH989060
Distance	5.5km/3.5 miles (to Coire Cas)
Ascent	400m/1500ft ascent, 500m/1700ft descent
Approx time	2.5hr
Terrain	Steep path

Note The path up Coire Raibert is steep and slightly rocky, making this more suitable as a way of *leaving* the Stone than of arriving at it.

Start by clambering downhill over boulders towards the Garbh Uisge, to find a path and cross the stream at its clump of islands. Turn right on a rocky path across a tiny spur to the head of Loch Avon.

At the loch head a small path forks left to slant up into the little stream valley below **Coire Raibert**. The path crosses the stream and goes up to its right, to emerge into the wide shallow Coire Raibert. The path continues to right of the stream, to about the 1050m contour. For **Cairn Gorm**, strike up stony ground northwards to the summit; for **Coire Cas**, keep ahead to the cairn at the top of the Fiacaill a' Choire Chais and head straight down the ridge beyond.

The Shelter Stone is the largest of the boulders behind the walker. Above the Shelter Stone is the Shelter Stone Crag. Just visible at top right, the Forefinger Pinnacle

29 From Coire Cas by Coire Domhain

Start	Coire Cas car park NH989060
Distance	5.5km/3.5 miles
Ascent	500m/1700ft
Approx time	2.75hr
Terrain	Small paths

The shortest and simplest way to reach the Shelter Stone.

*Descending Coire
Domhain towards
Loch Avon*

Start along Route 20 then 22 (see Cairn Gorm section), to follow the Goat Path to its arrival on the plateau at the col east of Cairn Lochan. Keep straight ahead down the shallow and damp **Coire Domhain** (pronounced 'Dawan'), staying left of the stream as it tumbles out of the

corrie and down the steeper slope below. A path forms to the left of the stream.

About 100m above the slope foot, the path slants away left, before dropping down a moraine to reach the Feith Buidhe. Cross using a cluster of river islands, and turn left, on a small path along a moraine top parallel with the stream. After 100m it joins a larger path leading right, to the **Shelter Stone**.

30 From Linn of Dee by Loch Etchachan

Start	Linn of Dee NO063897
Distance	15.5km/9.5 miles
Ascent	550m/1900ft
Approx time	5hr
Terrain	Good paths

A long route that, once past Derry Lodge, becomes ever more beautiful.

Start at Linn of Dee, and follow Route 39 (see Ben Macdui section) up Coire Etchachan to the outflow of **Loch Etchachan**. A good path crosses the outflow and a low col beyond, dropping spectacularly towards Loch Avon. Halfway down the slope it swings left and slants down to the **Shelter Stone**.

31 To Ben Macdui by Loch Etchachan

Start	Shelter Stone NJ001015
Finish	Ben Macdui NN988989
Distance	5km/3 miles
Ascent	550m/1900ft
Approx time	2.75hr
Terrain	Paths, stony plateau

Good paths and interesting scenery past bleak Loch Etchachan.

Descending to the Shelter Stone from Loch Etchachan. Above, the Shelter Stone Crag shows off its superb rock climbs. Note the stubborn snow patch in Castlegates Gully, beneath which it is scree-filled but spectacular

Start by reversing the previous route, taking the path that slants up the southern slope below the great crag of Carn Etchachan. It then turns right across a low col to cross Loch Etchachan's outflow. Route 39 (see Ben Macdui section) now leads to the summit of **Macdui**.

32 To Carn Etchachan by Pinnacle Gully

Difficulty	Scramble Grade 1
Start	Shelter Stone NJ001015
Distance	1km/0.75 miles
Ascent	400m/1200ft
Approx time	1.5hr
Terrain	A gully that's mostly stony, but with a short rock pitch at the top
Scrambling	Up to 200m but only 10m unavoidable

The scenery here is more spectacular than the scrambling, which amounts to only a few metres at the end. That is, unless you intend to try the Forefinger Pinnacle (Route 33). Pinnacle Gully forms the right-hand boundary of the imposing Shelter Stone Crag that's directly above the Shelter Stone. (The equally imposing gully further left, between Shelter Stone Crag and Carn Etchachan, is Castlegates Gully, a rugged walk.)

Start by contouring west over boulders for 50m; then head straight uphill, onto the strip of grass and stones left of the stonefield that runs down out of the gully. At the base of Shelter Stone Crag, slant up right, into the gully foot.

The gully is boulders and stones to start with. At a steeper section, it may be possible to scramble the watercourse in dry conditions, otherwise take to grass on the left, on traces of path. Gentle rock ribs provide an alternative to the grass in places.

Continue up stones to pass the Forefinger Pinnacle and reach the final dripping rock wall. Climb this on the right, on wet but good holds, for 5m. Above the wall, loose stones rest on rock, so for the last few steps onto the plateau either use handholds in the gully wall on the right or else use the bare rock exposed by the watercourse.

Head left, east, along crag tops, passing the top of Castlegates Gully, to the small cairn on the crag rim. This could be considered the true top of **Carn Etchachan**, though the highest point is a less interesting spot 300m to the south. Carn Etchachan is not a Munro, but a subsidiary top of Macdui.

33 Forefinger Pinnacle

Difficulty	Scramble Grade 3
Approach	Route 32
Scrambling	20m

A short but spectacular scramble, on excellent rock, well worth the journey to reach it. The technical difficulty is well within Grade 3 or rock-climbers' Moderate, but the exposure is so spectacular that most will want to use a rope. A sling and a set of nuts give good protection.

Approach from below by Route 32 (Pinnacle Gully). Seen from below, the Pinnacle is particularly intimidating. If arriving from above, Pinnacle Gully is instantly recognisable by the Forefinger Pinnacle inside, its top level with the gully exit. Descend into the gully along its left-hand (west) side, with care as loose stones rest on rock, so use holds in the gully wall on the left or else bare rock where water has flowed or is currently flowing. Descend the obstructing wet wall below on good clean holds (Grade 1).

Either way, cross the gully floor to the base of the Pinnacle (boulder belays).

Climb the pinnacle by the short arête joining it to the gully floor behind.

Forefinger Pinnacle, ascended by the arête of its right-hand edge. The drop behind the climber is about 40m

34 To Ben Macdui by Avon Slabs

Difficulty	Scramble Grade 1 or 2
Start	Shelter Stone NJ001015
Distance up	3km/1.5 miles
Ascent	600m/2000ft
Approx time	3hr
Terrain	Stream bed, then gentle slabs
Scrambling	300m

A long and natural scramble from Loch Avon to the Macdui Plateau that is, to my mind, the most intensely enjoyable route in this book. Equally good at Grade 2 (seeking out the steeper sections) or at Grade 1 (avoiding them).

The Garbh Uisge and the Feith Buidhe run down off the Macdui plateau, falling in cataracts and joining near the Shelter Stone to run into the head of Loch Avon. The ground between the two streams, from 900m to 1100m, is filled with an expanse of very easy-angled slabs. At their foot the slabs steepen into a very smooth wall, which must be avoided. The Grade 2 option will do this by a narrow rib of rock to left of the Garbh Uisge: the Grade 1 option walks up grass further to the left, though an approach from the Feith Buidhe onto the slabs looks to offer an alternative here.

From the Shelter Stone **start** up to left of the **Garbh Uisge** (Garruv Ooshgi: rough water; the English word whisky is 'uisge').

> At the level of the crag foot on the opposite side, enter the stream bed and scramble in or alongside the water to the foot of the main

waterfall just above. Here (Grade 2) take to the rib of clean rock on the left – easy-angled, but quite exposed and poor in handholds. Alternatively (Grade 1) take to grass left of the clean rib.

Above the two-stage main waterfall, you are level with the base of the gentle slabs on the opposite side. The stream runs down to this point as a cataract of white water. The crossing of the foot of the cataract is on good holds, but well splashed; Grade 1 with water low, impossible in spate when a higher crossing will have to be looked for.

Walk up and to the right across very gentle slabs and grass (see picture below), with superb views back along Loch Avon. A low band of steeper rock crosses from the right. This steep band becomes gradually even lower, to peter away to nothing at the centre of the slabs midway between the two streams. Surmount

On Avon Slabs, setting out on the slabby upper part of the scramble

upper steepening

the trickle

Feith Buidhe falls

middle steepening

terrace

lower steepening

⸻ Grade 2 variant
⸻ Grade 1 route

this lower steepening, where it's quite low, near its petering-away point (Grade 1) or choose a line further right (Grade 2); to reach an almost-level terrace above.

The right end of the terrace is Feith Buidhe waterfalls. Midway between there and its left end at the petering-away point, a smaller stream trickles down and forms mossy pools on the terrace. Above the terrace the rock steepens again – the middle steepening.

There are many routes up this middle steep-ening. A line from the terrace midway between its left end and the trickly stream gives a succession of mantelshelves and sideholds, good serious scrambling with some exposure (Grade 2). Alternatively (Grade 1) head to the right along the terrace, and go up immediately left of the trickly stream, on much easier ground, slanting left away from the stream as the angle eases.

Walk up and to the left on more gentle slabs to the low wall at their top. This, the upper steep-ening, can be surmounted at a ferny niche at its centre (5m, Grade 1) or at will.

Continue southwest up the gentle stony slope and across the grassy hollow of the **Garbh Uisge Beag**, then up the stony slope to Macdui North Top. Head south through the broad stony col to **Ben Macdui**'s large summit cairn with trig point on top.

SUMMIT SUMMARY

BEN MACDUI

Gaelic	Possibly from Beinn MacDuibh, Macduff's Hill: Macduff was Thane (later Earl) of Fife, and owned estates on Deeside. Alternatively Beinn Mhuic Dhuibh, hill of the black pig.
Altitude	1309m/4296ft, Scotland's 2nd highest
First recorded ascent	Dr George Keith, Church of Scotland minister and surveyor, 15 September 1810. He arrived from Braeriach, took barometer readings to determine that Macdui was not the highest in Scotland, and continued over Cairn Gorm. Queen Victoria and her prime minister Gladstone both made the ascent in the 1850s.
Maps	All routes are covered on OS Explorer 403 Cairn Gorm or Harveys Cairn Gorm; northern routes are on OS Landranger 36 Grantown and southern on 43 Braemar, the summit itself being on both maps.

Macdui was Scotland's highest until mean Dr Keith took his barometer up to discover that actually Ben Nevis had 35 extra metres. It's still satisfyingly big, and

Macdui from the north. In bad conditions, the simple wander across from Cairn Gorm (Route 41) can get very serious

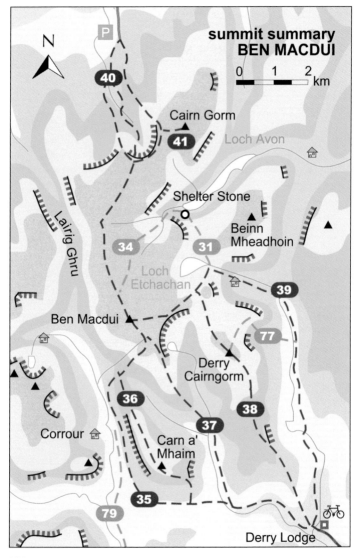

N

summit summary
BEN MACDUI

0   1   2 km

40

Cairn Gorm

41

Loch Avon

Shelter Stone

34   31

Beinn
Mheadhoin

Loch
Etchachan

39

77

Ben Macdui

Derry
Cairngorm

36

38

Corrour

37

Carn a'
Mhaim

35

79

Derry Lodge

MACDUI ROUTES

one of the hardest spots in Scotland to escape from if struck by a blizzard. In summer conditions, though, it can now be reached inappropriately quickly, by bike up Glen Derry or from the high car park on the side of Cairn Gorm.

Although the main paths are gentle – so much so that Queen Victoria rode her pony up Route 39 – there are large crags all around. The most intimate encounters with the crags are on routes from the Shelter Stone of Loch Avon. These include one superb scramble (see the Shelter Stone summary).

THE GREAT GREY MAN

Macdui is haunted by Ferlas Mor, the Great Grey Man, occasionally glimpsed through the mist whereupon the glimpser traditionally flees northwards over the stones and flings himself off Lurcher's Crag. Slightly less seldom he has been heard, his dreadful size indicated by the way he can keep pace with only one foot falling to the human walker's three.

35 From Lairig Ghru by Tailor Burn

Difficulty

Start	Linn of Dee NO063897
Distance up	16km/10 miles
Ascent	1000m/3300ft
Approx time up	6.5hr
Bike approach	To Derry Lodge (saves 1hr each way on all southern routes)
Terrain	Path, bouldery ridge and plateau

Less unpleasant than any other route up the steep western side of Ben Macdui, but still a tough haul up the boulders. If planning to return via Derry Lodge, you may prefer to walk in by Glen Dee on Route 79 (Dee and Derry) – this adds 30min.

Start out of the car park along a wide well-built path signed to Glen Lui. It runs through woods to join a track, where you turn left. (This path is not for bikes, which must start along the track itself from a point 400m east of the car park along the road.)

The track runs over Lui Water and upstream to the boarded-up **Derry Lodge**. Bob Scott's bothy was by the river on the left: burnt down in 2003 it is expected to be rebuilt soon. Next comes the boarded-up lodge among its trees and a wooden building with an emergency phone. Keep ahead to cross a footbridge beyond. ◀

Route 39 for Coire Etchachan turns right after this footbridge: **Route 38** (Derry Cairngorm) keeps ahead.

At once turn left, signed 'Lairig Ghru', under pines with Luibeg Burn on the left. After 2km, ignore a path that forks off right, ◀ instead bearing slightly left on the wider path, into a fenced enclosure. A small path turns off right, and leads to a ford of Luibeg Burn. Boulder-hop, or divert 400m upstream to a footbridge.

Route 37, to Macdui by Sron Riach.

Above the boulder-hop ford, the path continues through a gate in a deer fence. ◀ It is well worn and

Route 36 (Carn a' Mhaim) will turn off here.

stony as it bends right, around the base of Carn a' Mhaim, and into the wide deep valley of the Lairig Ghru. The path heads up-valley, to right of the River Dee, which is still quite large at this point.

Ben Macdui from Corrour bothy

You pass the turn-off for **Corrour bothy** on the other side of the valley. About 1km later, a small path forks off right. It slants up the heathery face, then turns uphill alongside the Tailor Burn, to peter out in a grassy hollow. Slant up right, to reach the level ground of Carn a' Mhaim's col. ▶

Route 36 rejoins.

Continue uphill on traces of paths, broken by stretches of boulderfield. As the slope eases, turn left (northwest) around the plateau rim, at once crossing the Tailor Burn (Allt Clach nan Taillear, named for three

IN DESCENT

This is the quickest way off Macdui to lower ground. However, it's easy to get carried down the unpleasant spur north of the Tailor Burn. From the summit start gently down southeast, being careful not to drop off the plateau until after you've crossed the Tailor Burn in its slight dip. Turn right (southwest) down the stony spur beyond.

tailors who tried to cross the Lairig Ghru on a winter night and died at the burn foot).

A very faint path passes a few unhelpful cairns and the ruined sappers' hut to the summit with its trig-topped cairn.

36 From Derry Lodge
by Carn a' Mhaim

Start	Linn of Dee NO063897
Distance up	15km/9.25 miles
Ascent	1200m/4000ft
Approx time up	6.5hr
Terrain	Path, bouldery ridge and plateau

It's not just that Carn a' Mhaim makes a bonus Munro on the way in. Northwards from Carn a' Mhaim runs the only ridge-walk in the Cairngorms. Regrettably, the ridge-walking ends abruptly below a 400m boulderslope onto the Macdui plateau.

On the ridge of Carn a' Mhaim

Start as Route 35 above, across the footbridge at Derry Lodge and up the Luibeg Burn to cross it at the boulder-hop ford or the bridge upstream. Above the boulder-hop ford, the path continues through a gate in a deer fence. After 500m and at the top of the path's uphill section, bear up right, on a small path through short heather, to ascend the southeast spur of Carn a' Mhaim. The small path runs up the crest of the wide spur to **Carn a' Mhaim**'s summit. The pathed ridge runs down north, quite narrow at one point, then drops right, to a wide col. Here you rejoin Route 35.

37 Sron Riach

Start	Linn of Dee NO063897
Distance up	13.5km/ 8.5 miles
Ascent	900m/3000ft
Approx time up	5.75hr
Terrain	Path, bouldery ridge and plateau

The easiest route from the south, and an attractive one, but no bonus Munro.

Start as Route 35 above. About 3km after Derry Lodge, with a deer fence starting down left, fork off right on a well built but smaller path that runs up right of the Luibeg Burn.

After 1.5km comes the burn that runs from Coire Sputan Dearg. Its crossing could be awkward in spate. The clear path runs straight up the nose of Sron Riach, passing just right of a tor. Above the tors the ridge steepens again, becoming bouldery as it swings right to the small cairn on **Sron Riach** (Gaelic Riabhach: brindled nose).

Sron Riach and Luibeg Burn

A slight drop crosses a narrow col with drops on the right, then comes another rise on bouldery ground. As the slope eases, keep ahead, away from the drops on the right, northeast. In 300m you dip slightly to cross the very top of the Tailor Burn, then rise gently up the stony slope, past the ruins of the sappers' hut to the summit.

38 Via Derry Cairngorm

Difficulty

■ ■ ■ ■

Start	Linn of Dee NO063897
Distance up	15km/9.25 miles
Ascent	1100m/3700ft
Approx time up	6.5hr
Terrain	Path, bouldery ridge and plateau

The extra Munro on the way up, Derry Cairngorm, is ferociously bouldery. A slightly more demanding way up Derry Cairngorm is Route 77.

Start as Route 35, to the footbridge at Derry Lodge. Cross, and keep straight ahead on a path across a meadow and up through trees. It crosses two ladder stiles to open hill.

The path (being rebuilt in 2004) runs up just right of the nose of Creag Bad an t-Seabhaig and onto the crest above. It runs up the broad ridge, then skirts right of the summit of Carn Crom across the top of a steep rocky slope: there's a scrambling move here and an exposed crossing above some slabs, and in windy or icy weather it may be better to cross Carn Crom's top.

After the following col (833m) the path fades. Keep north along the broad ridge, on grass then on boulders to the summit of **Derry Cairngorm**. Continue northwest over boulders through the col (1014m), and skirting the left side of **Creagan a' Choire Etchachan**, to join the good path on the back slope above Loch Etchachan.

Continue as Route 39.

39 Coire Etchachan

Start	Linn of Dee NO063897
Distance up	16km/10 miles
Ascent	900m/3000ft
Approx time up	6.5hr
Terrain	Path, bouldery ridge and plateau

Queen Victoria's route is sheltered most of the way, not steep, and has superb scenery of glen, corrie and loch.

Start as Route 35 above, to cross the footbridge just north of Derry Lodge. Turn right, on a path northwards up Glen Derry. It runs under mature pines to left of Derry Burn.

Loch Etchachan, and a helicopter removing contaminated snow after the aeroplane crash on Ben Macdui in winter 2001

After 2.5 km it crosses another footbridge, to join a path running up the valley to right of the burn. This well-built path soon runs along the line of a former track, now removed. It passes in and then out of a fenced regeneration enclosure.

In another 1.5km, fork left to a footbridge over Derry Burn. A good path heads up Coire Etchachan, past the **Hutchison Hut**, a small bothy, completely unfurnished last time I slept in it. The path crosses a side-stream here and continues up to left of the main stream to the outflow of Loch Etchachan. ◄

For Loch Avon/ Shelter Stone, continue north, passing right of the loch and through a wide col. For **Beinn Mheadhoin**, cross the outflow and take a zigzag path up ahead.

A clear path heads up left, slanting away from the loch on the slopes of **Creagan a' Choire Etchachan**. It continues slantwise southwest, keeping down to the right of the ridge crest that on the other side drops suddenly into Coire Sputan Dearg. At the slope top, with those drops immediately to your left, turn right, northwest, and cross gently sloping boulderfield to the summit.

Careful compass work may be needed. Head just south of east, ignoring cairns and being careful not to get carried down the first north-trending hollow, which is the Garbh Uisge Mor and leads eventually to Loch Avon. The ground rises very slightly, with the drop into Coire Sputan Dearg just beyond the rise. Turn down left at the beginning of the rise, finding a made path down northeast with a stream on its left. It descends easily to the outflow of Loch Etchachan.

40 From Coire Cas

Start	Coire Cas car park NH989060
Distance up	8km/5 miles
Ascent	700m/2300ft
Approx time up	3.5hr
Terrain	Paths and stony exposed plateau

These are the most convenient routes to Macdui. The Coire Cas route gives an enjoyable stroll atop the northern corries; the Goat Path an exciting ascent through the crags of Coire an t-Sneachda; and the Fiacaill Ridge a fine scramble.

Start using any of the routes 18–23 to the plateau of Cairn Gorm. At the col east of Cairn Lochan pick up Route 41 below, across the plateau southwards to Macdui summit.

41 Plateau route from Cairn Gorm

Start	Cairn Gorm summit NJ005040
Distance	6.5km/4 miles
Ascent	250m/750ft
Approx time	2.25hr (plus time to get up Cairn Gorm)
Terrain	Featureless plateau, on wide path then stony one

A gently undulating wander, splendid along the top of Coire an t-Sneachda but then with mere glimpses of the surrounding hills below the plateau edge. Route-finding is easier in this southward direction (which means, of course, that it's harder on the way back).

Reach Cairn Gorm's summit by any of Routes 15–24. From the summit weather station, head down west on no path into a level col, then slant out southwest below the cairn at the top of Fiacaill a' Choire Chais. A trodden path skirts the rim of Coire an t-Sneachda, south then west, to the cairn on flat slabs before the rise to Cairn Lochan.

Turn left in the col, on a clear southward path that contours around the shallow Coire Domhain and the head of the equally shallow valley of Feith Buidhe to **Lochan Buidhe**. Head south, gently uphill, on a fading path among stones. You should pass to right of Macdui's **North Top** (1295m). The North Top has only small cairns and no people; if you arrive there, just head south for another 500m to the main summit with its big trig-topped cairn.

PART 3

BADENOCH

The beauties of Scotland are mostly the mountains. Except that, alongside the upper Spey, they aren't. Cairngorm is the granite, but it's also the birch tree: and in particular, the birches of Badenoch. Here are miles of pathway alongside the silvery Spey, up rocky but rather small hills, alongside lochans left over from the Ice Age. At Kingussie you can slide in under the pines, emerge at Aviemore, skip into the Spey Way and wake up a week later alongside the Moray Firth.

As at Aviemore, Kingussie offers shops, bunkhouses and places to eat. Unlike Aviemore, Kingussie has charm as well as a chip shop. As a base for day walks in the big hills, Kingussie is inconvenient (although the hostels at Insh and Glen Feshie are better). As start point for an expedition, Badenoch is better: half a day of forest and river are the perfect preamble to the Braeriach Plateau. But the best of Badenoch is autumn under the birch trees, or winter below a blue sky and the white line of the mountains, looking across icy Loch Insh. Badenoch is the first choice for those whose tastes are low.

Badenoch is mostly low level. Birch and pignut on the Speybank Walk (Route 42)

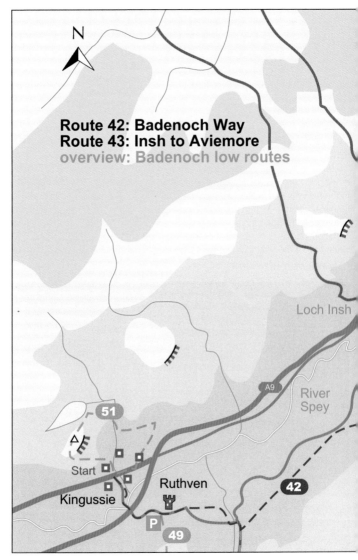

Route 42: Badenoch Way
Route 43: Insh to Aviemore
overview: Badenoch low routes

Loch Insh

A9

River
Spey

51

Start

Ruthven

42

Kingussie

P 49

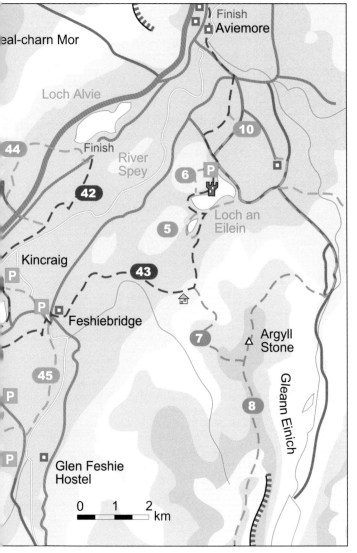

KINCRAIG

42 Badenoch Way

Start	Kingussie NH756006
Finish	Dalraddy campsite NH856083
Distance	18.5km/11.5 miles
Ascent	230m/750ft
Approx time	5hr
Max altitude	330m
Terrain	Tracks, paths, 4km of quiet roads
Map	OS Landranger 35 Kingussie; OS Explorers 402 Strathspey and 403 Cairn Gorm; route maps 49, 45, 44 almost cover this walk
Food on route	Restaurant Insh Watersports, grocer's shop Kincraig
Transport	Scottish Citylink coaches Edinburgh–Inverness link Dalraddy with Kingussie and Aviemore

Length

■ ■ □ □ □

Difficulty

■ □ □ □ □

This waymarked route, following the right-of-way of the old military road, is the backbone of low-level walking in Badenoch. With riverside, lochside, forest and open moor, it shows Badenoch at its best. Badenoch is pronounced 'Baid-noch' locally (though 'Baddenoch' is nicer).

While the official start is at Ruthven (also pronounced 'Riven') Barracks, I've moved it 2km down the road to Kingussie to allow bus transport between the two ends. Route 45 (Take an Insh) offers an alternative line through Inshriach, with forest lochans instead of Loch Insh. Route 43 (Insh to Aviemore) branches off by Loch an Eilein to Aviemore, whence it's tempting to continue the low-level walk to Loch Morlich, or even link into the Spey Way all the way to the Moray Firth.

Start at the bridge over the River Gynack in Kingussie centre. A signpost 'Badenoch Way' points south through a flower park. At its far end, exit right then turn left to cross the level crossing by the station. After a school, there's a footpath to left of the road, but rejoin the road through a kissing gate rather than veering away left on a dead-end continuation path. Follow the road across the Spey to Ruthven Barracks.

Continue east along the B970 for 1km, when a gated stretch of old road on the left leads into the car park of the Insh Marshes RSPB reserve. From its back take the waymarked path (RSPB white arrows and Badenoch Way green markers). This path has a fence on its right, and the drop to the Spey flood plain on its left. After a footbridge, a side path drops left to a hide, and this is a revelation for its sudden view across the flat marshes that had previously been concealed by trees.

The main path continues as before, to a junction where a viewpoint over the marshes is 100m away on the left. The main path turns right to cross a track, and heads northeast then southeast over hummocky ground with birches, then rejoins the top of the flood-plain bank. It goes through a small gate; 150m after this look out for the

Ruthven Barracks is worth visiting, open even at night under the floodlights.

Insh Church from Kincraig. The Badenoch Way is the route to follow to get away from the high snowfields

waymark where the path doubles back to the left down the banking, then turns back to the right alongside a wall. After a kissing gate the path joins the River Tromie on its left.

The path passes a small hut (water-level monitoring). In another 200m, watch out for where the RSPB path turns sharp right, but the Badenoch Way continues ahead for 150m on a green track, to exit onto the B970 beside **Tromie Bridge**.

Turn left across Tromie Bridge, then right at multiple signposts on a broad smooth track. After 300m turn left on a good track signposted 'Badenoch Way'. At Drumguish keep ahead onto a tarred lane that soon reverts to gravel. The track runs northeast into a plantation, and passes left of a clearing. After a gate, follow the main track ahead, bending right to a clearing under high-voltage wires. Here the track bends left, then left again along the plantation edge for 150m to a bench, where it bends back to the right. It heads northeast through heather, parallel with the high wires and then passing under them to a waymarked gate. Here join the smooth gravel track arriving from the right and continuing ahead through **Inveruglass**.

At the end of the settlement, the main track bends right, but continue ahead through an unwaymarked gate with a plantation on the right. The track gradually diminishes to a wide path, under the high wires, with two side-paths leading down left into Insh. The main path runs through overhanging birches to reach a road corner with houses.

Here a tall waymark pole marks the turn right, up a forest road, soon through a gate and in another 100m turning left at a waymarked track junction. Follow the new track for 400m then turn off left on a waymarked path into the trees. This contours northeast then climbs gradually past an artificial clearing with a picnic table, to meet an old track. ◄

Route 45 (Take an Insh) joins here.

Turn left, downhill northwest, past a waymarker pole. At the slope foot, with the high wires again above, turn right with a red-banded waymark. Where the track bends right into the trees keep ahead, waymarked 'Badenoch Way', down a stony old track under the wires. This soon joins a new track arriving from the right. Follow it down through a green barrier and past a path map, but just before reaching the B970 road, turn off right on a path. This runs alongside the road for 400m, to end at a gate. Cross diagonally to a gate into woodland on the other side.

The path runs through the wood for 200m to meet a green track. ▶ Here the Badenoch Way turns down left, waymarked: in 20m ignore another waymark with a white arrow, but continue ahead down the track to the shore of **Loch Insh**.

Turn right along the lochside trail for 500m, then bear up right (ignoring white-arrow trail markers but following green Badenoch Way ones) through open woodland to join the road.

Turn left, to pass Inshbreck house, where the path, now well surfaced, turns left back into the wood. It leads down to the Insh Watersports centre (restaurant here). Keep ahead out onto the road.

A tarred path runs along the roadside, first on the left, then on the right, then recrossing to the shore of Loch Insh and passing below Insh Church. It rejoins the road opposite a small car park. ▶ Turn left, along the road and over a long bridge, into **Kincraig**.

Ignore the first turn-off on the right, keeping ahead past the useful PO store to the next street on the right, Speybank Walk. The street becomes a track; where this bends left keep ahead on a good path. This runs above the River Spey through birchwoods for a delightful 1.5km.

The path exits through a gate onto a road corner (with a bridge over railway just left). Keep ahead along the road, and into its continuation track, which enters the corner of a pinewood (with the railway still alongside on the left). Just inside the wood turn right, with a waymark pole. The path bends back and forth through the wood, marked with many waymark poles, to emerge at a gate in the wood's southeast corner.

Here **Route 43** (Insh to Aviemore) forks off right.

Route 45 (Take an Insh) starts, and ends, here.

123

Turn left for 20m, through another gate, and turn left again alongside the wood edge, heading north for 250m. A waymark pole indicates the point to turn right, northeast, with a birch-grown dip on your right. Follow the edge of these birch trees, then head away half-left to a waymark pole. Here you can detect an old track running across the field, northeast, heading for the left corner of a plantation. Pass between the plantation and the railway to a bridge under the railway on the left leading into Dalraddy Holiday Park. Keep ahead through small gates to the car park that marks the end of the Badenoch Way. A few steps right is the entrance track onto the B9152.

43 Insh to Aviemore

Length
■ ■ ■ ☐ ☐

Difficulty
■ ☐ ☐ ☐ ☐

Start	Kingussie NH756006
Finish	Aviemore NH894118
Distance	28km/17.5 miles
Ascent	270m/900ft
Approx time	7.5hr
Max altitude	330m
Terrain	Tracks and paths
Map	OS Landranger 35 Kingussie plus 36 Grantown; OS Explorer 403 Cairn Gorm; route maps 45, 7, 3 almost cover this walk
Food on route	Snacks at Loch an Eilein Nature Centre hut
Transport	Frequent buses and trains Aviemore–Kingussie

Start as Route 42 (Badenoch Way), and follow it for about 10km into Inshriach Forest, then out again to cross

This branch route off the Badenoch Way takes you through to Aviemore. You lose the beautiful Speybank Walk, but you gain the beautiful Loch an Eilein, and you end up somewhere with both buses and trains as well as beer and plenty to eat. But after a beer and a hearty meal, you may be tempted to walk onwards at low level, through Rothiemurchus or even on the Spey Way right through to the Moray Firth.

A different link to Feshiebridge could be achieved by using Route 45 (Take an Insh) either clockwise or anticlockwise, but the line described here is quicker than either.

the B970 and go through the gate into the birchwoods around **Loch Insh** (NH830034).

After 200m the path meets a green track, with a waymark pointing left. But here bear right, away from the waymark's arrow, for 100m, to rejoin the road through a kissing gate. Turn left for 100m, then right into the road signed for Glenfeshie. Follow it for 400m, bending to the right as it passes a farm, and ignoring two tracks left into the farm. Just after trees restart on the left, take a third track sharply back left, running behind the farm and along the top of a clearing; then forking right to keep the forest and a low stone wall alongside on the right.

Still running northeast, the track enters woodland, with a blue-waymark trail joining from the right. Just before reaching the road at a forester's house, turn right (blue marker) up a broad forest road for 300m, looking out for a blue-marked path turning sharply back left and leading down to join the road opposite the tarred lane to the FC car park.

Turn right along the road, but at once step over the fence on the left to join the orange trail between the River Feshie (left) and road (right). It leads up-river to a grand pool and then up to the road at **Feshiebridge**.

Cross the bridge, and take a path ahead that climbs above the river to rejoin the road above. Keep left past a phone box, then turn sharp right on the road towards Glen Feshie hostel. After 200m turn left on a forest road northeast.

At the gravel road's first bend, ignore a tempting path running forward into trees. Stay on the track to a junction after 500m. Turn left on a track, northeast, for 1.2km to a four-way junction, signed to the left for Danavert. Here turn right, away from Danavert, roughly east. Ignore side-tracks first right and then left. About a mile from the four-way junction, a forest ride with wheelmark track turns off right, but ignore it and continue ahead for 200m. Now as the main track turns left, take a smaller one ahead to reach the edge of the plantation. Here several boulders have been experimentally carved with trial efforts at the SNH logo and Nature Reserve signs.

Keep ahead, on a wide path through regenerating woodland and boggy ground, passing the Inshriach bothy on your right. About 500m later the path fords a stream, then runs through low scrub of birch and pine, to join a bigger path at **Loch Gamhna**. Keep ahead, then turn left to cross a footbridge between Loch Gamhna (left) and Loch an Eilein (right). Continue on the main path ahead around Loch an Eilein. At the west corner of the loch, turn right onto a wider track, still alongside the loch. There is also a smaller path between track and loch. After a gate and a new house on the left, drop right, to the shore, to see **Loch an Eilein Castle**. Continue on the main track to fork left to the Nature Centre hut with ice cream, coke, crisps and toilets.

Pass the Nature Centre, forking left to pass through a car park onto the beginning of a tarmac road. Follow it for 800m to a house on the right, Milton. Just past it turn right on a track which after the next cottage becomes a wide path, and passes the Lily Lochan (formal Gaelic name is Lochan Mor, large lochan). It then bends left, northeast, and forks. Take the left branch, running gradually away from the right-hand one, then bending left, to reach the road triangle at **Inverdruie**.

Turn left then right to meet the main Glenmore road opposite the Rothiemurchus Visitor Centre. Turn left along pavement for 800m, then keep ahead on a cycle path with a footpath in woods on its left. A bridge crosses the Spey into Aviemore, where you turn right along the riverside, and take any bridge under the railway on the left to reach the village centre.

44 Druid Circle at Dalraddy

Start/finish	Kincraig NH834056
Distance	10.5km/6.5 miles
Ascent	40m/120ft
Approx time	2.5hr
Max altitude	250m
Terrain	Paths and tracks
Food on route	Small shop at Dalraddy Holiday Park
Transport	Scottish Citylink coaches link Dalraddy with Kincraig

Length

Difficulty

This walk is on tracks, some of them tarred, and as a 7.5km loop from Dalraddy could be done by bike. Starting from Kincraig is better, as it lets you add in the lovely Speybank Walk before visiting the farmland, forest and ancient ring cairn. And then you get to do the Speybank again in the other direction.

Start at Kincraig shop, and follow the waymarked Badenoch Way (Route 42) to its end at the car park near the entrance of **Dalraddy Holiday Park**.

Brown-arrow waymarks head into the caravan site towards reception, to a post with arrows pointing three ways. Turn right here, to enter the campers' enclosure by a gate, but after 20m bear right. After the next gate turn right, with fence on your right, on the pathless edge of a young plantation, to a ladder stile over a deer fence onto the B9152.

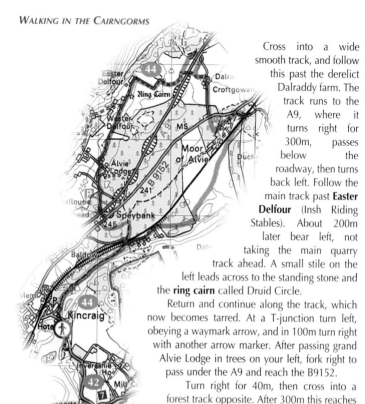

Cross into a wide smooth track, and follow this past the derelict Dalraddy farm. The track runs to the A9, where it turns right for 300m, passes below the roadway, then turns back left. Follow the main track past **Easter Delfour** (Insh Riding Stables). About 200m later bear left, not taking the main quarry track ahead. A small stile on the left leads across to the standing stone and the **ring cairn** called Druid Circle.

Return and continue along the track, which now becomes tarred. At a T-junction turn left, obeying a waymark arrow, and in 100m turn right with another arrow marker. After passing grand Alvie Lodge in trees on your left, fork right to pass under the A9 and reach the B9152.

Turn right for 40m, then cross into a forest track opposite. After 300m this reaches a track junction with waymarks pointing in various directions. Turn right, with a broken old

The Speybank Walk features once in Route 42 and twice in Route 44

fence on the right, to another junction with multiple waymarks. Here keep ahead on a track, which at once meets the railway and bends right for 50m to the road bridge over it.

Across the railway, turn right through a waymarked gate, to reverse the first part of this route along the Speybank Walk back to **Kincraig**.

GLEN FESHIE

45 Take an Insh

Start/finish	Insh Church NH836054
Distance	11.5km/7 miles
Ascent	170m/600ft
Approx time	3hr
Max altitude	340m
Terrain	Paths and tracks, mostly waymarked

Length

Difficulty

Give them an Insh – and they'll take seven miles! This is an example of joined-up walking, as it uses parts of the Badenoch Way, three forest trails, and two separate rights-of-way. The result is a superbly varied circuit, with lochside (under birches), riverside (under more birches) and forest lochans (under pines) as well as a cragtop viewpoint that gets above all the afore-mentioned trees.

Start at a roadside car park just north of Insh Church. Cross and bear right (Badenoch Way marker) to pass along the lochside below Insh Church and rejoin the road. Cross to the path to the left of the road for 300m.

At the entrance to **Invereshie House**, turn full left into a farm track (left of the house's entrance gateway) with a green signpost for Feshiebridge. The farm track bends right, with sign 'foot-path', and 300m later ends at a gate. Go through this on a path up into

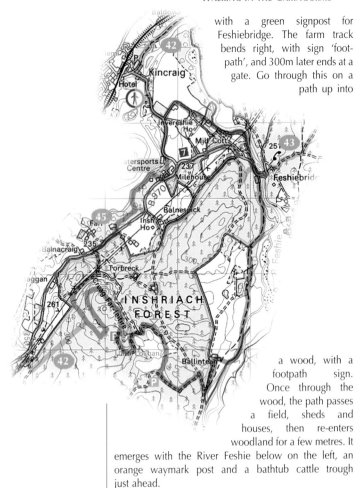

a wood, with a footpath sign. Once through the wood, the path passes a field, sheds and houses, then re-enters woodland for a few metres. It emerges with the River Feshie below on the left, an orange waymark post and a bathtub cattle trough just ahead.

Here turn sharp left between two rocks, on a mown path (Orange Trail) that doubles back right to follow the river upstream. The path runs under low-voltage wires; where high-voltage wires cross overhead, it turns right over a footbridge then back left. After another footbridge it reaches the Forestry Commission car park near **Feshiebridge**.

Go through the car park, onto the Orange/Yellow Trail, which runs between the river (left) and the minor road (above right) to a fine pool below the bridge at Feshiebridge, then up to the road at the bridge end.

Cross the road but not the bridge, keeping ahead into a track with Scottish Rights of Way Society sign for Glen Tilt. The track runs close to the river, past a yellow-topped post, then keeps on south, the river on the left being temporarily hidden by pine and birch. Just before a gate ignore the yellow trail turning off right; but go through the gate, and in 20m fork down left, signed as a footpath. The track drops to the flood plain, becoming a wide green path through scattered birches. The path

Uath Lochans from Farleiter Hill, with the Feshie Hills behind

heads south, crossing a small steam with waymark just beyond, and reaches the riverbank.

Just before the buildings at **Ballintean**, turn right (waymark arrows) at the corner of a trestle-fenced paddock, and left before an unpainted stone building onto a track. Follow this ahead (south) out past buildings, with pine on the right and birch on the left, to join a back road above the Feshie.

Turn right on the tarmac for 300m, then turn left into a forest road marked as 'X-C Ski Trail 3'. In 400m turn right, still on the ski trail, to reach the first of the **Uath Lochans**.

Turn right on a wide smooth path marked as 'White Trail +'. It runs along the south side of the loch, then turns left along its east side, to a path junction on duckboards in a marsh. Paths ahead and left are marked as 'White Trail –'. Keep ahead, as the trail runs past a second Uath Lochan and then along the side of a third to a Forestry Commission car park with trail map.

Head west out of the car park, on the combined Red/Green Trail that immediately joins a track. This bends left then right, to pass the fourth lochan, with crags above on the right. Soon after this ignore the 'White Trail –' forking off left. The track of the Red/Green Trail turns right twice (now heading northwest) to a junction. Here the Green Trail follows the track ahead, but take the wide path off to the right, Red/Green Trail. This follows the top of the crag already walked below, then bends left to **Farleiter Hill**'s summit with cairn and bench. It continues bending left to a junction. Here the Green Trail forks off left, but our route keeps ahead, now waymarked as Red Trail. The path at once bends right to meet a track. Turn right, downhill, with the Badenoch Way soon arriving from the left.

Keep ahead, downhill, now switching to the Badenoch Way (Route 42) for the last 3km of the walk. Finally, where the Badenoch Way follows the lochside below Insh Church, you can pass through a gate above to visit the church itself and descend a stepped path beyond to the start-point car park.

46 Carn Dearg Mor

Start/finish	Achlean NN852985
Distance	20km/12.5 miles
Ascent	600m/2000ft
Approx time	6.5hr
Bike approach	To Carnachuin, from west Feshie road (saves 1hr)
Max altitude	857m
Terrain	Tracks and paths

Length
■ ■ ■ ▫ ▫

Difficulty
■ ■ ▫ ▫ ▫

This Corbett (2500-footer) is on the 'wrong' side of Glen Feshie, separated from the main range. Accordingly, it offers particularly fine views in almost all directions. The approach, on an easy track, takes you deep into the lovely glen; the descent on a faint track is also easy except in mist. The Gaelic for Glen Feshie is Gleann Feisidh, with a slender vowel either side of the 's' changing its sound to 'sh', and 'dh' silent.

NOTE

The bridge across the Feshie at Carnachuin is marked as unsafe. Originally sturdy enough for Landrovers it is now somewhat decayed. Most hillwalkers judge that the crossing is justified, though I won't cross when the river below is in spate. To avoid the bridge, start from the road barrier near Tolvah (NN843995, very limited parking) or, better, cycle in along the tarred track to Carnachuin from the car park at NH842009.

Start from the car park at the edge of the forest north of Achlean. About 800m south along the road, a sign on a stone points left 'Carn Ban Mor', but keep ahead on the road for another 100m to **Achlean**. A footpath sign to the left of the building indicates the well-built path with waymark poles. It leads down to a gate in a deer fence.

Immediately beyond is a small river. This is most easily crossed at an island 50m downstream. Continue along the left-hand edge of the large riverside field, then bear right on a grassy track to reach (but not cross) a bridge over the River Feshie.

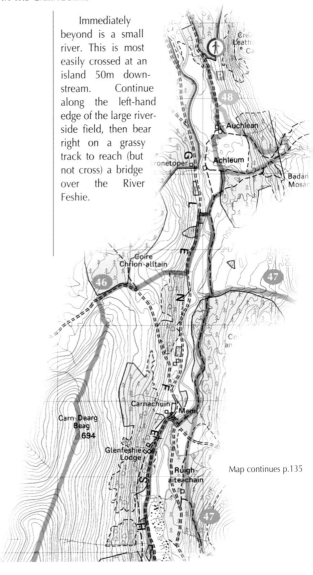

Map continues p.135

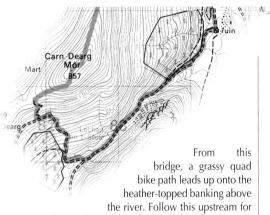

From this bridge, a grassy quad bike path leads up onto the heather-topped banking above the river. Follow this upstream for 300m only. As the river curves to the right, leave the quad track that stays alongside it and take a path heading slightly left, south, across the heathery moor, to reach the **Allt Garbhlach**.

Cross the river, which may be awkward and require a short or long diversion upstream. On the opposite bank, head downstream for 100m, where a clear path turns left into a tree gap. It heads south, after 100m crossing a rough track, and in another 50m joining a track that continues ahead. Ignore two small side-tracks on the left, keeping with the main track south. After 1km it leaves the plantation and joins the River Feshie on the right. In another 300m it forks; bear right along the river to cross the bridge at **Carnachuin**.

Turn left on the tarred track beyond. At **Glenfeshie Lodge** bear left on an unsurfaced track across the valley bottom meadow. Beside a pair of pines and a low ruin the track bends right, fords a small stream, and heads up into the sharp little valley southwest.

At the top of the valley, the track passes little **Lochan an t-Sluic** (An Tlik: lochan at the hollow) and in another 500m the track forks. Turn right, dropping slightly then climbing to the right of a plantation in zigzags. From the track's highest point, now above the plantation, turn off right: it's gravelled for a few metres, then becomes a peaty wheelmark track that reaches the ridge between Carn Dearg and Carn Dearg Mor.

The wheelmark track turns right, to the summit cairn of **Carn Dearg Mor**, and a smaller cairn 200m beyond that's a better viewpoint. The wheelmarks, gradually getting fainter, still provide a guide down the long gentle ridge to **Carn Dearg Beag** with its concrete cylinder trig. (Carn Dearg Mor/Beag:greater/lesser red stonepile.) Faint paths in the heather give good going down to the knoll at 540m. Here turn north (towards the front left corner of the plantation ahead) finding the least uncomfortable way down the last 300m to the track below.

Turn right, across the base of the ridge, with the track dipping slightly after the end of the plantation. Before its next slight rise, turn off to the left, heading down a slope of grass and heather northeast. Join a stream, with woods on the right, to find grassy going on its right bank down to the tarred track below.

Turn left to cross the stream, then fork off right on a grass track that crosses the meadow between road and river to the bridge (NN851964) near **Achleum**. Cross this to rejoin the outward route. Note Route 48 (Badan

River Feshie near Ruigh-aiteachain bothy

Mosach) which now offers you a short diversion to a woodland waterfall.

In Glen Feshie near Ruigh-aiteachain bothy

47 Mullach Clach a' Bhlair
by Coire Garbhlach

Start/finish	Achlean NN852985
Distance	19.5km/12 miles
Ascent	750m/2600ft
Approx time	6.75hr
Max altitude	1019m
Terrain	Some rough heathery ground (and quite a lot more if you fail to find the correct path down)
Map	OS Landranger 35 Kingussie (or 36, with map for route 46 above); OS Explorer 403 Cairn Gorm
Scrambling	50m (optional) Grade 1

Length

Difficulty

Clach a' Bhlair is often dismissed as a boring hill. This is because it's usually ascended by a boring route. Bike to Carnachuin, cross the dodgy bridge and take the Landrover track opposite all the way up – that's really all the route description you need if you want to be bored by Clach a' Bhlair.

But if you prefer to stay alert and interested, the route below offers an approach through the long hollow of Coire Garbhlach – an approach that's tough, and also at the top mildly terrifying as there's a scrambling option for the final waterfall, though this can be avoided. The descent route takes a forgotten stalkers' path that, if you can find it, treats you to a close-up of the Caledonian Forest: intimate enough that you'll find juniper in your socks and pine twigs lodged under the lid of your rucksack.

Start from the car park at the south edge of the forest north of Achlean, and follow Route 46 above (Carn Dearg Mor) to reach the **Allt Garbhlach**.

Head upstream – this is easier if you cross the river first as there's grass alongside the plantation. Rejoin the river as the plantation becomes scattered pines. Now it's rough heather and grassy patches, but the going gets easier as you penetrate **Coire Garbhlach**. This deep valley bends left, to show a fine waterfall. A deer path on the left avoids this, leading into the grassy upper valley.

Schist rocks, less poor in minerals, ring the Cairngorm granite. Globeflower and roseroot grow at 900m at the top of Coire Garbhlach

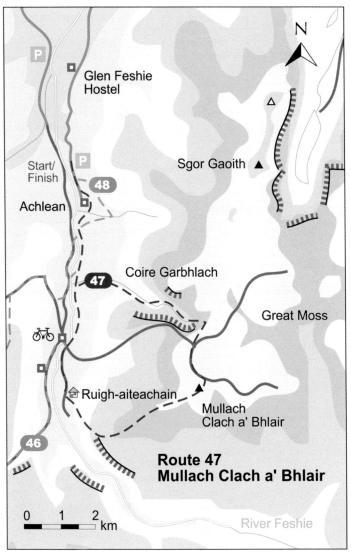

139

Here a branch stream on the left (**Fionnar Choire**) offers a grassy escape if required.

Continue up the main valley to its head, where it divides. The easy option is on the left, where a dry valley runs up northeast as grass and stones, leading into a little stream hollow just below the plateau. The right-hand branch (running southeast) is a succession of small cascades, offering some easy scrambling (Grade 1, but not much of it). The gill bends left to the final cascade, immediately below the plateau. Here are many wild flowers. The final fall can be bypassed by heading left, just below a small pinnacle, onto a steep and rather nasty slope of scree and earth, with the plateau 10m above.

Turn right, around the corrie rim, on a small path with big views down into the corrie. From the rim's highest point, head away from the corrie, south, to meet a track. Follow it to the right to a junction, where you turn sharply back left on a more-used track. This curves across the plateau, with wheelmarks from its highest point running up to the summit of **Mullach Clach a' Bhlair** (Vlair: humpy-hill of the plain, ie of the flat plateau).

Head down the southwest ridge, which is smooth-topped and gentle with low arctic vegetation and traces of wheelmarks. Head along the level Druim nam Bo (wide ridge of the cattle, though the reference is probably to red deer), down to another levelling below, and pass to the right of Lochan nam Bo to a well-built cairn on Creag na Gaibhre.

Head down northwest in calf-high heather. You should see the groove of the old stalkers' path crossing the moorland below, not far above the top of the trees. Look closer at hand to find the same path descending the slope you're on in wide, gentle zigzags that give a view up Glen Feshie at the southern angle of each zig.

Below, the old path has a small modern trod along-side it, giving passage through the heather. A little stone bridge marks where the old path crosses a stream (NN853918 Allt Coire nam Bo). Turn downhill alongside the stream, but once in the trees the path bends to the right to slant very gradually down the forested slope, heading directly for the bothy soon visible below. Keep alert to the groove of the old path and the small trod of the modern one, usually coinciding but sometimes a metre or two apart.

A wheelmark track joins the path from above, then turns directly downhill to reach the grassy valley floor 100m south of **Ruigh-aiteachain** bothy. ▶

Turn north, passing the bothy on a grass track. It runs over open grassland with the bridge of Carnachuin 300m away on the left, crosses the grassy track that's the dull way up Clach a' Bhlair, and in another 400m reaches the River Feshie.

The track is now clear, climbing slightly into forest away from the river. Ignore two minor tracks on the right. The track climbs briefly again to pass through a slight col, then drops to ford a small stream. In another 200m, the track bends left; here take a path ahead into the trees. After 50m this crosses another rough track; 100m later it emerges on the bank of the **Allt Garbhlach**.

Turn upstream to find a crossing point, and return along the outward route along the heathery riverbank and the riverside meadow.

About 75m before the river crossing near Achlean, note the ladder stile on the right; cross this onto **Route 48** (Badan Mosach) if you want to visit a fine waterfall.

> **Ruigh-aiteachain** (Rui Aitchechan), known as the Island House, is a beautifully sited and very popular bothy.

48 Badan Mosach Waterfall

Start/finish	Achean NN852985
Distance	4km/2.5 miles
Ascent	80m/250ft
Approx time	1.5hr
Max altitude	400m
Terrain	Rough little path beside a waterfall

Length
■ □ □ □ □

Difficulty
■ ■ ■ □ □

The waterfall tumbles down between the tree trunks on gentle granite slabs. It makes an excellent excuse for a bike ride up beautiful Glen Feshie, or can be tacked onto the end of Walk 47 (Mullach Clach a' Bhlair) or 46 (Carn Dearg Mor).

*The main route crosses the river twice. With the river in spate the waterfall becomes all the more worthwhile: an **alternative** is given without river crossings.*

Badan Mosach in Glen Feshie

Start from the car park north of **Achlean** at the south edge of the forest. Walk 800m south along the road, past a sign on a stone that points to a path on the left for Carn Ban Mor. Ignore that for now, but keep ahead another 100m to Achlean. A sign to the left of the building indicates the well-built path with waymark poles. It leads down to a gate in a deer fence.

Immediately beyond is a small river. This is most easily crossed at an island 50m downstream. From the river continue along the left-hand edge of the large riverside field, beside a deer fence. After 75m there's a decrepit stile over this fence. Cross, and take the path straight ahead (or the path slanting right, slanting back left to rejoin). The path runs through open woodland, with the waterfall soon visible ahead. The path rejoins

the river to cross a very ramshackle stile over another deer fence, and reach the foot of the Badan Mosach (scruffy thicket) falls, where the river tumbles down through the forest on a series of granite slabs.

Cross the river below the falls. Ahead now is a path, with a deer fence to its left, which could be used to short-cut out to Achlean. The current route heads up to the left of the water, on a rough path or bare waterworn granite, to the top of the falls. Here the forest gives way to smaller trees. A small path heads left, away from the river, gently uphill then contouring to meet a large stony path. Go down this to a gate and ladder stile. After another 300m, bear right, to reach the tarred road at the 'Carn Ban Mor' sign stone.

ALTERNATIVE TO AVOID CROSSING THE RIVER

From the car park walk 800m south to the sign stone, and take the path to the left 'Carn Ban Mor'. It crosses heathery moor to pass through a gate in a deer fence with a ladder stile alongside. Now turn right on a smaller path alongside the deer fence to the falls' foot. Continue up to the left of the waterfalls as before.

KINGUSSIE

49 Summer Road to Ruthven

Start/finish	Ruthven Barracks NN764995
Distance	9km/5.5 miles
Ascent	200m/600ft
Approx time	3hr
Max altitude	400m
Terrain	Moorland path, sketchy for a short distance, then tarred track and good path

Length

Difficulty

143

The route used by Hanoverian troops to reach the security of Ruthven Barracks from the south is still visible across the moors, though a little care is required right at the top. Those seeking to follow it further than this route does will find no onward path and a missing footbridge. Instead, this route drops into wooded Glen Tromie, with a choice of a heathery hill beyond (Route 50, Croidh-la) or a tarred track down the valley, for a finish through the Insh Marshes bird reserve.

Start at the car park at Ruthven Barracks. Above the west end, a gate with a green waymark leads onto a short fenced track. After 150m is a second gate. Here the right-of-way turns right, on a rough track, turning up left at the next field corner to cross the crest of a field to an abandoned house. Pass to left of the house to a gate and ladder stile onto open hill.

Cross the stream beyond at a stream junction, and take an inconspicuous green track ahead south-south-east. The track is much clearer as it curves around the western flank of **Beinn Bhuidhe** (Ben Vui: yellow hill – this hill has radio masts: the obvious track leading up to these isn't part of our route).

The track crosses a damp dip behind Beinn Bhuidhe, still south-southeast, and climbs the next slope as a sunken dip in the heather, with a modern path alongside on the right. Before the crest of the slope, and just before a small cairn, the sunken dip of the old road bears slightly right while our path bears left. It passes two more cairns over the crest of the moor, then goes down to a ladder stile to enter birch woods.

Above **Glentromie Lodge**, a signboard marks the start of a diversion to the path, where it turns left, with white-topped marker poles. It runs down to a stile, then follows a deer fence on its right to join the tarred access track of the lodge. The bridge over the River Tromie is just ahead. ◄

Route 50, Croidh-la, now turns right, up-valley.

Turn left on the tarred track for 3km to the B970. Turn left over **Tromie Bridge**, and in a few more steps turn off right through a gate into Tromie Bridge Meadow.

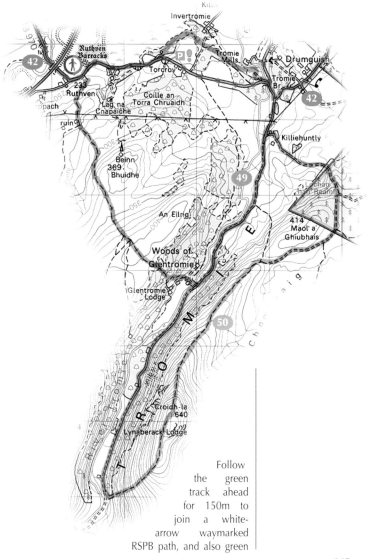

Follow the green track ahead for 150m to join a white-arrow waymarked RSPB path, and also green

The Summer Road to Ruthven Barracks provides the moorland path of Route 49

Badenoch Way arrows. Keep ahead on a path that joins the River Tromie. Follow it downstream to a kissing gate, and continue with a wall to the right for 200m. The path now zigzags up left and (at waymark) back right at the top of the slope.

The path now follows roughly the top of the flood-plain banking that defines the edge of Insh Marshes, over hummocky ground northwest then southwest. At a fence corner turn right for 50m, and cross a track to a gate opposite. In 100m, at a second gate, a viewpoint over Insh Marshes with a picnic table is on the right, while the wide green path continues on the left.

A branch path on the right leads down to a hide, with the sudden open view out over the marshes. The main path crosses a footbridge and continues as before along the top of the Insh-edge bank to a car park with another hide.

Leave the car park, turn right along a gated stretch of old road, and join the B970 for the last 1km back to the **Barracks**. Having walked the Summer Road to Ruthven, a visit to the place itself is now implied.

50 Glen Tromie: Croidh-la

Start/finish	Ruthven Barracks NN764995
Distance	16.5km/10 miles
Ascent	550m/1800ft
Approx time	5.5hr
Max altitude	640m
Terrain	Steep hillside, then path and track

Length

Difficulty

This extends Route 49 (Summer Road to Ruthven) to take in a steep-sided little hill above Glen Tromie. There's a steep rough ascent, but then a deer fence and small paths guide through the heather.

Start at Ruthven car park, and follow Route 49 (Summer Road to Ruthven) to the bridge over the River Tromie. Now turn right on the tarred track up Glen Tromie for 3km. A hut building is passed on your right, and 400m later the river rejoins the track. Here turn off left, up a steep slope of grass and stones, with paths made by cows, and a deer fence nearby on the left.

Above, the slope becomes less steep but also more heathery. A small path is alongside the deer fence. On reaching the first summit cairn the going becomes very much pleasanter. A small path leads through low arctic vegetation across the gentle plateau for 500m to **Croidh-la** cairn and a concrete cylinder trig point just beyond.

A path continues down the ridgeline, with the deer fence still nearby on left, the path becoming wheelmarks as the heather deepens. Where a deer fence crosses ahead, the wheelmarks head through a gate at its left-hand end.

Once through this gate the wheelmarks turn away east and are no longer helpful, but a small path continues down the crest of the ridge, with a plantation down on the left whose topmost trees are visible. At a sharp little col, the path continues confidently ahead, but turn down to the right, to the wide **Allt Chomhraig** stream just below, and a clear track starting just ahead. Follow this northeast as it climbs gradually up the valley side to a gate into a forest plantation.

Immediately inside the forest, fork left on the main track. It leads across a crest and down to a junction. Here it bends right towards a green barrier, but take the smaller, older track ahead. This runs down north, to a gate out of the plantation, then through two more deer-fence gates as it passes above the small **Lochan nan Reamh**. The track carries on down through **Killiehuntly** farm to rejoin the tarred track below. Here you rejoin Route 49 as you turn right towards **Tromie Bridge**.

51 Creag Bheag

Length
■ □ □ □ □

Difficulty
■ ■ □ □ □

Start/finish	Kingussie NH756007
Distance	7km/4.5 miles
Ascent	260m/900ft
Approx time	2.5hr
Max altitude	486m
Terrain	Waymarked paths, with one steepish descent

Creag Bheag is a rocky little hill with big views. Add a little loch hidden round the back, and this is just right after an afternoon arrival, as a preview of river and hills ahead.

Start at the Ardvonie car park, reached 100m up Gynack Road (not Gynack Street) from the bridge at the centre of Kingussie.

At the back of the car park is an information signboard (path map is on the *back* of the board) and toilets. Here a signpost 'Creag Bheag' points up along the top edge of a small park to its top corner. Emerging onto a street, with a signpost for Creag Bheag both ahead and up to the right, turn up the street to the right. After 200m there is woodland on the left, and in another 50m, at a street sign 'Middle Terrace', fork left into a track signposted 'Creag Bheag'.

In another 50m, turn left through a gate. The path heads northwest for 50m, through another

On Creag Bheag, looking across the Spey to the Monadhliath mountains

149

The Spey and Newtonmore from Creag Bheag, Kingussie

gate, then bends left, southwest. After a zigzag, ignore an unused path off right, instead turning left on the main path to contour around the slope under pines with a crag outcrop just above.

The path turns uphill, north, with two mauve-arrow waymarks, and a small stream flowing down the path, to a gap in a deer fence. Here it emerges onto the open hill, with a signpost just above. The clear path continues up through heather, with a broken wall on its right at first, and with occasional waymark posts, to the wide knolly summit of **Creag Bheag** (small crag; correct Gaelic would sound 'Krek Vek', but local pronunciation is 'Craig Beg').

The path continues northeast over a second cairned top to a stone shelter with outlooks over Kingussie. With waymarks still indicating 'Creag Bheag' (though that's now behind), it continues quite steeply down the spur beyond, towards the head of Loch Gynack. You'll see a gate into a plantation down below; the path will be passing through that.

The path drops into birchwoods above the loch. A signpost indicates 'Golf Course Circular Kingussie' both ahead and to the right. Keep ahead, now with yellow arrows on waymarks, to turn right, through the gate seen from above, into the plantation beside the head of **Loch Gynack**.

The path runs through the plantation to emerge at the top edge of Kingussie golf course. Bear left, leaving the plantation through a fence gap with gateposts but no gate. The unclear path passes left of an abandoned cottage, then along a little wooded ridge eastwards along the golf course top. After passing above a green, look out for a waymark post indicating a new and inconspicuous line for the path, turning down left away from the golf course for 30m to a section with a wooden handrail above the River Gynack. Turn left across a wide footbridge – here watch out for golf carts, whose drivers may be blinded by the sudden shade of the trees. Follow the golf-cart path for another 50m, then turn right down a tarmac track signposted 'Kingussie'. ▶

Follow the tarred track down, ignoring turn-offs on the left and a footbridge on the right. About 80m after passing the footbridge, a signpost 'Tom Baraidh' points left on a tar track through a gate. Immediately through the fence, green waymark arrows point up left into the wood. Follow the path, close to the wood top for 400m, then to a path junction inside the wood. Here keep ahead, signed 'Kingussie'. The wide path descends southeast, still with green waymarks.

At the wood's edge, a signpost points ahead for Kingussie. Leave the wood by a stile and a gate, then with a house (**Kerrow**) ahead turn right to a second gate. A green track leads down to join the house's access track. Turn right, away from the house, and follow the track down to the 30mph sign at the eastern end of **Kingussie**. Walk through the village to the start point.

Short cut This track could be followed down the river, at the first houses turning down right, to a footbridge, then continuing down-river to the walk start.

SUMMIT SUMMARY

BRAERIACH

Gaelic	From Braigh Riabhach, the speckled hill-slope
Altitude	1296m/4252ft, Scotland's 3rd highest
First recorded ascent	17 July 1810, by Dr George Keith, minister of Kinkell parish, on a survey trip; he poured an offering of whisky into the Wells of Dee and continued to Cairn Toul
Maps	OS Landranger 36 Grantown; OS Explorer 403 Cairn Gorm; Harveys Cairngorms (any of the three maps for all routes)

BRAERIACH ROUTES

52 From Glenmore by Chalamain Gap and Sron na Lairige

53 From Rothiemurchus by Sron na Lairige

54 Gleann Einich and Coire Ruadh

55 Gleann Einich and Coire Dhondail

56 Coire Dhondail scramble (scramble Grade 1)

57 South ridge of Coire Bhrochain

58 Ridge route from Cairn Toul

From Aviemore or the A9, Braeriach lives up to its name as the 'brindled slope', appearing as a gently sloping and smooth-topped mass. If you approach it from the west, across the Great Moss, that impression is only confirmed. Here is an undulating plain of stones, a dreich moorland dating back to before the Ice Age. The Dee emerges from mossy hollows among the stones and wanders away like meltwater over a permafrosted tundra.

Arrive at the summit, though, and any such impressions of smooth gentility will be blown away – and so, quite possibly, will your hat. On the southeast side, the great hollow of Coire Bhrochain drops in crag and pinnacle for 300m towards the Lairig Ghru. The name means porridge or gruel, and commemorates the fate

152

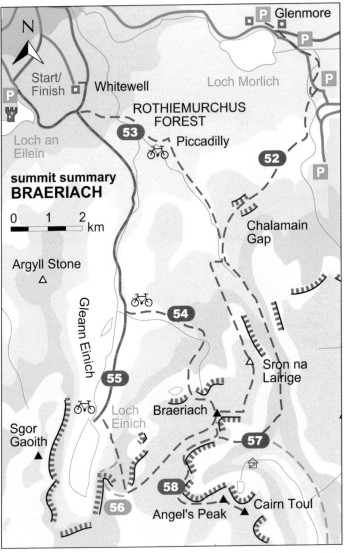

N

Start/Finish

Whitewell

P

Glenmore

P

P

P

Loch Morlich

ROTHIEMURCHUS FOREST

53

Piccadilly

52

P

Loch an Eilein

Chalamain Gap

summit summary
BRAERIACH

0   1   2
km

Argyll Stone
△

Gleann Einich

54

55

Sron na Lairige
△

Braeriach ▲

57

Loch Einich

Sgor Gaoith ▲

56

58

Angel's Peak ▲

Cairn Toul ▲

Ascending Coire Bhrochain's south ridge, with Cairn Toul and Lochain Uaine behind (Route 57)

of some unlucky cattle that wandered too far across the summit plateau, and ended on the corrie floor as ready-made soup.

More fine corries drop northwards. And south across the plateau, all the way to Cairn Toul, drops on the left-hand side are into the Garbh Choire, surrounded by Scotland's biggest ring of cliffs.

So Braeriach could be called a hill of two halves. Except that the eastern half has been carted away by the glacier, leaving simply one huge hole.

52 From Glenmore by Chalamain Gap and Sron na Lairige

Start	Glenmore village NH976097 (or Sugar Bowl car park NH986074)
Distance	12km/7.5hr
Ascent	1100m/3700ft
Approx time	5.75hr
Terrain	Paths, short rocky gorge at Chalamain Gap, exposed stony ridge to finish
Transport	Using the Cairngorm Link bus to the Sugar Bowl allows a return by any of the routes to Coylumbridge

Difficulty

The standard route, and a good one, with a fine finish along the rim of the Lairig Ghru. But unless you get clever with the bus, it leaves little choice but a return the same way.

Start at the Forest Enterprise information centre. Head southeast just above the road, then beside it, to cross the Allt Mor at Heron's Field (small car park here). At once turn left, on a path to right of the stream, to reach the corner of another car park and a long footbridge.

Cross this and turn right, up the well-made new path of the Allt Mor Trail. It crosses the road, and after another 1km reaches a long footbridge. ▶ Turn right across this, signed for Chalamain Gap. The path climbs the bank above the river and turns upstream, wide and clear. Soon it bends right, west, above the valley of a smaller side stream, and then drops to cross this. The path continues southwest, to enter the **Chalamain Gap**.

If starting from the **Sugar Bowl car park**, just drop south from the car park to this foot-bridge. Combining outward and return, this saves 4km and 1.25hr.

For 300m the way passes through a dramatic little canyon, walled with crags and floored with boulders. At its top, continue ahead on a clear path southwest. This slants down around the end of Lurcher's Crag, then drops with engineered steps to the **Allt Druidh**. ◀

Route 53 joins this route.

Turn left, upstream with the river to your right, for 200m, when the path crosses a natural boulder bridge and slants up the opposite bank. At the first bend, a smaller path ahead would continue through the Lairig Ghru (for Route 57). But keep to the main path zigzagging uphill, recently resurfaced in gravel with stone steps here and there.

At 750m altitude the path bends left, up the steeper north ridge of Sron na Lairige. Resurfacing soon ends, but the way is clear as there are large crags dropping on the left all the way up. As the ridge broadens, the now unclear path drops very slightly, then contours round the left (Lairig Ghru) flank of **Sron na Lairige**. In mist it's simpler to head south to the cairn on the 1180m north top, then across the slight dip to the main summit of Sron na Lairige; then drop slightly east of south across stony ground with no clear path. On the way down, the path reappears from the left, into a wide col just below. Follow the path up southwest onto what becomes a clearly defined ridge,

Reindeer of the Glenmore herd on Braeriach

with long drops into **Coire Bhrochain** on the left. Follow the corrie rim west to a cairn.

After the first cairn, the ridge dips slightly. Here you could divert to the top of Braeriach Pinnacle, which is on the left, 10m out from the plateau rim and 5m below. A short and easy boulder arete (scramble, Grade 1 for exposure rather than for any difficulty) leads out to the summit. There are very much harder routes up the back, the South Face giving fully 800ft of climbing (Diff). Further down the face is the multi-topped Black Pinnacle, also reachable by a technically easy but impressive mountaineering-style route (500ft to the plateau, Mod).

About 200m from the first cairn the crag rim rises again a much larger cairn that's the summit of **Braeriach**.

53 From Rothiemurchus by Sron na Lairige

Start	Whitewell NH916087 (or Loch an Eilein NH897085)
Distance	12km/7.5 miles
Ascent	1000m/3400ft
Approx time	5.5hr
Bike approach	To Piccadilly (save 1hr over return journey)
Terrain	Paths, and stony summit ridge

A dramatic and satisfying route, from the shelter of the forest up to the harsh stony plateau.

From **Loch an Eilein**, cross the loch foot and head clockwise round the loch for 1km, to a junction at its eastern corner. A bench with a stone boulder for its back is just ahead. Here turn left on a cycle path signed for Lairig Ghru and Gleann Einich. In 1km, at Lochan Deo, keep ahead, still signed for Lairig Ghru, for another 2km to the Piccadilly path junction.

From **Whitewell**, take a small, rough, path east for 300m, and turn right on a track through two gates to reach Lochan Deo. Turn left on the cycle path signed for Lairig Ghru, for 2km to the Piccadilly path junction.

At Piccadilly, turn right onto a smaller path. This runs to the top of the forest and into the Lairig Ghru. The path drops to join the **Allt Druidh** and goes up left of it into the jaws of the Lairig Ghru. The clear, rebuilt path out of the Chalamain Gap arrives from the left down a steep bank. Keep ahead, upstream, now following Route 52.

54 Gleann Einich and Coire Ruadh

Difficulty

Start	Whitewell NH916087 (or Loch an Eilein NH897085)
Distance	12km/7.5 miles
Ascent	1000m/3400ft
Approx time	5.5hr
Bike approach	To ford of Beanaidh Bheag (saves 2hr over return journey)
Terrain	Pathless slope of stones and short heather

A remote and rugged route, not popular. Coire an Lochain may only be Braeriach's second finest corrie, but it's still well worth a visit.

Starting from **Whitewell**, take a small, rough, path east for 300m, and turn right on a track through two gates to reach Lochan Deo. ▶ Keep ahead, south, signed for Gleann Einich.

To reach Lochan Deo from Loch an Eilein see **Route 53**.

After 2km the track divides: you can take either, the one on the left being more attractive. The tracks rejoin, cross the river Am Beanaidh by a small bridge, and in another 1.5km reach the ford of Beanaidh Beag.

Don't cross, but turn upstream on a clear path. But be careful: this path is formed by people looking for a crossing place of the river. After just 40m, opposite the first island in the river, look out for a much smaller path forking off left into the heather. Once found, this is clear and helpful, slanting away from the stream onto the flanks of **Carn a' Phris-ghiubhais** (Frice-hewish: the stone-hill of the price of pines). Continue up grassy slopes, keeping above the heather band that's next to the stream. At 600m altitude, bear right, above the top end of the heather band, to cross the stream at about NH940024. Head up slopes of heather and boulder onto the clear ridge between Coire Ruadh (left) and Coire an Lochain (right).

The ridge is pathless moss and rock, with crags on the left dropping into Coire Ruadh. It leads up easily to the plateau.

Follow the steep drop on the left-hand, Coire Ruadh, side for 200m to the highest point of the corrie rim, then head southeast, dropping across a very small col and rising to the summit cairn of **Braeriach** poised above the east-facing crags of Coire Bhrochain.

In Gleann Einich, with Braeriach ahead

55 Gleann Einich and Coire Dhondail

Difficulty

Start	Whitewell NH916087 (or Loch an Eilein NH897085)
Distance	16km/10 miles
Ascent	1000m/3400ft
Approx time	6.5hr
Bike approach	To head of Gleann Einich (saves 3.5hr over a return journey)
Terrain	Track, then path, then pathless grassy slope and stony plateau

A track along the length of Gleann Einich, and a dramatic stalkers' path onto the plateau. The 3km up Einich Cairn and across the plateau is path-less, and exposed to the weather. In mist it requires careful navigation.

Start as Route 54 from Whitewell, Loch an Eilein or even Aviemore, to reach the ford of **Am Beanaidh Beag**. This can be impassible in spate; otherwise it is crossed most easily at an island 100m upstream.

Continue on the track for another 3km, where it bends right towards the foot of Loch Einich. Here a cairn marks the start of a path climbing left. This passes below a waterfall burn then climbs to the flat floor of **Coire Dhondail**. ◄

Turn off the path here for the scramble of **Route 56**.

The path now climbs left up the left-hand corrie wall. It is clear and well rebuilt, but as it slants up the steep headwall, one section is very easy scrambling on the outer rim of a rocky groove. The path crosses the head of the first waterfall, ◄ to join the stream that forms the second of them and follow it up onto the plateau.

An alternative, rougher but with finer views, goes up to left of this stream, next to the brink of Gleann Einich, onto **Einich Cairn**.

Here turn left, up grassy slopes with no path. Head straight uphill, or follow the stream on the left. Heading

The source of the River Dee, at over 1200m on the Braeriach plateau

straight uphill will lead to the summit of Carn na Criche (1265m point on Landranger) which is fine, so long as you don't mistakenly believe you're on Einich Cairn; following the stream on the left will lead to the col between Einich Cairn and Carn na Criche. Continue northeast through this wide flat col to descend gently to the **Wells of Dee**. Follow the Dee stream down to the sudden edge of the Garbh Choire.

Turn left up along the crag top, but where it bends away right and levels, keep ahead uphill northeast. You'll probably regain the crag edge on the right just before the top. This is good, as it lets you look over the edge of Coire Bhrochain and admire its granite pinnacles. Follow the brink around the head of West Gully, turning east for the last 20m to the summit cairn perched close to the brink.

56 Coire Dhondail scramble

Difficulty	Scramble Grade 1 or less
Approach	Route 55
Scrambling	100m

A short and easy scramble, made spectacular by its views across Loch Einich to the Sgorans.

Follow the previous Route 55 as far as the floor of Coire Dhondail. Leave the path to cross the burn on the right and reach the top of the steep slope dropping to Loch Einich.

Scrambling on the west ridge of Coire Dhondail

Ahead (south) a sharpish ridge of scree, with a rocky crest, rises towards the plateau. Follow the crest of the ridge. There is some firm clean rock, and also some mossy boulders. All difficulties can be avoided on loose moss on the left. Either way, you quite suddenly reach grassy slopes at the ridge top.

Turn left, around the rim of Coire Dhondail, to cross a stream and rejoin Route 55.

57 South Ridge of Coire Bhrochain

Start	Sugar Bowl car park NH986074
Distance	12.5km/8 miles
Ascent	950m/3200ft
Approx time	6hr
Terrain	Rough slopes, mostly heather, then a bouldery ridge

According to the old climbing guide, Coire Bhrochain is the most imposing in the Cairngorms. I shan't argue with the hard men with the ice axes, though noting that the corrie does lack a lochan. This route takes you into the corrie, then up its left bounding ridge.

Start as Route 52 from the **Sugar Bowl**, and once through the Chalamain Gap drop to Allt Druidh and follow the path just above it southwards to the top of the Lairig Ghru pass. Alternatively (if your planned descent lies westwards) use Route 53 above, from **Whitewell** or **Loch an Eilein**. More ambitiously, you can enter the Lairig Ghru from the south by way of Derry Lodge and Glen Lui (Route 35), and use this route to start a loop over Braeriach with Cairn Toul.

Coire Bhrochain is the finest of Braeriach's thirteen corries

If approaching from the north, pass through the top of the Lairig Ghru path, to pass the **Pools of Dee**. Keep on the path for another 500m. If approaching from the south, follow the path past the wide entrance to the Garbh Choire opposite, to where it rejoins the northward Dee. From either start-point, head up steep heather and stones, with soggy grass options alongside streams, into the entrance to **Coire Bhrochain**.

At the back of the corrie floor is a stone shelter alongside a spring, a delicious lunch spot. But a direct line from the corrie floor onto the ridge is steep and uncomfortable, so return to the corrie entrance to start the ridge.

Turn west along a boulder moraine, and cross a field of large jumbled boulders to the foot of the ridge. It rises fairly steeply to start with, with boulder-clambering options. Soon the ridge eases, with increasing drops on the right down into Coire Bhrochain. The ridge eases further into a pleasant walk, with a view of the corrie headwall developing on the right. Finally swing around the corrie rim to the turning at the top of West Gully, with the summit just beyond.

58 Ridge route from Cairn Toul

Start	Cairn Toul summit
Distance	5.5km/3.5 miles + ascent of Cairn Toul
Ascent	350m/1200ft
Approx time	2hr from Cairn Toul
Terrain	Stony plateau, mostly with sketchy path

Difficulty

Given clear weather, this is one of the finest high-level walks in Scotland

From Cairn Toul's main (north) summit, a steep spur runs down west, with big drops on the right and a worn path, to reach a gravelly col. Go straight up northwest, still with drops on the right, to the summit of **Angel's Peak**. Again a steep spur with rough path and drops on the right leads down to a col. ▶

Keep following the crag tops on the right that drop into the Garbh Choire – this is straightforward, even in

Cairn Toul can be reached by **Routes 52–57**, as well as **80** and **81**.

Escape route 200m before the col, there's a safe escape into the Garbh Choire: **Route 63**.

The Falls of Dee

Walkers approach Braeriach summit

mist, but not if there are large dangerous snow cornices. The corrie rim rises gently, west and then north, to a high point below the 1265m top of Carn na Criche – no need to visit this, just keep following the corrie rim. It bends right, northeast, then turns back quite abruptly left, to northwest. At this point there is a view ahead to the **Falls of Dee**, where the infant river emerges from a snow patch to tumble down into the corrie below. Follow the rim round and gently downhill to reach the stream and cross it.

Now head up stony ground northeast, to regain the corrie rim on the right. At the slope top turn right, round the top of West Gully, to the large summit cairn.

SUMMIT SUMMARY

CAIRN TOUL

Gaelic	From Carn an t-Sabhail, stone-hill of the barn, describing the shape of the hill seen from the east or west, with steep ends and horizontal top.
Altitude	1293m/4242ft, Scotland's 4th highest
First recorded ascent	17 July 1810, by Dr George Keith, having just made the first recorded ascent of Braeriach
Maps	Harveys Cairn Gorm; OS Explorer 403 Cairn Gorm; OS Landranger 36 Grantown (from the north) or 43 Braemar (from the south), the summit being on both maps

Forget about its being a barn. Seen from the southeast, down the Dee, Cairn Toul is spectacular, soaring to a fine point against the sky. Seen from the northeast up

The refuge in the great Garbh Choire under Cairn Toul (start-point for Routes 62 and 63)

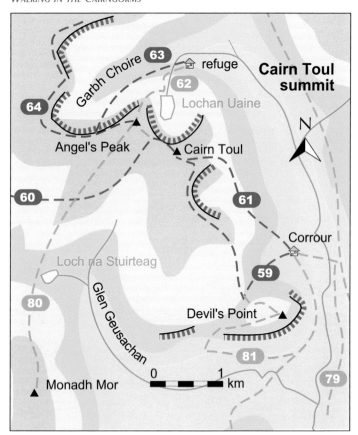

the Lairig Ghru, or from Braeriach across the great Garbh Choire, it's even better as its shapely satellite the Angel's Peak comes into the picture. Cairn Toul's two scrambling ridges, though not difficult, are almost alpine in atmosphere.

But then approach Cairn Toul across the Great Moss, and the barn comes back to mind. Cairn Toul is, quite simply, the accidental high point at the edge of a rolling grassland plateau. It's the last bite-mark of the glacier before the ice lost its teeth. And yet the barn has its charm; that way in from the west is invigoratingly long, and quite beautifully bleak.

CAIRN TOUL ROUTES

Near the top of Cairn Toul's south ridge (Route 59)

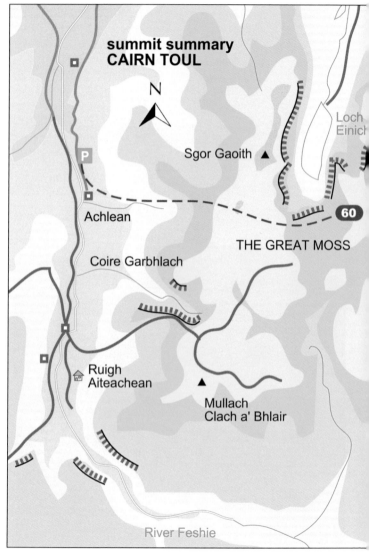

summit summary
CAIRN TOUL

N

Loch
Einich

Sgor Gaoith ▲

P

Achlean

60

THE GREAT MOSS

Coire Garbhlach

Ruigh
Aiteachean

Mullach
Clach a' Bhlair ▲

River Feshie

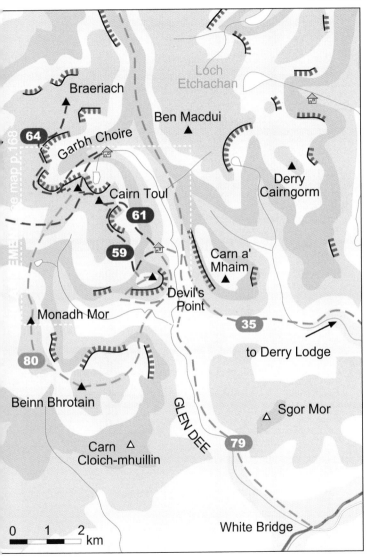

see map p.168

Braeriach

Loch Etchachan

Ben Macdui

64

Garbh Choire

Cairn Toul

61

59

Derry Cairngorm

Carn a' Mhaim

Devil's Point

35

to Derry Lodge

Monadh Mor

80

Beinn Bhrotain

GLEN DEE

Sgor Mor

79

Carn Cloich-mhuillin

White Bridge

0   1   2 km

59 Coire Odhar

Start	Corrour Bothy NN981957
Distance up	3.5km/2 miles
Ascent	750m/2500ft
Approx time up	2.5hr from the bothy
Terrain	Good path, then boulderfields

The standard route, and the safest and simplest descent (though the boulderfields can be awkward in gales). A downhill description is at Route 80.

CORROUR BOTHY

The start point is reached from Linn of Dee by Derry Lodge (Route 35, 3hr) or by White Bridge (Route 79, 3.5hr); or down the Lairig Ghru from Glenmore, starting at the Sugar Bowl (see Route 52, 5hr), at Whitewell or Loch an Eilein (Route 53, 5.5 or 6hr).

Start up the well-made path behind the bothy. It heads straight up Coire Odhar (Corrour: Dun-coloured Corrie)

Cairn Toul from Devil's Point

to the col northeast of Devil's Point. Turn north along the rim of Coire Odhar to join a path up ahead. There are in fact two paths: a clear stony one follows the tops of crags and the steep drop into the Lairig Ghru – much of the way is bouldery, but the views are superb. Alternatively, a grass path forks off left and goes straight up the slope to the cairned top of **Stob Coire an t-Saighdeir**.

A bouldery ridge leads down across a slight col, and up more boulder slope to the cairned south top of **Cairn Toul**. Ahead, a level ridge runs for 150m to the main top with its shelter cairn.

60 Great Moss

Start	Achlean, Glen Feshie (NN852985)
Distance up	13km/8 miles
Approx time up	6hr
Ascent	1150m/3800ft
Terrain	Pathless grassland

On the Great Moss

The approach across the full width of the Great Moss is normally a back-packing trip. The going is easy, the ambience is terrific, but in mist the navigation is a challenge.

From the car park, **start** down the road towards **Achlean**, but turn off on the path with a stone sign for Carn Ban Mor. A good path (actually two of them) leads onto the plateau, where you skirt the south flank of Carn Ban Mor and then head east between lochans onto the rising slope of **Angel's Peak**.

Either go up Angel Peak's southwest ridge, or bypass Angel's Peak by slanting up the right-hand flank of the ridge to the col between it and **Cairn Toul**.

61 East Ridge

Difficulty	Scramble Grade 1
Start	Corrour bothy NN981957
Distance up	2km/1.5 miles
Ascent	750m/2500ft
Approx time up	2.5hr
Terrain	Grass and heather slope, stony and rocky ridge
Scrambling	100m

Splendidly direct, a beeline from the bothy to the south summit. The lower slopes are not quite as arduous as they appear. The scrambling is very easy (only just Grade 1) but becomes serious at the top, where the pinnacle cannot conveniently be avoided. In a stiff westerly, this can provide a surprisingly sheltered descent route.

Route 59 summarises routes in to Corrour. **Start** by slanting up northwest, a beeline from the bothy towards Cairn Toul's south summit. This straight line avoids most of the boulderfields, while the wet grass and heather is fairly short at this altitude. Cross two streams to reach the foot of the ridge at the northern corner of Coire an t-Saighdeir (Corran Tighter: corrie of the soldier).

The pinnacle on the East Ridge of Cairn Toul

Go straight up the ridge. At 1100m, level with the floor of Coire an t-Sabhail on the right, a slabby band across the ridge offers the first scrambling. Above this, a bouldery wide ridge leads on up to another rocky section at about 1200m. Here the ridge rises into a slight tower (conspicuous from the bothy below). The tower has a gently sloping slabby front face: go straight up the middle of this for maximum scramble.

Now the ridge is narrower, mostly bouldery but with gentle rock slabs under the boulders. The pinnacle at the top gives a taste of exposure but is easy (except in high wind). Climb straight over its crest, then up the last few metres to **Cairn Toul**'s south summit.

62 Northeast Ridge of Angel's Peak

Difficulty	Scramble Grade 1
Start	Garbh Choire refuge NN959986
Distance up	2.5km/1.5 miles
Ascent	500m/1800ft
Approx time up	3hr from refuge to Cairn Toul
Terrain	Steep rough slope, bouldery then rocky ridge
Scrambling	100m

Tough but lovely, with two notable moments in the sudden arrival at Lochan Uaine and, equally sudden, at the summit of Angel's Peak. This makes an enjoyable evening ascent from the refuge, with a continuation not over Cairn Toul but westwards to descend by the Corrie of the Chokestone Gully (Route 62, 3.5hr for the circuit) or by Coire Bhrochain's South Ridge (Route 57, 4.5hr).

GARBH CHOIRE REFUGE

The small shelter in the Garbh Choire (Garra Churrie: Rough Corrie) sleeps three in scenic discomfort. From the south it is reached up the Lairig Ghru main path to the 670m contour opposite the Garbh Choire. From the north, the map suggests a path vestige from higher up the pass, just below the Pools of Dee.

Either way, cross the infant Dee, and contour into the Garbh Choire above the deepest heather, dropping to join the **Allt a' Gharbh-choire**. Cross it near the Bhrochain confluence, to find a small path beyond leading upstream to the refuge, which stands on a gravel knoll above the burn, and is covered in stones. (From Linn of Dee by Derry Lodge 4.5hr; from Sugar Bowl car park above Glenmore 4.5hr; from Loch an Eilein 5.5hr).

Start from the Garbh Choire refuge and head straight uphill, 100m to the right of the stream issuing out of Lochan Uaine. Up on the left, that stream comes down over steep slabs; on the right is more craggy ground. Head up through the gap between, finding a small zigzag path as the route choices diminish at the slope top. Arrive suddenly at the outflow of **Lochan Uaine**.

Turn right and head up the clearly defined ridge. At first it's bouldery, with some scrambling if you choose the larger boulders. Above 1100m it steepens, with a fluted block providing the start of the real scrambling. This block could be avoided on exposed slabs on the left, but better to surmount it and know that the technically hardest move of the ascent is now done.

The crest is jammed large boulders and little ledges, with small trodden paths weaving left and right to link the short scramble sections. Finally the ridge levels for a couple of metres to arrive in fine style at the cairn on the summit of **Angel's Peak**. Continue to Cairn Toul as Route 64.

Lochain Uaine under Angel's Peak, and Cairn Toul

63 Corrie of the Chokestone Gully

Start	Garbh Choire refuge NN959986
Distance up	4km/2.5 miles
Ascent	500m/1800ft
Approx time up	3hr
Terrain	Path, grassy slopes and gentle ridge

Difficulty

In all the 6km rim of the tremendous Garbh Choire, this is the only comfortable way up to, or down from, the Braeriach–Cairn Toul plateau.

For the approach to the Garbh Choire Refuge, see **Route 62**.

Start up to the left of **Allt a' Gharbh-choire**, on a small path and then on gravelly moraine tops alongside the stream. Unseen from the refuge, a little side-corrie appears high on the left, with a C-curved gully, the

Frosted rocks in August at the summit of Angel's Peak.
Four weeks earlier I was being bitten by midges at the same spot

Chokestone Gully (150m, Mod, winter grade III) dropping down its left-hand wall. At about 900m, bear left away from the stream, to walk up gentle rock slabs to the stone-slope emerging from this corrie.

Go up the right-hand edge of this stone-slope, passing below a small crag. From the corrie entrance, you need to get up to the right onto the crest of the low ridge above the small crag: this ridge forms the corrie's right-hand, northern boundary. You can scramble this ridge from its foot, on grass and rocks; or stay on the stone-slopes of the corrie floor and later head right onto the low ridge. The ridge runs up easily to the plateau, joining it at a wide, well-built but low cairn (NN948976). Continue left over Angel's Peak to **Cairn Toul**.

DESCENT

The ridge is invisible from immediately above, and so it is crucial to find that wide, well-built but low cairn on the plateau rim. The main plateau path is some 50m in from the rim at this point, which is probably why the cairn remains undisturbed.

From the cairn head down on magnetic bearing 40°, finding a small path. In a few steps the ridgeline appears below. The foot of the ridge ends on the left in crag: bear right, into the bottom end of the Corrie of the Chokestone Gully, then descend without difficulty to the **Allt a' Gharbh-choire**.

64 Ridge route from Braeriach

Start	Braeriach summit (NN953999)
Distance	5.5km/3.5 miles + ascent of Braeriach
Ascent	350m/1200ft
Approx time	2.25hr
Terrain	Stony paths, some bouldery bits

Around the rim of the Garbh Choire: magnificent.

Routes 52–57 in the preceding Summit Summary get you up Braeriach.

From Braeriach's cairn, head west for 20m around the head of West Gully, then drop southwest over stony pathless ground to rediscover the crag edge. Turn right (west) along the crag top, with Garbh Choire Daidh now down on the left. Soon you cross the stream that's the infant River Dee, about to drop over the edge in some fine falls. (In mist, descending too far to the right from the top of West Gully will mean you meet the Dee stream before the crag rim: in which case turn left and follow it downstream to the crag top.)

GARBH CHOIRE

The northern lobe is Garbh Choire Dhaidh (Dee); the southern is Garbh Choire Mor (Great), whose high corner holds snow patches that have completely melted just four times in the last century.

Follow the crag edge, now uphill, soon with a fine view back to the falls of Dee. Diverting up right for the 1265m Munro top Carn na Criche will mean missing some of the corrie rim; it's simpler just to stay on the edge. Continue around the rim of Garbh Choire Mor, dropping to a col on its south side. About 200m after this col is the escape into the Garbh Choire by Route 63. Otherwise, keep ahead up a stony path onto **Angel's Peak**.

A clear path leads down southeast to a col, then up east over boulders to the summit of **Cairn Toul**.

On the plateau edge above the
Garbh Choire, with Angel's Peak ahead

PART 4

GLENLIVET AND TOMINTOUL

Distillery visits and 1200m peaks make a dodgy combination. So it's just as well that Tomintoul's walks are mostly at a lower level. After a taste of The Glenlivet (or Glenfiddich, or Cardow) wander Glenlivet Estate. Here is a network of marked and signposted walks among the fields where the barley used to grow golden, through the woods from which peat smoke rose out of small-scale illicit stills. Amplify the route selection here with the free leaflet from the Crown Estates. And above the woodland and moorland rise gentle hills, criss-crossed with the paths of the whisky smugglers and the Landrover tracks of today.

The highest hills lie back from Tomintoul. The big-booted and serious minded tend to pass this corner by. They miss just two things: but each of the two is tremendous. The gorge walk of Ailnack, either along the rim or down in the clattering linn; and the back way in to the interesting side of Ben Avon.

River Avon at Tomintoul. Great low-level walking on Glenlivet Estate, or big hills up the river (Route 67)

GLENLIVET

65 Hills of Cromdale

Start/finish	Ballcorach, Strath Avon NJ155265
Distance	19km/12 miles
Ascent	900m/3000ft
Approx time	7hr
Max altitude	722m
Terrain	Tracks and rough grassland

Length

Difficulty

These are grassy hills, unfenced and largely unpathed, with Landrover tracks up and down the rough heather of the sides. Though low, they are higher than anything nearby, with fine views of Straths Avon and Spey as well as the big hills. This must be a fine tour on cross-country skis.

Cross the Avon on a very minor side road to a parking place on the right.

Walking north along the Cromdale Hills

Start along the minor road upstream for 2km to **Milton**. Opposite the house, a gate leads onto a grassy track uphill. The track bends left over a ford, and continues uphill as an ugly white flat surface carved by an over-enthusiastic bulldozer. The track passes up to the left of a tin hut marked as 'bothy' on Explorer maps, and ends at 500m altitude. Quad bike wheelmarks continue up to the plateau, reaching it at a fallen stone grouse butt (Carlag 698m).

Pleasant pathless walking continues for 1km to the summit of **Creagan a' Chaise**, with its trig and grandiose cairn with

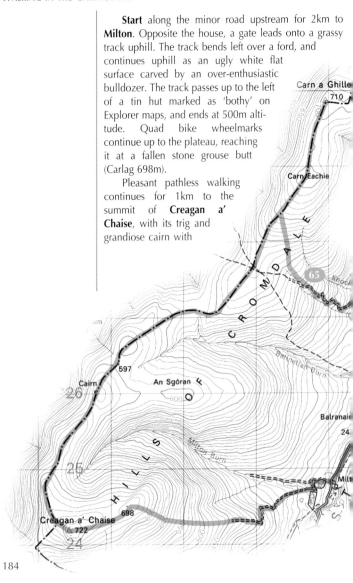

visitor book. Creagan a' Chaise means 'the craglet of steepness or difficulty', a serious misnomer for this flat hill.

Once off the stony summit knoll, a small path leads northwest and then round northeast, passing the top end of a fence running down to the left, to the tall pointed cairn at 635m. This commemorates the coronation of Edward VII. Pleasant going continues over a 610m hump, but rough grass-heather mixture is harder going through the 531m col and onto Reidh Lean. On your way along this flattening in the ridge you'll cross a right-of-way path, visible on the ground. Continue up northeast, still on quite rough ground, to **Carn Eachie**. It has a small summit cairn, and further cairns at viewpoints just down the eastern slope.

Rather than the obvious straight line, head left (north) to rejoin the rounded crest line for easier going on a small path through short heather, to the trig point on **Carn a' Ghille Chearr** (Stonepile of the Left-hand Lad, or the Wrong Lad).

Return along the ridgeline, keeping right of Carn Eachie summit. Retrace steps for halfway back down the slope to the levelling Reidh Lean. Now head down half-left, south, on ground becoming rougher. White posts mark future grouse butts, and among them you'll find quad bike wheelmarks, running down to a track top that's just to left (north) of Allt Balnabeinne stream. This track runs down and soon joins the track on the right bank that's marked on the OS maps.

Again this track has been 'improved' by a rampaging bulldozer, as far down as the 450m contour. But then it goes down as a pleasant one with a grassy middle. At **Knock** farm, turn right along a track that bends left to a junction near the Avon. Turn right to the car park.

66 Carn Daimh

Length

■□□□□

Difficulty

■■□□□

Start/finish	Tomnavoulin NJ207265
Distance	10.5km/6.5 miles
Ascent	350m/1200ft
Approx time	3.5hr
Max altitude	570m
Terrain	Waymarked paths

This adds together two of the waymarked routes laid out by Glenlivet Estate – though in the reverse direction to the main waymarking. It combines a wild little wood with the high-point (not terrifically high) of the Spey Way, and would make an excellent sobering-up exercise after a visit to Glenlivet distillery.

At the north end of Tomnavoulin, turn up into a small and unsignposted lane. The start-point car park is inconspicuous, but has a small notice board and a Glenlivet Estate stile onto the forest road at its back.

Start along the track behind the car park through a pine plantation, ignoring a waymarked path on the left (it's the return route). At the plantation edge, the track turns up right alongside the trees. At the first junction, waymark arrows point in all directions except to the right. Turn right, however, along a forest road. After a gate the track narrows, encroached by broom, and surrounded by self-seeded wild forest of larch, spruce and pine.

The track slants uphill, then bends left and steepens, soon with a deer fence just above. The track turns left, contouring back through the wood, through another gate, then descends to rejoin the track at the forest edge.

Turn right for 100m to a gate with a stile. Here bear left on a green track that fades as you cross a field to the

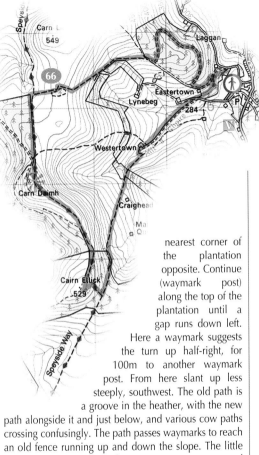

nearest corner of the plantation opposite. Continue (waymark post) along the top of the plantation until a gap runs down left. Here a waymark suggests the turn up half-right, for 100m to another waymark post. From here slant up less steeply, southwest. The old path is a groove in the heather, with the new path alongside it and just below, and various cow paths crossing confusingly. The path passes waymarks to reach an old fence running up and down the slope. The little peat path passes through this at an empty gateway, and turns uphill alongside it in short heather.

At the brow of the hill turn left alongside a new fence, and follow this as it bends right, down the western slope.

Path and fence reach the corner of a track where many paths meet. Don't cross a stile right onto the track, but keep ahead, obeying a Spey Way marker. A path to the left of the fence runs forward boggily, to the corner of a plantation. Turn left on the eroded path of the Spey Way, with the plantation on your right.

As the ground levels the path improves. At a signpost, an escape path marked 'Tomnavoulin' runs off left, but keep ahead signed for Tomintoul. The path gradually becomes a clear gravelled track, and runs up with a fence on its right to the summit of **Carn Daimh** (locally Carn Dye, stonepile of the stags). The viewpoint indicator claims to see Morven 100km north and Lochnagar southwards.

Various paths meet here at Carn Daimh summit. Keep on the track ahead, with a fence to its right, downhill now across open ground, to a gate into a plantation. The track runs just inside the plantation, with open ground out on the right. Where the track turns left, downhill, you can if you wish take a rutted ride on the right to visit the summit of **Cairn Ellick**. At the ride's top, with open hill ahead, bear left through a tree screen to another patch of open hill to find the summit cairn half-buried in heather.

Return down the rutted ride, and follow the main track as it bends downhill to a signposted T-junction. Here turn left 'Tomnavoulin'. A green track runs down through, then along the bottom edge of, the forest, to a gate with a stile. The track ahead crosses heather, gently downhill, but becomes a watercourse, so now take a new parallel track just below. Pass through two empty gateways with stiles alongside, then a stile beside an actual gate onto a clear track.

This track runs down to a ford with a plank footbridge, through a short plantation, and then down to another ford with footbridge below **Westertown** farm. Follow the track down to where the Eastertown track joins from up left. Here keep ahead, across two stiles, into woodland. The path runs along the foot of the wood, then up to join the track of the outward walk.

TOMINTOUL

67 Around the Brown

Start/finish	The Square, Tomintoul NJ167187
Distance	13km/8 miles
Ascent	300m/1000ft
Approx time	4hr
Max altitude	400m
Terrain	Tracks and paths
Food on route	Cafe at Bridge of Brown

Length

■■□□□

Difficulty

■□□□□

This walk is based on Glenlivet Estate's Walk 8, and gives views up and down Strath Avon, and a crossing of the historic military bridge. It can be shortened by starting at White Bridge (NJ133209), or lengthened to include Ailnack Ravine in Route 68.

Start at the Square in Tomintoul, and head north out of the village. (Tomintoul rhymes with foul, not fool; Gaelic is Tom an t-Sabhail, hill of the barn.) Just after a derelict garage, and 50m before the parish church on the right, turn left into a side street. At a T-junction, cross Cults Drive into a farm track. It bends right, and where it immediately bends back left keep ahead through a narrow gate onto a fenced path. This reaches the bank above **River Avon**, then bends right and up steps to cross the A939 to a track above.

Turn left to **Campdalmore** farm. Pass to right of the buildings to a stile with a signpost, ignoring the gate and continuing gravel track on its right. Instead, take a green track just below, which is the old military road. It slants downhill to a gate, then swings left around a field edge with views north, to a narrow gate. Keep ahead into a path descending through woodland nettlebeds, with wooden steps, to a road.

189

Turn right, away from the main A939, and in 150m turn left, with Scottish Rights of Way Society signpost for Dorback, to cross the old **Bridge of Avon**. Take the path beyond up to the A939, cross it, and turn left into a tarred driveway. Before the gateway to **Kylnadrochit Lodge**, bear right, on track now dirt. In 100m there's a lay-by on the right. Either turn up just beyond this between trees for 50m to a clear path above and turn right; or continue up the track for 200m and turn sharp right over a little ditch bridge, onto the waymarked path.

The path contours through the plantation then becomes less clear, turning up left along the plantation edge to leave it by a stile. Contour north above a fence, across a stile, then still above the fence to a second stile. Across this, a fenced track turns uphill, left, for 50m. From its top continue contouring above a fence, and then across open ground with juniper. After crossing a small stream, bear left, uphill, past a waymark to a bench. A faint green track now contours forward, passing 50m above a pylon, towards the closest corner of a plantation. Just before it, you join the uphill track of the old military road.

Turn left, uphill, and follow the track across a col and down to White Bridge on the A939. ▶ Turn left along the verge. As the road drops to the valley floor, with the cafe 400m ahead along the main road, bear left around the back of a crash barrier on a path down to a damp stony track.

Turn left on the track, which passes through a plantation then heads slightly up the valley side to ruins (NJ120193) marked as a dangerous building. ▶ Just before it, a waymark points up left. Obey its arrow, southeast, to pass above the building and then

Alternative Starting and ending here gives a circular walk, missing out Tomintoul, of 7km/ 4 miles.

Route 68 (Brown and Ailnack) forks off.

slant uphill across an open field to a waymarked gatepost. Continue ahead on a track that crosses moorland to the edge of a forest. The track turns down right, along the forest edge, around its corner, and down to a forest road.

A waymark arrow points left down this road. After 1.5km follow the main track slightly right, ignoring the side-track climbing to the left. Soon afterwards Glenlivet's Walk 8 forks off left on a path, but continue down the main track to rejoin the outward route.

Retrace the outward route across the **Bridge of Avon**, up the military road, and past **Campdalmore** farm. The farm track leads on to a car park at a corner of the A939.

A path beside the road leads back into **Tomintoul**.

ALTERNATIVE FINISH

Alternatively (but only slightly interestingly), you can take the stile on the left, and follow the track of the Spey Way for 300m to the signposted 'Tomintoul Circular Path' on the right. The path leads across the back of the village to an information board where you turn right and pass through a plantation to reach the southern end of the village. This adds 2.5km/1.5 miles to the walk.

68 Glen Brown and Ailnack Ravine

Length

Difficulty

Start/finish	Tomintoul: the Square NJ166188 or Queen's View NJ164175
Distance	19.5km/12.25 miles
Ascent	450m/1500ft
Approx time	6hr
Max altitude	530m
Terrain	Tracks and paths, with a short section of rough moorland

The Water of Ailnack flows out to Tomintoul through a ravine that's very large, and quite unlike anything else in the Cairngorms. Even the geography is astonishing: the gorge formed when a glacier blocked the River Avon (which was at the time the head of the River Don) and diverted it backwards up Glen Loin. Route 72 explores the ravine floor; this one visits its rim without such rock-and-boulder adventure.

SHORTER VERSION

The route can reduced by 4km by staying on the track after Kylnadrochit Lodge (reversing Route 67) and following it to the Burn of Brown.

Start in Tomintoul and follow Route 67 to the dangerous ruin at NJ128189. Here a waymark points up to left of the ruin, but the old right of way passes below the ruin and slants down alongside a broken fence to a second ruin.

Keep ahead for 100m to a gate in an old fence. Beyond it, the old path slants gently uphill, becoming clearer as it enters heather. When it joins a track, turn right, gently downhill. The track bends back before a fenced plantation, down to a gate near Burn of Brown with a green waymark arrow.

Head up the **Burn of Brown**, crossing to the track on the opposite bank if convenient; quite soon this track fords back to the east bank. After 1km, there's a stream junction where the valley divides. Cross to a grassy nose opposite, and go up this by a slanting path on the left. Keep uphill through heather for 200m to find a track.

Turn left up Glen Brown. The track gradually gets closer to the Burn of Brown, and joins it at a shooters' hut (NJ123167). The track fords the small burn ahead (Allt na Farraidh) and turns uphill alongside it. It climbs to about the 500m contour, then turns left around the slope of **Carn Tuadhan**.

Stay with the track as it passes just above a small pool (NJ135153) and turns uphill alongside a stream. The track ends at a stream junction 400m above (NJ133148).

*The lower ravine of
the Water of Ailnack*

Now it's easy to cross the stream on the left, and head west across the shorter heather of the flat-topped spur (530m). Keep down east to pass between two ends of fences to the turning area at the top of a track (NJ141148).

Head north along the track, with the Ailnack ravine down to the right. At the track's highest point, a single post on the right marks a good viewpoint into the ravine, with a grassy path continuing along the brink for more views down in. Return to the track and continue along it. It drops through a deer fence gate, with a ladder stile alongside, then passes above **Delnabo** house. Keep ahead down the avenue driveway and between gateposts to a bridge over the Avon. The tarred lane beyond leads up, past the track to Queen's View car park, and into the top end of Tomintoul.

GLEN AVON

69 Ben Avon by its River

Start/finish	Queen's View car park Tomintoul NJ164175
Distance	40km/24 miles
Ascent	1000m/3300ft
Approx time	12.5hr
Bike approach	To Builg Bridge (saves 3.5hr)
Max altitude	1171m
Terrain	Tarred track, hill path, and smooth plateau
Map	OS Landranger 36 Grantown; Explorer 404 Braemar

Ben Avon is often approached by Landrover tracks from the south, through Glens Slugain or Quoich. To do this is to miss out on the true nature of this big and remote hill by making it seem almost small. More seriously, it's to miss all but one of the many distinctive tors, and not to see the knobbed and stony northern corries.

So here's the route that starts at Tomintoul to give you almost all of Avon, including several miles of its same-named river. River and hill are pronounced Aan: from Ath-fhionn, the bright ford, or the ford of the mythic Fingalians. Route 70 scrambles over the larger tors, all of which can be reached from this walk. The same route on the hill – but with a slightly shorter walk in – is Route 75, Avon from Don.

To find the car park head south through Tomintoul to the top end of the village. Turn right on a tarmac lane down towards the Avon. In 1km fork left onto a track signed for the car park.

195

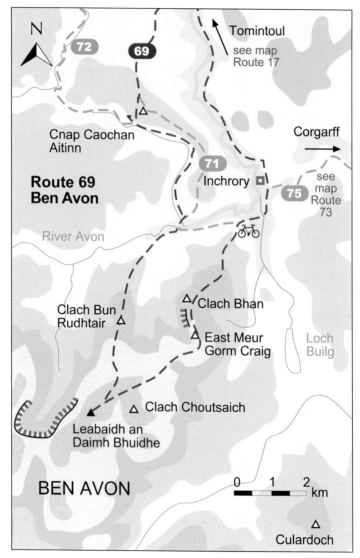

Start along the continuation of the track as it passes through woods above the Avon, with the Queen Victoria viewpoint 30m above.

The track drops to the **River Avon** and joins a tarred track arriving from the right over a bridge. It's tempting to use unsurfaced tracks on the right-hand, west, side of the river; but note that the footbridge marked upstream at Dalestie (NJ162111) does not exist. So follow the east bank's tarred track all the way to **Inchrory** (2.5hr from the car park).

At Inchrory, ignore the main entrance track forking right and pass round to the left of the grand house. A track turns up left, ▶ but keep ahead. The track drops and turns right onto a bridge over Builg Burn. After 300m turn up left on a new track to grouse butts. Continue on a quad bike track, then join the heather groove of the old path, as marked on the Landranger map, as it zigzags up west towards Carn Fiaclach.

Turn left up the broad north spur of **Meall Gaineimh**. This is easy going, but with no particular path. Meall Gaineimh summit has a crag outcrop, but to find the continuation path you must skirt this summit on the right.

Route 75 from Cock Bridge arrives along this track.

Tor blimey! Towards Clach Bhan on the way up Ben Avon

So look out for a pointed cairn on the high right-hand skyline. Here the path restarts, contouring into the col Gaineimh/Clach Bhan.

To the right now is the interesting rock tor of **Clach Bhan**, ◄ but the path keeps southwest, slanting gently uphill below the coxcomb crest of East Meur Gorm Craig, eventually joining that crest at its final and highest point.

The big blocky tor far ahead is not the summit of Ben Avon but is Clach Choutsaich, not visited on this walk. ◄ Bear right (west), to slant up the left flank of the first hummock to the shallow col beyond, and up the ridge of

For easy scrambling on Clach Bhan and East Meur Gorm Craig see **Route 70**.

Unless you want to **scramble** on it: again see **Route 70**.

Potholes in Clach Bhan, ground out by pebbles under wind action

Mullach Lochan nan Ghabhar to its top. As the ridge forks, turn right (west) for 200m then turn back southwest to skirt a low tor to **Leabaidh an Daimh Bhuidhe**, the summit tor of Ben Avon. A path leads up to a col just right of the summit block, with an easy scramble (less than Grade 1) up gentle slabs to the top.

Return northeast, past the insignificant tors at 1147m and 1136m, then walk north across the head of a small stream of fresh cold water and up to **Stob Bac an Fhurain** (Ooran: peat-bank peak of the springs). This is only a small outcrop at a plateau corner, although appearing from below as a fine summit.

Direct descent northwards offers a little easy scrambling on boulders and cracked slabs, or avoid it on the left. Head down the rounded ridge to the three rock towers of **Clach Bun Rudhtair**, ▶ passing to left of them. Keep down the ridge northwards, crossing a long gravelly col to the very minor top **Da Dhruim Lom**. The ridgeline continues down, just east of north, on short walkable heather and grass. As it steepens at its foot the heather gets higher, but some of it has been burnt away and there is also a very small path.

At the ridge foot cross the stream on the right (named on OS maps, presumably incorrectly, as Caol Ghleann, the Narrow Glen). A small fishermen's path leads downstream along the south bank of **River Avon** for 600m to a bridge.

Cross here, and head north into **Glen Loin**. A sheltered track runs along the valley floor, which after 2km bends from north to northeast. In another 2.5km, just before the crossing of Caochan Aitinn burn, a track branches up to the right. It climbs in a big zigzag onto the high slope of **Cnap Chaochan Aitinn**, then descends gently northwards for 3km. It fords Allt Bheithachan and descends its birchwooded valley to cross the **Avon**. Here it rejoins the tarred track of the outward route, 3km from the car park.

Fine **scrambling** here: see Route 70.

70 Tors of Ben Avon

Difficulty	Scrambles Grade 1–3
Approach	Route 69 (from Tomintoul) or 75 (from Donside)
Scrambling	80m or more

Scramblers will want to include some, or even all, of the distinctive tors of Ben Avon in any walk on this hill. Four of the groups offer climbs that can be considered more than mere bouldering. While the central pillar of Clach Bun Rudhtair was recorded as still unclimbed as late as 1938, the others are at most Grade 1 by their easiest lines. This allows attempts to be made on their longer or steeper sides with confidence that there will be a straightforward descent.

All four of these scrambles can be included in Route 69 or Route 75, although in Clach Choutsaich's case with a slight diversion.

Clach Bhan and East Meur Gorm Craig

Clach Bhan ('white stone') has various easy lines (Grade 1 or 0), but is worth visiting for the interesting potholes on top. As late as the 1860s pregnant women bathed in these holes, believing this would bring an easier childbirth.

Head south over two or three more small tors, onto the rocky crest of East Meur Gorm Craig (Meur Gorm: blue finger, referring to the piling of the grey granite rather than the cold-weather climber). By keeping strictly to the crest, some mild scrambling (Grade 1) can be had, with a slightly exposed step on sloping holds leading onto the second tower. Just before the final and highest point of the coxcomb ridge the path of the walkers' route rejoins from the left.

Clach Bun Rudhtair

The three fine rock towers offer a wealth of scrambling possibilities, with even the easiest routes not being altogether easy.

The northern, downhill, one can be climbed over blocks from the uphill end, but demands an exposed final move onto the summit. The central and most impressive tower has a most tempting line, by a through route from west to east, followed by a steep move on big holds and a gentler groove above. Two grooves at its downhill (northern) end also offer possibilities. (Each of these appears to be Grade 2, but I was alone when I visited the tors and omitted the final steps.)

At the uphill end of the group, the southern tower (at *its* uphill end) offers an open corner followed by one awkwardly steep move to finish. An alternative route just to the right takes a holdless but easy crack onto a platform at half height. Cross this to the right, and descend across a large jammed boulder, to finish by a ferny slope on the eastern side. Either of these lines is Grade 1.

Clach Bun Rudhtair's middle tower, unclimbed to the 1930s. The suggested route passes through a hole above and left of the walker

If heading uphill up the slope behind the tors, the final ridge to Stob Bac an Fhurain can be taken direct for some very easy scrambling on slabs and boulders.

Ben Avon's true summit consists of the tor **Leabaidh an Daimh Bhuidhe** ('lebbie an dye vooie': the bed of the yellow stag). The col to the north of the summit block is reached by an easy groove from the west or a path from the east. From this little col it's a walk up on slabs, straightforward when dry and not too windy, though slightly less straightforward in descent even then. More interesting (Grade 1) is the continuation across a gap to the lower south summit of the tor.

Clach Choutsaich turns out to be a reasonably easy ascent, up a gentle but holdless groove on the west side to a col, and then by cracked slabs, again holdless but very easy angled, to the summit. Grade 1.

71 Cnap Chaochan Aitinn

Length

Difficulty

Start/finish	Queen's View car park NJ164175
Distance	29km/19 miles
Ascent	500m/1700ft
Approx time	8.5hr
Bike approach	To bridge below Gaulrig (saves 1hr)
Max altitude	714m
Terrain	Tracks, and short grass hilltop

A long but otherwise remarkably easy walk, that could be undertaken on mountain bike. Still, it has a remote turning point below the great northern ridges of Ben Avon.

Start at the Queen's View car park. The onward track passes below Queen's View, drops to the valley floor, passes above a cottage called Keppoch, then joins with a tarred track that arrives from across the river. This continues through a gate at Birchfield. About 800m later is a ricketty looking track bridge on the right.

Cross and take the main track ahead across a field. At a junction, take the main track left across a tiny stream and uphill alongside it. The track passes abandoned **Wester Gaulrig**, goes through a field, and then into birchwoods. Ignore a faint track

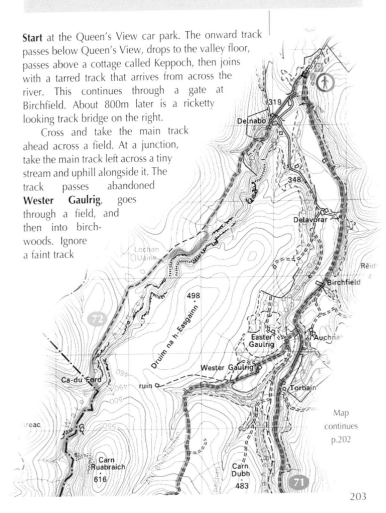

Map continues p.202

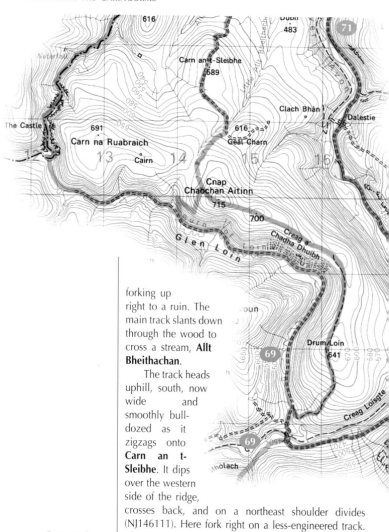

forking up right to a ruin. The main track slants down through the wood to cross a stream, **Allt Bheithachan**.

The track heads uphill, south, now wide and smoothly bull-dozed as it zigzags onto **Carn an t-Sleibhe**. It dips over the western side of the ridge, crosses back, and on a northeast shoulder divides (NJ146111). Here fork right on a less-engineered track. This heads south across a stream and up the north ridge of Cnap Chaochan Aitinn. At 650m it divides again, ◄

Route 72 keeps ahead here

Descending into Glen Avon from Drum Loin

the left branch heading uphill to end just right of the summit of **Cnap Chaochan Aitinn** with its anemometer and quartz-topped cairn. Cnap (krap) is lump; Caochan a local word for stream.

Head southeast, through a gentle col with some small peat hags passed on their right, to Cnap Eas Chaorach (699m – hillock of sheep waterfall). Pleasant ridgewalking on short vegetation continues southeast along the ridge, past a couple of erratic granite boulders. After 1km, a track starts. Follow it over **Drum Loin** and down to a junction near the River Avon. Cross the ford ahead, then head down left to the bridge over the Avon.

A wide track heads downstream, on the right bank – the path marked on the left bank is unusable, being cut by deer fencing. This fencing also prevents close approach to Linn of Avon. After a bridge over the Builg Burn, the main track turns left and passes **Inchrory**. It becomes tarred for the easy and scenic 10km down Glen Avon to the start point.

72 Ailnack Upper Ravine

Length

Difficulty	Scramble Grade 1
Start/finish	Tomintoul, Queen's View NJ164175
Distance	21.5km/13.5 miles
Ascent	400m/1300ft
Approx time	7hr
Max altitude	650m
Terrain	Tracks lead to rocky river bed, and rough heather
Scrambling	1.5km

This river scramble is only possible after a dry spell, as it requires the Water of Ailnack to be crossable at virtually any point. Given such conditions, it's a scenic and entertaining ravine route, with surprisingly good rock and going on for over a mile. For the adventurous, a continuation down the lower gorge is worth attempting.

Extension For an extra 8km/5 miles (and a close-up of Ben Avon) continue Walk 71 down into Glen Avon, doubling back up Glen Loin on Route 69.

Start as the preceding Route 71, and follow it to the track junction just before the summit of **Cnap Chaochan Aitinn**. ◀

Here take the main track that contours ahead, then drops in a big zigzag into **Glen Loin**. Turn right on the track up the valley floor. The track ends at a sign about access and deer stalking. Now don't take the wheelmarks forking left but the small path forking right, along the right side of the valley floor, to reach the Water of Ailnack at the top of its upper ravine.

The ravine downstream should only be attempted if the water is low enough to show plenty of river-bed stones, and to be crossable almost at will. In which case, head downstream between rising ravine walls. Progress is made by frequent crossings of the stream. Where walls drop directly into the water, the rock is often surprisingly good, with handholds, and a line immediately above the water may prove easier than it looks. At one point where steep walls drop on both sides into a deep pool, I escaped briefly up a 5m rib of clean rock on the left, returning to the stream down heather.

After 1.5km the steep side walls withdraw. Continue downstream, with quite rough going on grassy or heathery riverbank or on river-bed stones. There are a couple more short but interesting scrambling moments just above the water, one on the left then on the right.

Entering the top end of Ailnack's upper ravine

AILNACK LOWER RAVINE

The lower ravine is even more spectacular but also more serious, requiring swimming certainly, and somewhere between Grade 2 and impassible.

Straight away below the **Ca-du** stream junction comes a pleasant scramble on the left, followed by a section on the right with an underwater shelf for footholds. One section with steep walls on both sides required a 2m swim right to left across the stream. A boulderfall on the left offered a through route.

As the walls on either side steepened and got higher, a first small waterfall had a groove on the left dropping into a swimming pool, and so was avoided by a wooded ledge 15m up on the right. The single fencepost viewpoint, mentioned above, is visible from the riverbed; below it the stream passes among conglomerate pudding-stone boulders. A waterfall slide is followed by a zigzag linn (this useful Scots word means a channel between rock walls). Here progress was made along a ledge on the right, followed by a 2m wall onto a higher shelf (Grade 2). Further progress, if possible at all, required swimming, and I wasn't ready to damage my camera, so I escaped up a scree spur on the right (NJ149153). In glimpses from above, the river below the zigzag linn seemed to be straightforward.

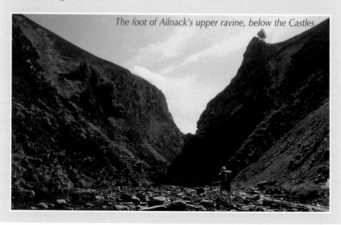

The foot of Ailnack's upper ravine, below the Castles

After 1.5km a large stream arrives from the left out of a little green gorge: there is a pinnacle on the right opposite. This is the **Ca-du Ford**. Having crossed the side-stream, head up the left bank of the main river on a small path through the heather, gradually rising above the river and crossing the top of a hollow filled with juniper scrub. The going is rough, unless you find one of the useful sheep paths along the brim of the ravine. Contour forward, with views down to the river on the right, to cross a fence near a small pool (NJ140146). Head north, slanting away from the ravine, to pass the head of a little dip and find a track starting just beyond.

The track runs north above the lower ravine. At its highest point, a post on the right marks a 'don't-miss-it' viewpoint into the lower ravine. Follow the grassy brink on for 200m for a view down to the zigzag linn (mentioned below) that ended my attempt on the lower ravine. Rejoin the track, to descend past **Delnabo** house and cross the Avon to the car park.

Pine and birch in Ailnack ravine

209

PART 5

DONSIDE

Some time in the last 10,000 years, an incident of river burglary took place at Inchrory. The waters of Loch Avon – that should be the source of the Don – were stolen by the Spey. And ever since, the top of the Don has been an ignored corner. There's one hotel, one bunkhouse, and no public transport at all.

This is the quiet corner of the Cairngorms. Unlike at Glenlivet, no friendly estate has laid stiles and signposts for the low-level stroller. For those prepared to anatomise the map, there are some fine mountain bike routes to be worked out. For the rest of us there's a day or two of walking on mid-height hills of heather and grass, and no fewer than 13 castles to visit. Corgarff is where the walking routes start: of the other 12, Kildrummie is the finest and most historic. Meanwhile, for the ambitious, this is the best start-point for the exciting and remote northern side of Ben Avon.

*Corgarff Castle, the first of thirteen along the Don
(start point of Routes 73–75)*

73 Carn Ealasaid

Start/finish	Corgarff Castle NJ294089
Distance	16.5km/10.25 miles
Ascent	550m/1900ft
Approx time	6hr
Max altitude	792m
Terrain	Track ascent, then rough heather/grass

Length

Difficulty

> Carn Ealasaid could be done as an up-and-down taking about 3hr; the track is quick and comfortable, and offers a fine view across to Corgarff Castle. The continuation ridgewalk is rather rougher than the one on Brown Cow Hill (Route 74), having some small peat hags and rough heather.

Just south of the River Don, turn off on a dirt road signed for **Corgarff Castle**. A large parking area is on the left below the castle.

Start by returning down the track to the A939, and turn left across the **River Don**. Immediately above the Allargue Arms hotel, turn left up a section of old road, leading to a gravel track. Follow this below a plantation, through a gate marked 'no unauthorised vehicles', then across the Burn of Loinherry.

Just before **Loinherry**, turn up the grassy hillside on a small sheep path, to join a track 200m up the slope. Follow this up to the right, as it slants up the side of the Loinherry Burn's little glen. After 1km, the track turns back on itself. As it contours back across the slope, it gives a fine view of the top of Don and the castle opposite. It regains the southeast ridge of Carn Ealasaid above its steep lower section, and turns right to go straight up the ridge.

The ridge levels, and even dips a little, across the minor top of **Cairn Vaich**. During the next gentle rise the track

wanders off to the left: simply keep uphill on short heather and lichen. The track rejoins to lead across the plateau to the summit cairn of **Carn Ealasaid** (Elizabeth's hill).

In mist, the descent to the next col requires a little technical navigation. Ignoring various unhelpful wheel-mark tracks, descend northwest for 400m. At this point – discovered by counting paces, by timing at about 5min, by an altimeter reading of 720m or a GPS reading of NJ225122 – you need to turn west, to find the rounded spur leading down to the 639m col and **Tolm Buirich** beyond.

Again, a little technical sophistication is called for, as you must descend west for 300m to find the wide ridge running southwest. There are some peat hags to avoid or clamber through on the final climb to the trig point on **Craig Veann**. (Veann and Vaich are odd names: Gealic doesn't use the letter V.)

Descend the south ridge on comfortable short heather, bending left (southeast). Keep rather to the left, towards the stream, to be sure of picking up the track below. The map marks a continuation path towards the Eag, but this path does not exist, so if you pass to the west of the track end you'll just carry on down to the valley floor. Assuming you do find the track, turn left, briefly uphill, then down across the valley floor to join the main track opposite.

Follow this track out down the valley. At the second house, the track bears right and becomes tarred: here take a grass track ahead, which bypasses **Delnadamph Lodge** before rejoining the tarred one. In another 3km you regain the car park.

74 Brown Cow Hill

Length

Difficulty

Start/finish	Corgarff Castle NJ255089
Distance	19km/11.5 miles
Ascent	500m/1700ft
Approx time	6.25hr
Max altitude	829m
Terrain	Tracks, short heather and grass, a short shallow peat hag

'About as exciting as the name suggests' says the SMC Corbetts guide drily. The walking is smooth and straightforward, at least in clear weather: and the views are huge, east to the sea and west to Ben Avon and Cairn Gorm – hills which are, of course, considerably more exciting than Brown Cow. In thick weather, however, you may not even get to see the summit cairn: it needs a bit of navigation.

Just south of the River Don, turn off on a dirt road signed for **Corgarff Castle**. A large parking area is on the left below the castle.

Start by heading back down the dirt track to the A939, and turning right for 300m to a farm. A track passes between the buildings, becoming grassy beyond them. A footbridge on the right lets you across the **Cock Burn**, which the track fords 50m further on, below Corgarff Castle.

Follow the track uphill, not steeply. Ignore a smaller track forking up right, and pass below a small plantation (all that remains of a large forest marked on the Landranger). The track turns up to the col south of **Carn Oighreag** (stonepile of the cloudberry). Here turn up left, with small paths made by mountain hares and the occasional walker, passing to the left of a line of grouse butts to a flattening above. Here there are some small peat hags to avoid. Head southwest to the cairned summit at **823m**, marked as Brown Cow Hill.

From here to the true summit at 829m has proved impossible for at least one experienced walker in mist. Head west across a broad, level col and up the slight rise beyond. A wheelmark track joins from the right and leads you within 10m of the 829m cairn that's the true summit of **Brown Cow Hill**.

The helpful wheelmarks continue across the next col to a point 50m north of the summit of **Cairn Sawvie**. The actual summit of this is an unmarked point in a swamp,

The source of the Don

so scarcely worth seeking out. Instead turn down right, on a small heather path, northwest to the next top, **Meikle Geal Charn** (big white stonepile) which, as the name suggests, is capped with pale quartzite stones.

A broken fence shows the way northwest to **Little Geal Charn**, then northeast over its smaller 709m top. Head down northeast to the start of a rough track: just above it is the mossy puddle that's the source of the River Don. The rough track guides up the next slope to **Cairn Culchavie**. Head down north, with fence remains at first. The spur is comfortable short heather, becoming tiresome right at the foot, but the track is only a short distance below.

Turn right, and follow the track down the valley past a cottage at **Inchmore**. Just after a second building, some abandoned stables, the track bends right and becomes tarred: here keep ahead on a grassy track for 300m, when it rejoins the tarred one. After 3km this finally arrives back at the car park below **Corgarff Castle**.

75 Don to Ben Avon

Length

Difficulty

Start/finish	Corgarff Castle NJ255089
Distance	32.5km/20 miles
Ascent	750m/2500ft
Approx time	10hr
Bike approach	To Builg Bridge (saves 3hr)
Max altitude	1171m
Terrain	Tarred track, hill path, and smooth plateau
Map	Route map 74 plus OS Landranger 36 Grantown; or OS Explorer 404 Braemar

Apart from the approach, this is identical to Route 69 to Beinn Avon from Tomintoul. The distance is the same either way: the Glen Avon way is more beautiful, but is mostly on tarmac: accordingly it may be preferred by cyclists rather than walkers.

Just south of the River Don, turn off on the dirt road signed for **Corgarff Castle** to a large parking area below the castle.

Start up the Don valley on the same track, which is now tarred, but marked as a private road only. After 3km, just after a plantation on the right, you can fork right, to avoid the last 300m of tar. The rougher track continues up the left, south, side of the Don valley. After another 4km, the track fords the **Feith Bhait** (perhaps a misprint for Feith Bhaith, bog of drowning), which is the head-water of the Don itself. A few steps later, keep ahead (not up left) on a more-used track.

In 400m, at a gate, a sign 'Inchrory' indicates a pebble path on the right. This bypasses **Lagganauld** before rejoining the track beyond. The track zigzags down a valley with odd outcrops of the lime-rich schist that supports wildflowers, notably rock rose, to the junction above **Inchrory**. Here turn left to the bridge over the **Builg Burn**, joining Route 69.

Route 69 (with scrambling options in Route 70) takes you up Ben Avon by its northeast ridge and down by its north one. Once back in Glen Avon, take the track along the right, south, side of the river back to **Inchrory**.

ALTERNATIVE RETURN ROUTE

If you have the energy and the inclination to take in Brown Cow Hill on the return, note that there's a comfortable descent off Ben Avon over Carn Dearg to the foot of Loch Builg, and the track marked up east from NJ186050 does exist.

PART 6

DEESIDE BRAEMAR

Braemar ought to be – and to some extent still is – the place of the long walk in. Several hours of striding under the pines or by the riverside are to be enjoyed before you even get to the bottom of some of Britain's biggest hills.

But Braemar is where the mountain has been spoilt, just slightly, by the mountain bike. For this the Landrover landowners must take much of the blame. Long dusty tracks make for a boring walk to the foot of Macdui or Beinn a' Bhuird, or worst of all westwards to White Bridge. The mountain bike makes the track shorter, but also brings Ben Macdui closer to the car park.

But Braemar is not altogether bad. Mar Lodge Estate now belongs to Scotland, or at least to the Scottish National Trust; and the dreary tracks are, bit by bit, being unbulldozed out of existence. Meanwhile, in between the tracks, find such lovely spots as Linn of Quoich, or the Fairy Glen of Slugain, or the birkwood of Morrone. Or else, take to the track, on two wheels or on trudging feet. At track's end are the grey stony slopes, and the granite crags, and the ice floes of Loch Etchachan. Here are the peat-pickled stumps of Glen Geusachan, the evil-gleaming slabs of the Devil's Point, the rock blobs and the gravel lands of Beinn a' Bhuird.

Braemar itself is a bright little tourist village, earning its living by selling tartan stuff and shortbread to coach parties. The Queen comes once a year to Braemar Games. She arrives by helicopter; you could reach Braemar by bus, but only if you started out from Aberdeen.

In the Sneck of Beinn a' Bhuird. Deeside gives the longest walks to the biggest hills

LINN OF DEE

76 Clais Fhearnaig

Start/finish	Victoria Bridge (NO103895)
Distance	16km/10 miles
Ascent	250m/800ft
Approx time	4.5hr
Max altitude	520m
Terrain	Tracks and path

Length

Difficulty

Quite a lot of fine pinewood, a strange little slot in the hills, and the banks of Quoich: every office worker at Mar Lodge should take a very long lunch-hour to enjoy this walk around the block. In case you've already walked Quoich Water on Route 82, there's an alternative return over Craig Bhalg.

Don't park in the small spaces either side of the lodge: these are needed by large lorries turning across the bridge. Verge parking is nearby in the Braemar direction.

Start by crossing the white-railed **Victoria Bridge**. At once turn down left to a small gate onto the riverbank, and head upstream with the river on your left. After ducking under some fir trees, follow the riverbank round to the right until a ladder stile crosses the deer fence on your right onto a tarred track. Nearby now is **Mar Lodge**: an ugly red-roofed building that replaces two earlier ones burnt down. Turn left, away from Mar Lodge, and follow the tarmac up to a road above.

Keep ahead (west) for 200m, then fork right up a little-used Landrover track. At an X-junction go straight across, with the track now contouring through open woodland with self-seeded small pine and birch along its verge. After 1km the track passes through a gate with a ladder stile; this deer fence marks the end of forest

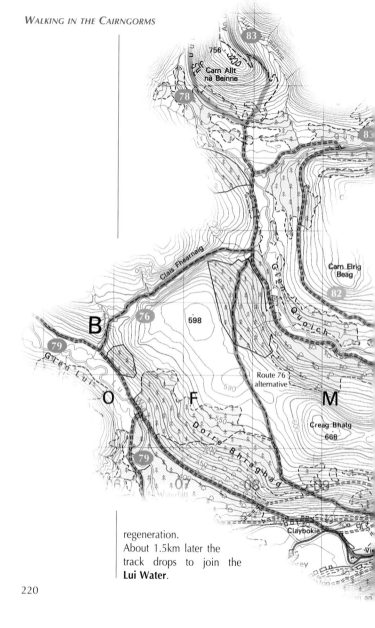

regeneration.
About 1.5km later the
track drops to join the
Lui Water.

A wide smooth track arrives from the left across a bridge. Follow this new track ahead, right of the river, through open grassland with low ruins of a former township. After 1km, the corner of a fenced plantation is on the right. Here a small but clear path turns off uphill, but it's nicer to continue along the track for 100m more, to just before the Allt a' Mhadaidh (fox burn) stream. Here turn right on a grass path to right of the stream, past ruined shielings in the sheltered hollow. After a section slightly eroded by the river, the path rises to join the clearer one.

The combined path is repaired in places as it rises alongside the stream, past one small cairn to another at the top of the slope. Now it heads through the odd hollow of **Clais Fhearnaig** – Clash Yarnik: the notch of the alder trees (though none grow here today) – with two long little lochans sprinkled with schisty boulders. The path contours out of the notch along the left-hand heather slope, and turns downhill alongside a fenced pony paddock to reach the wide, smooth track in the bottom of **Glen Quoich**.

Turn right, crossing the Allt Clais Fhearnaig. ▶ The track runs into open woodland. After 1.5km, it drops to the Quoich Water side. In another 1km, it again runs alongside the river; as it turns uphill, look out for a new-built path running down left to a half-hidden footbridge. Don't miss this!

For now a delightful path, restored in places, runs down the left side of Quoich Water.

After 1.5km you reach a shuttered lodge near Linn of Quoich, with the Earl

A rough track forking right is the **alternative return route**: see below.

of Mar's **Punch Bowl** (a natural pothole) in the river below. About 20m downstream, turn right across a long footbridge. Take the wide path up to the right, then back left along the top of the pinewood. The path now becomes wheelmarks in heather. It bends right, away from the trees, passing under power lines then crossing a branch track to meet the main track previously walked on. Turn left, curving round the spur of Creag Bhalg and descending past a barrier to join the road.

Cross a cattle grid ahead, and fork left into a track signed for Craggan. Pass to the left of the buildings to a gate in deer fencing, onto a rough track. This passes through open field and plantation, to a junction with **Victoria Bridge** 100m to the left.

CREAG BHALG ALTERNATIVE

If you've already walked Glen Quoich, this moorland continuation takes you across the shoulder of Creag Bhalg on a rough but clear track. Creag Bhalg (locally 'Krek Vallaig') means the crag of the tummy or the blister – it's rounded and gently bulgy.

After walking down the wide, smooth Quoich track just long enough to cross the culvert of the Allt Clais Fhearnaig, fork off right on the rough track. It rises through a plantation, passing a cairn at the slope top. It continues southeast as it crosses the moorland of **Creag Bhalg**, ◄ dropping to the edge of woodland on the Dee slope.

After 400m the track passes through a deer fence and slants downhill through open woodland. At an X-junction, keep ahead onto a less-used track, that drops to the road opposite **Mar Lodge**.

Cross onto a tarred track marked 'walkers welcome', turning right to pass estate buildings. The track crosses an open meadow to a junction under trees. About 100m ahead is **Victoria Bridge**.

Diversion Walk up left to the summit itself if you don't mind tramping some pathless heather, then descend west and southwest to rejoin the track above the deer fence.

77 Derry Cairngorm by Lochan Uaine

Start/finish	Linn of Dee car park NO063897
Distance	23km/14.5 miles
Ascent	900m/2900ft
Approx time	8hr
Bike approach	To Derry Lodge (saves 2hr)
Max altitude	1156m
Terrain	A steep, rough climb out of the corrie
Map	Harveys Cairn Gorm; OS Explorer 403 Cairn Gorm; OS Landranger 43 Braemar

This vigorous and unused route avoids most of Derry Cairngorm's boulders; but it has difficult ground of its own, climbing out of Coire an Lochain Uaine. The lochan in that corrie is tiny, but the waterfall is quite large.

EASIER ALTERNATIVE

For an easier ascent of Derry Cairngorm, the descent part of this route is described, in the uphill direction, as Route 38 to Ben Macdui. Leave Derry Cairngorm, still on Route 38, to Loch Etchachan; and turn down right, to its outflow, to pick up Route 39 in reverse.

Start along the path out of the car park signed for Glen Lui. After 700m it meets a track, which you follow to the left, up Glen Lui, to **Derry Lodge** (5km, 1.25hr).

Beyond the buildings cross a footbridge, and turn right on a wide path that follows the Derry Burn upstream and crosses it after 2.5km. Now it joins a new-built path along the line of a track now removed. After

223

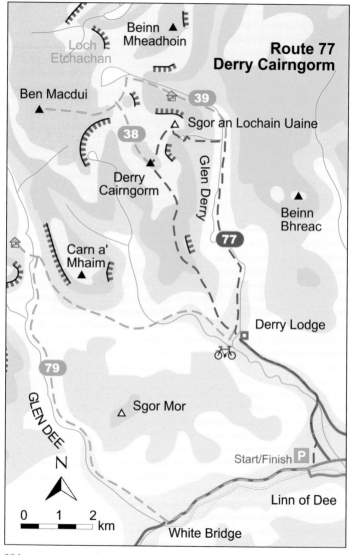

Beinn
Mheadhoin

Loch
Etchachan

**Route 77
Derry Cairngorm**

Ben Macdui

39

38

Sgor an Lochain Uaine

Glen Derry

Derry
Cairngorm

Beinn
Bhreac

Carn a'
Mhaim

77

79

Derry Lodge

GLEN DEE

Sgor Mor

N

Start/Finish

Linn of Dee

0   1   2 km

White Bridge

Exploring the waterfall above Lochan Uaine of Derry Cairngorm

1.5km the path enters a fenced enclosure, and 500m later leaves it again. At once head down left to cross the Derry Burn at boulders.

Now two streams run down out of Coire an Lochan Uaine far above. Go up heathery slopes, using grassy patches between the two streams, then joining the right-hand one to reach the small **Lochan Uaine** (green lochan, the smallest of the four so named in the Cairngorms).

Go round the lochan to the waterfall above. Head up to right of the fall, zigzagging but always within 20m of the stream, on steep ground between small outcrops. ◄ At the plateau, head round right, to the summit of **Sgurr an Lochain Uaine** (983m). It's a plateau corner rather than a true peak.

Alternative An easier line is by the corrie's northern spur, up steepish heather onto Sgurr an Lochain Uaine.

Head southwest across the shallow valley that drains into the waterfall. The slope of Derry Cairngorm ahead can be slanted up, bottom right to top left, on a grassy strip, giving the only boulderless ascent to the summit of **Derry Cairngorm**.

Descend southeast, down boulders, to the cairned lesser top at 1040m; then south, down more boulders, to pick up path traces on grassy levels below. Keep right of a slight top on the eastern edge, and drop into the col north of Carn Crom. A path climbs out of the col then contours across the eastern slope of **Carn Crom**. This passage is slightly exposed across the top of a slab, then scrambles downwards for 3m, somewhat rounded and holdless. If that's not fun, cross Carn Crom's summit instead.

The path regains the spur crest southeast of Carn Crom, descending to the small outcrop of Creag Bad an t-Seabhaig. In a little col in this outcrop, a path currently being built turns down left, then slants down the eastern face of the outcrop. It crosses deer fence, twice, by ladder stiles. Then it winds down through pines and across a meadow to the footbridge at **Derry Lodge**.

78 The Happy Face
of Beinn a' Chaorainn

Start/finish	Linn of Dee car park NO063897
Distance	29.5km/18.5 miles
Ascent	1000m/3300ft
Approx time	9.75hr
Bike approach	To Quoich track end, omitting Clais Fhearnaig (saves 2hr)
Max altitude	1082m
Terrain	Pathless glen, peaty moorland and tracks
Map	OS Explorer 404 Braemar; OS Landranger 36 Grantown plus mapping for Route 76
Scrambling	50m (optional) Grade 1

Beinn Bhreac is my least-compelling Cairngorm. Beinn a' Chaorainn isn't much better. Somehow the peaty Moine Bhealaidh has all the bleakness of the Great Moss but none of the fun. The going is just that much wetter and blacker; the view is of Beinn a' Bhuird's less interesting side; there are no crags round the edge.

The standard way over these two Munros is to cycle and walk all the way up Glen Derry (using Route 39, Coire Etchachan) and simply to continue up the northward path to its highest point. Then hack northeast up a rounded spur of rough heather followed by soft squelchy grass; then head south from Chaorainn across that peaty moor. I've done it, and it's dull, and I didn't want to do it again.

But then my eye turned to the Dubh Ghleann, the Black Valley round the back, wooded below and darkly shady above. At its top was a little wiggly stream that

227

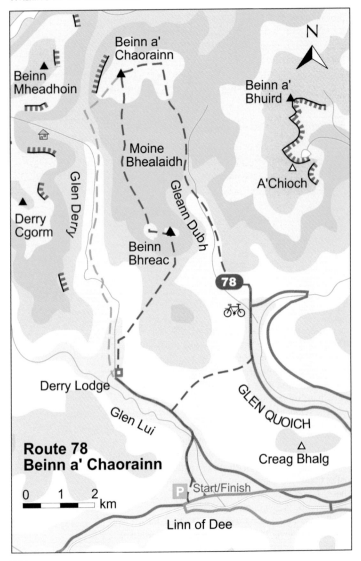

N

Beinn a'
Chaorainn

Beinn
Mheadhoin

Beinn a'
Bhuird

Moine
Bhealaidh

Gleann Dubh

A'Chioch

Glen Derry

Derry
Cgorm

Beinn
Bhreac

78

Derry Lodge

GLEN QUOICH

Glen Lui

**Route 78
Beinn a' Chaorainn**

Creag Bhalg

0   1   2
km

P Start/Finish

Linn of Dee

provided a brief but delicious scramble on granite scrubbed pink by the water. It was just chance that the stream turned out to translate as 'honey face'; but here is the smiling side of Beinn a' Chaorainn. The route starts through the charming hill slot of Clais Fhearnaig, and finishes with that standard crossing of the Moine Bhealaidh anyway.

CYCLISTS' ROUTE

Cyclists should be able to come in from Linn of Quoich for a shorter route omitting Clais Fhearnaig: 32km/20 miles (of which 15km in the saddle) and 1000m/3000ft of ascent (7.75hr).

Start along the path out of Linn of Dee car park signed for Glen Lui. After 700m it meets a track, which you follow to the left, up **Glen Lui**, after 1km crossing the Lui Water.

About 1km past the bridge, the corner of a plantation is on the right. Here a path turns up right, but continue along the track for another 100m and turn up a smaller path alongside the Allt a' Mhadaidh. The two paths join up, and lead through the loch-filled slot of Clais Fhearnaig.

At the slot's end the path drops to the track in **Glen Quoich**. Follow it to the left, north, across a ford, to its end (NO079955). Here a path turns off left, contouring through the wood and along the right (east) side of the **Dubh Ghleann**. The path peters out under the east spur of Beinn Bhreac. Old shieling land gives grassy patches alongside the stream, and there are also deer paths assisting the feet to the fallen buildings at a stream junction northwest of Beinn Bhreac (NO066977).

Between the two streams a couple of old cairns mark a small path running north, to left of the main stream. After 600m the path runs up onto a moraine at the valley head, to left of the ravine of the **Allt an Aghaidh Mhilis** (Aggy Villis: stream of the sweet face).

If you don't want the ravine, the grassy slope now above leads onto the plateau moorland north of Point 858m.

RAVINE ROUTE

Alternatively, from the moraine contour right, to the foot of the ravine, entering it by a rowan tree.

Stroll up inside the ravine on bilberry and boulder between rising walls. Once the walls are high enough to prevent escape, the first obstacle is a boulder-choke. Climb it on the left with footholds on both sides of the stream, which is awkward, or more easily 2m to right of the stream on large holds in the line of a temporary overflow stream.

The pool above can be traversed on the left, tricky on sloping holds, or walked round on the right. The ravine is now twisting. Pass below an overhang on the right to confront a fierce-looking 3m fall. This is climbed on large comfortable holds to the left of the water.

This is the last necessary difficulty. The runnel above gives further scrambling up a small cataract. The walls of the stream valley are now grassy and lower, but stay in the stream as half a dozen more small cataracts give a little scrambling here and there, and the moor above is not a place to hasten onto.

Whichever route up, head north across the moorland plateau. It's peaty and rough, with coarse grass next to the stream possibly the least uncomfortable option. Once on the cone of **Beinn a' Chaorainn Bheag** (small hill of the rowans), stony going is easier. The slope rises gently up to its summit cairn, with views of Glen Avon.

Descend west over boulders, into a col where the large pool drains north to Spey Bay, the smaller pool drains south to Aberdeen, and the third pool doesn't drain at all. A stony slope leads up to **Beinn a' Chaorainn**.

Two ways offer themselves across the peaty grassland of the **Moine Bhealaidh** (Moina Valley: moor of the broom). One could head back east, then down the stony southeast ridge, to cross the rough yellow grassland of the top of the moor. Slightly more direct, and offering a

bit of a view, is a line down the stony south ridge. As you descend the going gets worse but the weather possibly gets less bad. There's rough grass and some dissected peatland to cross just above the cut-out hollow of **Glas Allt Mor**.

Once past this stream slot on the right, head directly for the stony hump of misnamed **Craig Derry**. Once on the stones of this cragless 'Craig', going is easier again (although the weather will, very probably, get worse). A small cairn marks the isolated 900m contour ring. From it you can head up onto the 927m cairned west top (a Munro top) or directly into the 906m col, then up to the 931m main summit of **Beinn Breac** (speckled hill).

Paths lead down variously. The best way is down the south ridge, broad and gravelly, for about 15min until it steepens at the 800m contour. ▶ Now head down the damp grass slope west, towards the top of Beinne Brica stream. The col here is an odd double one that's rather west of where it really belongs. On the 707m knoll between the two colettes, a path starts, that runs down confidently southwest towards Glen Derry. When it peters out, head straight down in deep grass and heather, then through open woodland with less bad going, to the

Beinn a' Chaorainn from Glen Avon

For cyclists heading for Glen Quoich, small paths now lead southeast towards Poll Bhat lochan.

floor of Glen Derry. Here you join a path that runs along the line of the removed track.

Turn left down this well-made path, which reverts to track just before Derry Lodge footbridge. Pass the footbridge, and (to avoid the first bit of the Derry track) keep along the foot of woods near the river. The faint path crosses a side-track, and runs alongside Lui Water past the burnt-out Bob Scott's bothy; then it rises to join the main track down Glen Lui. In 1.5km you rejoin the outward route, reaching the car park in another 2.5km.

79 Dee and Derry

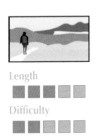

Length

Difficulty

Start/finish	Linn of Dee car park NO063897
Distance	25km/15.5 miles
Ascent	250m/800ft
Approx time	6.5hr
Max altitude	610m
Terrain	Tracks and paths, with 8km of rough path up the Dee
Map	Harveys Cairn Gorm; OS Explorer 403 Cairn Gorm; OS Landranger 43 Braemar. Sketch map with Route 77

This walk may have almost no uphill, but it's still a long and serious hike into remote country. In the huge empty valley of the Lairig Ghru, below the granite slabs of the Devil's Point, you're a long way from anywhere at all – apart from the small and sometimes squalid Corrour. The bothy offers no facilities apart from a waterproof roof, but even so provides lunchtime shelter and a chance to scrape the peat off your gaiters.

Start by crossing the road opposite the car park to visit the gorge that's the Linn of Dee. Head upstream to the road bridge. A few steps right, a track is signed for very distant places like Blair Atholl and Kingussie. This wide, smooth track heads up the open Dee Valley, right of the river, for 5km to **White Bridge**.

Just before the bridge, turn off right on a well-made path. This heads upstream to right of the Dee, which runs down to here from the north. After 800m, the path reaches **Chest of Dee**, a slab-stepped waterfall above a wooded pool. Now it reverts to a narrow trod, through heather but also grassy ground and the low ruins of former shielings (summer huts). In another 1km the path runs delightfully alongside the Dee – on the opposite side you'll see another path built on top of a former track painstakingly unbulldozed by Mar Lodge Estate.

The path is small, and in a few places wet. Views up the Lairig Ghru become more and more impressive. On the left is, first, the gentle cone of Carn Cloich-mhuilinn. 'Cloich' is from Clach, a stone: Mhuilinn from Muileann, straight from the French, a mill. Cloich-mhuilin: millstone. Is Gaelic starting to make sense? Next you pass the slabbed end of Beinn Bhrotain; the blind valley of Glen Geusachan; and the great granite cone of **Devil's Point**.

Heading down the Dee, with Devil's Point and Lairig Ghru behind

DEVIL'S POINT

The English name for Bod an Deamhain was supplied by a quick-witted ghillie when Queen Victoria asked 'What does that mean?' It's actually Demon's Prick.

Opposite Devil's Point you emerge onto a rather clearer path. (3.5hr to this point). If you want to visit **Corrour** bothy 800m ahead, keep ahead at this junction to cross some peaty swamp to a little metal bridge, with more swamp leading to the tiny building. If you don't want to visit the bothy, turn sharp back right at the path junction, in 50m joining a newly resurfaced path just above.

Keep ahead on this new path, back down the Dee Valley at a higher level. But soon the path swings left, east, around the base of Carn a' Mhaim. It drops to a deer fence above **Luibeg Burn**.

The path drops to a ford of the burn, which is here quite wide and can be impassible in spate – so note the footbridge 400m upstream. The path continues down Glen Luibeg to the buildings at **Derry Lodge**. Cross a footbridge on the right to the lodge building: a wooden hut has an emergency phone mounted on its end.

A track runs down-valley: you can avoid it at at first by passing through trees next to the river, crossing a side-track, and taking a riverside path ahead. This leads past the ruins of Bob Scott's bothy, accidentally burnt in 2003, before rejoining the main track.

The track runs down the Luibeg valley through pastureland, past the ruins of a township cleared to make way for deer 150 years ago. About 3km from Derry Lodge the track turns right across a bridge. In another 800m, look out for a wide path on the right leading back to the car park.

80 Around Glen Geusachan

Start/finish	Corrour bothy NN981958
Distance	19km/12 miles
Ascent	1400m/4700ft
Approx time	8.75hr
Max altitude	Cairn Toul 1293m
Terrain	Steep heather and boulders, then grassy and bouldery plateau
Map	Harveys Cairn Gorm; OS Explorer 403 Cairn Gorm; OS Landranger 43 Braemar

The standard route to Bhrotain and Monadh Mor is by bike to White Bridge; then up the footpath that replaces the unbulldozed track (and which the NTS doesn't want cycled on); and up over Carn Cloich-mhuillin. Such an approach is, to my mind, brisk but rather boring.

Bothy life, on the other hand, is cramped and uncomfortable – especially when that bothy is over-popular, litter-sprinkled Corrour. Still it has a certain aura, as when an impressionable young person I was too scared to go out to the stream for teeth cleaning because of the roaring of a stag. And that stag is still there – I met him coming round the corner of the bothy at dawn the day after I surveyed this route.

So sleep fitfully on the concrete floor, rise to a chilly breakfast of oats and stream water – and then step out into Deeside and do this walk. It's a grand circuit of five summits around Glen Geusachan.

REACHING THE BOTHY IN THE FIRST PLACE

For an approach to Corrour bothy via the Derry see Route 35 (Ben Macdui). It's 3hr to the bothy, or 2.25hr using a bike to Derry Lodge. Glen Dee, slightly rougher, takes 30min longer (Route 79, Dee and Derry).

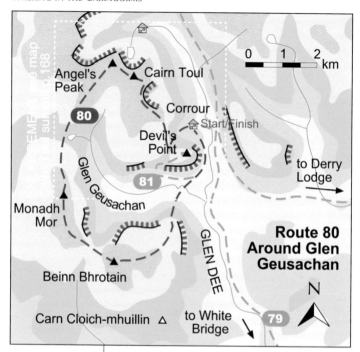

Map legend:

map 168

SUBLIME SUMMIT

Angel's Peak

80

Cairn Toul

Corrour

Start/Finish

Devil's Point

81

Glen Geusachan

0 1 2 km

to Derry Lodge

Monadh Mor

Beinn Bhrotain

GLEN DEE

Route 80 Around Glen Geusachan

N

Carn Cloich-mhuillin △

to White Bridge

79

Start along a small path heading south around the base of the Devil's Point and into **Glen Geusachan** (don't start in the dark, or you'll lose this path and make things a lot harder). Once in the glen's mouth, look at the sharp northeast corner of Beinn Bhrotain opposite. On the right-hand (Geusachan) face of this corner are granite slabs, gleaming evilly. A stream, not marked on any map, splashes down the slabs to fall off their bottom corner (NN967936). Our route will slant up to the right from this bottom corner.

So slant down to cross the **Geusachan Burn**: in normal water conditions this can be done barefoot across gravel beds. Slant to the right up the steep heather slope, heading for the stream where it falls off the lowest point of the slabs.

Cross the stream and slant up to the right, to reach the foot of a boulderfield. Go up the boulders, with care as some are loose. More slabs are above the top of the boulderfield, so now slant up left on grass, to rejoin the stream above the top of its slab waterslide. Follow the stream up to the shallow corrie at the top of the northeast corner (NN971935). ▶

The rest of the route is straightforward but strenuous. Head up slopes of grass then of gravel and stones to the cairned east top, then 1km west through a wide col to the main summit of **Beinn Bhrotain** (Vroten: hill of the mastiff dog). There is a cylindrical trig point here, and a large cairn to the southeast indicating the line to the descent towards Carn Cloich-mhuilinn and White Bridge. Our route drops northwest over pathless boulderfield, then picks up a small path through a col and up northwest. The path vanishes again, but going is easy on gravelly grass across level plateau to the summit of **Monadh Mor** (Mona More: the great moor-hill).

Follow the broad flat ridge north till it steepens, then slant down northeast, keeping to the left of craggy ground. Pass above the bogs around **Loch nan Stuirteag.** ▶ The

Beinn Bhrotain's northeast corner. Route 80 takes the slope on the right

In descent, a safer way is just to the right of the Coachan Roibidh, 2km round to the south.

Escape route into Glen Geusachan: head down to the left of the stream and along the left side of the valley floor on a very small rough path.

ridge rising opposite looks uncomfortably bouldery; however, keep slightly right of the ill-defined crest and you may find a tiny earth causeway, just wide enough for the path that has formed on top of it. At its top you reach the brink of Garbh Choire Mor. Turn up right on the stony path to the summit of **Angel's Peak**.

The path continues down southeast with big drops on the left, and up a bouldery spur to the summit of **Cairn Toul** with its shelter cairn. About 200m beyond is the smaller cairn on the south top. ◀ Descend the bouldery spur southwest, across a narrow col to the cairn on **Stob Coire an t-Saighdeir**.

The descent of Cairn Toul's East Ridge (Route 61) is a direct but rather demanding way to the bothy.

There's now a choice of descents. Following the brink on the left, with a sketchy path, is bouldery and windswept but with very fine views down into Coire an t-Saighdeir. Alternatively, a beeline for the rim of Coire Odhar soon gets you off the boulders onto grass. Either way, descend to where the stream drops over the edge into Coire Odhar.

From here, a path continues across the col. It slants up left, across a short bouldery section, then easily up to the cairn of **Devil's Point** on the very southeast corner of the plateau.

Descend the same way to the stream where it drops to the right into **Coire Odhar**. Paths start down on either

Cairn Toul and Loch na Stuirteag

side of the stream, with a third one almost in the water. The left-hand (northerly) one of the three is the easiest. They join 30m down the slope, and a well-made path zigzags down to the left of the stream to the floor of the shallow corrie. Here the path crosses the stream, and goes down to its right, to reach Corrour bothy.

81 The Devil's Back Side

Start/finish	Corrour bothy NN981958
Distance	6km/4 miles
Ascent	500m/1600ft
Approx time	3.25hr
Max altitude	1003m
Terrain	Steep heathery slope, then ravine with a nasty earth pitch (Scramble Grade 2) or a moderate heathery ridge
Map	Harveys Cairn Gorm; OS Explorer 403 Cairn Gorm; OS Landranger 43 Braemar. Sketch map with Route 80; enlarged at Cairn Toul Summit Summary
Scrambling	20m (optional) Grade 2

Devil's Point, so sinister and slabby from below, is always approached by the rather tame Route 59 up Coire Odhar. Here's an alternative way up that gives the real feel of the hill. Calling this damp and rather unwholesome cleft 'the Devil's Back Side' may be a bit too forceful. It's a delightful ravine walk, marred by an earthy pitch of scrambling to avoid a waterfall. The easier route up the bounding spur is less romantic, but you don't have to rinse out your jacket.

The outing could well continue with an ascent of Cairn Toul (Route 59) and a descent of its East Ridge (Route 61, 5hr for the circuit). For the 3hr approach to Corrour bothy via the Derry see Route 35 (Ben Macdui) or via the Dee see Route 79 (Dee and Derry).

Start southwards from the bothy, on a small path around the base of Devil's Point. It gradually dwindles: make efforts to stay on it as long as possible as it greatly eases the way. It curves around the Devil's southeast corner and up into **Glen Geusachan**. Here the path runs along the foot of the steep right-hand slope, where that slope levels to the valley floor. (Another small path runs up the left-hand, southern, side of Glen Geusachan).

Devil's Point Burn. The awkward waterfall is at the top of the picture

About 1km up the valley, the **Devil's Point Burn** (NN965945, named only on the Explorer map) runs down ahead in a series of small waterfalls. Further up, it runs down top-right to bottom-left in a **ravine** behind a fold in the slope. The continuing route will follow either the ravine or that **fold ridge** on its right.

Slant up to cross the burn below its waterfalls, and head up to the left of them. At the 660m contour the ravine runs to the right up into the hill.

The ascent of the ravine is a charming walk, except that one short waterfall will require an awkward scramble on earth and mossy rock to avoid it. The alternative is to cross the stream here at the very foot of the ravine, where it is gentle and stony. A short and very easy scramble (not even Grade 1) leads onto the fold ridge to right of the ravine. Go up this, beside the ravine, for 250m vertical height to the plateau edge.

RAVINE ALTERNATIVE

The fold ridge is pleasant, but the **ravine** is more romantic. A first small fall is avoided by an eroded deer-path on the right. Above this, a grassy gash heads up to the right: this becomes very steep at the top and is not advised as an escape from the ravine. Further up the ravine, the right wall overhangs impressively, and a bend in the stream reveals the 3m-high chockstone fall that proves problematic. Head up the left-hand ravine wall for about 10m, on earth and heather, looking for handholds in the half-buried rocks. Contour across to regain the stream 5m above the waterfall (Grade 2).

The rest of the ravine is a walk. Go up grass to the right of the final waterfalls, and emerge onto the plateau on the right.

Follow the plateau edge, with the slabby rockface dropping on your right into Glen Geusachan. Gently uphill for 800m reaches the **Devil's Point** summit cairn poised at the plateau corner.

Return along the Geusachan edge for 50m, and bear down right on a gravelly path that has one short bouldery section on the way down. Head north along the rim of Coire Odhar to the stream that falls into it. Ahead now is the standard route up **Cairn Toul** (Route 59). For the bothy, turn down right just before the stream, or on an easier path just after the stream. After 30m the two paths join, and run down to left of the stream. This well-made path crosses the stream halfway down and arrives right behind **Corrour bothy**.

LINN OF QUOICH

82 Glen Quoich

Length

Difficulty

Start/finish	Linn of Quoich NO118912
Distance	13.5km/8.5 miles
Ascent	200m/700ft
Approx time	4hr
Max altitude	500m
Terrain	Tracks and path
Map	See map for Route 76

Quoich is a beautiful wooded valley with fine hills at its head. The walk, on small tracks and a restored path, heads up the glen through moorland heather with wide views, and returns by the riverside under the pines. Two fords at the turn of the walk provide the only problem. They require agile boulder-hopping, or a pair of sandals in the pack, and will be impassible after heavy rain. To keep feet out of the water, it could be cycled, with the eastern outward track being rough and demanding.

Car parking at Allanquoich is across a wooden bridge at the road's end. **Start** up right of the river, past a boarded-up lodge and along the brink of Linn of Quoich (from Cuach, a cup), to a second boarded-up lodge near a footbridge. The Earl of Mar's **Punch Bowl**, a natural pothole in the river, is just upstream.

Don't cross the bridge but turn right, away from it, up through the trees to a track at their top edge. Turn left along this pleasant rough track through luxuriant heather. After 1.3km, passing along the top of a wood, ignore another track forking off right (marked as a path on maps). The main track continues above the wood, with views across to the wooded slope of Creag Bhalg and back to Lochnagar. In another 3km the track runs into open woodland. It swings right, into the upper valley, becoming narrow and little used and dropping to a ford through the **Quoich Water**. ▶

The track turns back downstream, following the valley floor with several small fords to give fun to mountain cyclists. After 1.5km it reaches a wider track, where you turn left for 100m to the ford over Allt an Dubhghlinne. Stone spits upstream give easiest crossing.

The wide, smooth track runs down-valley, south, first in the open then entering woodland. About 2.5km from the ford it drops to the riverside, and in another 1km once again runs alongside the river. As it turns away uphill, look out for a new-built path running down left, to a half-hidden footbridge (NO101922). Don't miss this bridge, as now a delightful path, restored in places, runs down the left side of Quoich Water. After 2km it reaches the Earl of Mar's **Punch Bowl**, with the car park just downstream.

This route is identical with the following one, except that **Route 83** adds in one of those fine hills, Beinn a' Bhuird.

Route 83 (Beinn a' Bhuird) keeps ahead here.

Earl of Mar's Punch Bowl. He filled it with whisky, honey, and a little boiling water for several hundred hunt followers

243

83 Beinn a' Bhuird

Length

Difficulty

Start/finish	Linn of Quoich NO118912
Distance	28.5km/18 miles
Ascent	950m/3200ft
Approx time	9.5hr
Bike approach	To ford of Allt an Dubh-ghlinne (saves 2hr)
Max altitude	1197m
Terrain	Tracks, paths including some rough ones, stones, heather, upland grass, and optional scrambling
Map	OS Explorer 404 Braemar; OS Landrangers 43 Braemar plus 36 Grantown
Scrambling	100m (optional) Grade 1

Imagine you're a mouse on a bothy table. A walk across the tabletop is fairly uninteresting, at least unless some human's after you for nibbling its biscuits. It's when you look over the edge to the concrete floor so many centimetres below that it gets exciting ... Beinn a' Bhuird means Table (Bhuird is from Buird, a board or table – Gaelic isn't always incomprehensible). Its edge is what's exciting.

That edge is on the east. Go right into the corrie with the lochan: a corrie that those who like their climbs remote and eagle-inspected call the loveliest rock playground of the area. And leave that corrie by a spur that's sharp but not steep, and offers some easy scrambling. Then follow the table's edge around that corrie and a bonus one to the north.

After all that, you can descend the standard route southwest. The standard route is gentle and easy and (like the Tourist Route on Ben Nevis) avoids all the interesting bits.

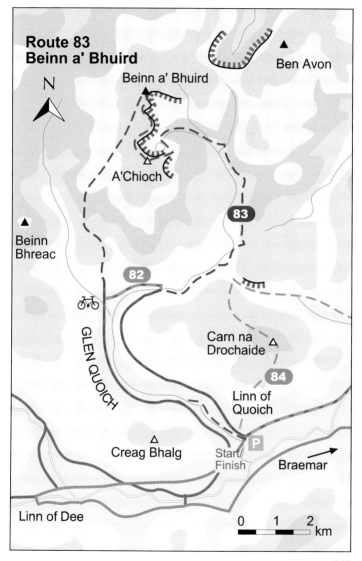

Route 83
Beinn a' Bhuird

N

Beinn a' Bhuird

Ben Avon

A'Chioch

83

Beinn
Bhreac

82

GLEN QUOICH

Carn na
Drochaide

84

Linn of
Quoich

Creag Bhalg

Start/
Finish

P

Braemar

Linn of Dee

0   1   2 km

CYCLISTS AND CORBETT-BAGGERS

Cyclists don't have to go out and back along the western track: try the tough one on the east side of Glen Quoich for the outward run. Corbett-baggers: Route 84 over Carn na Drochaide looks like a logical short-cut into this route. And it won't add anything to the overall time, though it may to the overall tiredness.

Short cut Across the ford on the left, an old path heads uphill, northwest, onto Carn Fiaclach for a shorter route up Beinn a' Bhuird.

Start along the previous Route 82 (Glen Quoich) to the ford of the Quoich Water. Cyclists will have walked the last bit from the ford of Allt an Dubh-ghlinne; they will need to cross the ford of the Quoich Water.

Head upstream, to the right of the river, on a rough, peaty path (another path is on the left side of the river). After 2km, and 200m after the final tree, comes an unobvious path junction. ◄

The path we want is the most noticeable one, bearing slightly right, away from the stream. After 500m it emerges back above Quoich Water on a high bank. Here it turns sharp right, away from the river. After 50m, turn left up a small peat path, northeast. ◄ This rises to join a clear and well-made path just above.

The main path, southwards, leads to the 'Fairy Glen', allowing a transfer into **Route 84**.

This comfortable path runs north up the right-hand side of the wild and heathery upper glen. At a stream crossing under Creag an Dail Mhor it reverts to its wild state, though further reconstruction is apparently planned for it. After 1km, at the valley head, the path crosses a stream.

Visible on the skyline just above is a square boulder, the **Clach a' Cleirich** (the clerk's stone), and the main path heads towards this. However, just above the stream turn left on a smaller path northwest. It peters out after 500m near a stream fork. Cross Allt Dearg, and go up to right of Allt an Dubh-lochain. The going is rocky and heathery, but not unduly rough. Pass the long pool of the Dubh Lochain (Black Pools), with the Dividing Buttress rising directly ahead, and bear left beside the main stream to the **Dubh Lochan** (same name, but in the singular) above.

From the outflow turn left around the lochan, and at its corner contour out left towards A'Chioch's northeast ridge. (A'Chioch means the breast, complete with granite nipple on top.) Make sure there's no uphill in your contouring, or you may miss some of the scrambling and end up on the wrong flank for the outflanking walk.

> The well-defined spur has as its crest a rocky rib for scramblers, with walking to its left. The rib steepens to a tower. There's a steep and slightly awkward path trace to left of the tower; scramblers can take the lower rib direct, then outflank the tower on the right on sloping and slightly exposed ledges, then back up left for 3m to the tower's top. The top has a small pothole, holding cool water to dampen the fevered brow.

> Walk up the gentler ridge above, to the rock knoll at the ridge top. This can be scrambled up, to left of a grassy streak. The final cupped boulder proves impregnable in windy conditions, and even the move leftwards along the crest requires the sophistication of a hand-jam hold. Descend the rock-knoll to the slightly higher one to the south, the true summit nipple of A'Chioch. This is scrambled easily up its facing side, with longer and rather harder routes up the southern face behind.

Unless you want to visit the 1179m South Top, whose tiny cairn rises 20cm above the stonefield and gravel, simply follow the corrie rim round westwards and then northwards, starting 3km of glorious walking along the Table's edge. Coire nan Clach (a double corrie) follows, to find the summit cairn of **Beinn a' Bhuird** 200m in from the crag edge.

Head back south on stony grassland past the top of Coire nan Clach, then down a grassy gentle southwest spur. At the 1180m contour pick up a new-made path

On the plateau of Beinn a' Bhuird, the Table

along the line of the removed track. Romp down the spur to **An Diollaid**. At the shelter marked on the Explorer map (NO075973), the path strikes down left across the sheltered valley wall of Alltan na Beinne, rejoining the former track line at a zigzag. It runs along the former track again onto the southeast spur of Carn Allt na Beinne, then at another zigzag keeps ahead, running down into woods.

At the floor of the Dubh Ghleann (NO079955) the path reaches the end of the surviving track. Follow it south out of trees to the ford of **Allt an Dubh-ghlinne**. After another 4km of track, as it turns slightly uphill away from the river, look out for a footbridge on the left. Don't miss it, as it leads to the delightful path on the left bank of Quoich Water back to Linn of Quoich.

84 Carn na Drochaide and the Fairy Glen

Start/finish	Linn of Quoich NO117910
Distance	15km/9.25 miles
Ascent	500m/1700ft
Approx time	5hr
Max altitude	818m
Terrain	Heather slope, then short easy heather, path and tracks

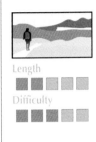

Length

Difficulty

Elsewhere in Scotland, a Corbett (2500-footer) counts as a considerable hill. Carn na Drochaide, however, is quite overpowered by the twin bulks of Beinn a' Bhuird and Ben Avon immediately to the north. The start at over 300m also helps make it seem distinctly middle-sized.

As a surprise contrast, the upper part of Glen Slugain is little and intricate. It's most untypical Cairngorm country in that it could be called pretty, or even sweet. Its nickname of Fairy Glen doesn't refer to the rather grim 'Sithean' of the Celts, but rather to the kind of fairies with twinkly slippers and outfits stitched from two bell-heather cups and a strategically placed birch leaf.

Start at **Linn of Quoich**, with a grass car park just over the Quoich Water.

Just after the car park the track forks, with the lesser left branch blocked against vehicles with large stones. Follow it to a boarded-up lodge and take the path beyond, up to right of the Quoich Water. Pass along the brink of the Linn, to a footbridge. The Earl of Mar's Punch Bowl is visible upstream from the bridge. This natural pot now has a hole in the bottom and no longer can be used for mixing drinks after deer hunts.

Don't cross the footbridge, but turn back sharp right away from the river, past another boarded-up lodge, onto

For a woodland way to the top of Glen Slugain use **Routes 82** and **83** – the circuit of 17.5km is again about 5hr.

249

a grassy track. A stony track joins from the left and runs towards **Allanaquoich**. At a gate just before it rejoins the larger track you started on, turn up left alongside a plantation. There's grassy going to the left of the trees, past the intake chamber for the house's water supply, then up a former ride in a patch of plantation now just stumps. At the highest scattered trees, take a small path slanting up to the right (20° magnetic). This path gets you through the worst of the deep heather, but when it peters out head straight uphill onto the shoulder called **Carn Dearg**. A path forms for the last slope onto this knoll.

Continue northwest, on an intermittent path, to the cairned summit of **Carn na Drochaide** (stone-hill of the bridges). Deeside is now out of sight but there are imposing views of the big hills to the north.

In the Fairy Glen of Gleann an t-Slugain

Head down on comfy short heather, passing a small pool on the ridge and the following a small rise, to the final rise to the cairn of **Carn na Criche**. Head down northeast, on ankle-high heather that becomes knee-high for the final 200m. Cross a col with small peaty hollows to a clump of big granite boulders, where you join a crossing path.

Turn right, down this good path, which drops into the green little Fairy Glen. You pass the ruined Slugain Lodge (Slugain means a gullet or throat – I think I prefer 'Fairy Glen'), then waterfalls and birches, before the valley widens and the path runs into a rough track.

The track runs down-valley with the river on its right. It enters forest through a deer gate, and 350m later joins a slightly larger track. Here turn back sharp right, signed by SRWS for Linn of Quoich.

The track crosses the river, then a cattle grid. Just after the grid is a junction where a small track continues ahead but our main one bends round left, again signed for Linn of Quoich. At the next grid, with a mobile phone mast alongside, ignore a track turning back left, and keep on ahead.

The track now runs close to the River Dee, with Braemar visible opposite. At **Allanmore** fork right onto a lesser track, thus passing to the right of the house. The track passes Allanaquoich to the bridge over Quoich Water at the car park.

BRAEMAR

85 Morrone Birkwood and the Dee

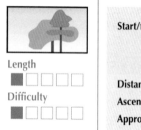

Length

■ □ □ □ □

Difficulty

■ □ □ □ □

Start/finish	West of Braemar on the Linn of Dee road, a small pull-off just outside the 30mph limit (NO144913)
Distance	9km/5.5 miles
Ascent	150m/500ft
Approx time	2.75hr
Max altitude	450m
Terrain	Paths

Ancient forest doesn't have to mean pines. Here are beautiful birches, views of the high mountains, and a wander along the banks of the Dee.

Start off down grassy banking to the River Dee. Follow it downstream to the right, to its confluence with the Clunie, and turn upstream alongside this new river. After 1.2km a footbridge leads across to the Invercauld Hotel.

Turn right, and cross the bridge towards **Braemar**'s centre, but at once turn left onto a minor road. It heads upstream with the ruins of the old Braemar castle on the right. After 1.2km it crosses a cattle grid, to a track on the right with a blue waymarker.

Head straight uphill under trees to a ladder stile. A faint path leads on uphill, bearing right to a gate. Now it gets easier to follow, to the top of the birchwood. Take a track ahead for 200m to a viewpoint indicator cairn above **Tomintoul** house. ▶

Keep on the main track ahead, contouring southwest through birchwood with juniper. After 1.5km, the track reaches a gate at the end of the **Morrone Birkwood** reserve.

Don't cross the ladder stile alongside, but turn sharp right on the Blue Trail's small path. Paths back through the birkwood are complex: keep gently downhill then level, northeast, and eventually you'll reach the duck pond above Braemar. Or closely follow the next two paragraphs:

The small path stays close to the plantation fence for 100m, then bears right for the same distance. Now it bends right again, and passes to the left of a damp grassy patch. Opposite the far end of this green patch, a small path turns up to the left, across a low knoll and down towards the Dee.

The path descends a slight spur, passing to the left of a small pool in the trees, then bearing right. The path now runs level, roughly east, and crosses a stream. A wider path joins from the right and stepping stones lead across another stream. The path now is wide and clear through a kissing gate to a track junction near the duck pond. ▶

Before the duck pond car park, turn sharply down left, on a stony track with a brown-topped waymark post. Cross the road below to a stile, and go down to the corner of a deer fence. Turn right to find a waymarked green path. This becomes a rough track, with the River Dee across grassland on the left. At a curve of the Dee, head up the banking on the right, to the car park pull-off.

The path up Morrone, **Route 86**, sets off left here.

Start and end of **Route 86**.

253

86 Morrone and Glen Ey

Start/finish	Braemar, the duck pond (NO144910)
Distance	20km/12.5 miles
Ascent	700m/1700ft
Approx time	6.75hr
Max altitude	859m
Terrain	Path, tracks, and short heather, with a rougher grassy descent

Length

Difficulty

At the back of Braemar rises a hill that's 50m too low to be a Munro. It also quite lacks the long walk in; you simply set off uphill between the birch trees. Morrone is a popular ascent, with a nice clear path, and a rough track leading off down the back (circuit of 11km/7 miles and 600m/2000ft; 4.25hr). For a slightly longer day on the hill, forget about the rough track and instead head west into lonely Glen Ey, the 'place of Gladness and Grief'. It's so-called from the 1840s when its inhabitants were cleared to make space for deer.

West of Braemar centre, Chapel Brae forks up left, signed for the Duck Pond. At the top of the road, there's a large car park.

Start up a track that runs uphill to right of the duck pond, forking left towards Woodhill (named as **Tomintoul** on the Landranger map). Before the house a path forks off right past a small quarry, rejoining the track above the house. Go straight on up it to a viewpoint cairn at a crossing track.

Cross this contouring track slantwise left, onto a clear path heading up Morrone. At about the 700m contour the path passes a clump of cairns, the turning point for the Morrone hill race that's part of the Braemar

Morrone summit

Games. The path continues less distinctly to **Morrone** summit with its cairn, radio mast, radio shack, and marker for the Birkwood Nature Reserve.

Behind the radio shack, a stony track, indistinct for the first few metres, runs gently down southwest. After a slight rise the track turns southeast towards a lower col. As the track turns down left, ▶ keep ahead to cross the col for the 60m of height gain to the cairn on **Carn na Drochaide**. This 825m summit doesn't have the 150m of drop needed for Corbett's list. It's the 818m Carn na Drochaide above Linn of Quoich (Route 84) that's a Corbett.

Shorter walk Follow the track to the back road in Glen Clunie. Turn left for 2km; just past the golf clubhouse turn up left (blue waymark) to viewpoint cairn above **Tomintoul**.

THE COLONEL'S BED

In the gorge of the main river at the foot of this stream is the **Colonel's Bed**: a ledge where John Farquharson of Inverey, known as the Black Colonel, hid out when the redcoats came to burn his castle after the Battle of Killiecrankie. Access to the ledge is now blocked by a loose landslip, but the gorge top is worth a visit anyway. The bridge further down the valley track is at the point on the gorge where the Black Colonel leapt across, stark naked, while his mistress Annie Bhan (fair-haired Annie) hurled the first of the soldiers down the castle steps with 'Cabh an Donus thu', 'Haste thee to the Devil, thou'.

Head down west, on short tundra vegetation, then climb slightly to a small cairned knoll at 760m on the Explorer (759m on Harveys). Follow its southwest spur down into Glen Ey (pronounced 'Glen Eye'). The Ey Burn is more like a river, but there's a track bridge just upstream.

The track runs down to the left of the river through the ruins of cottages. About 600m later the track crosses a stream (culvert, not bridge).

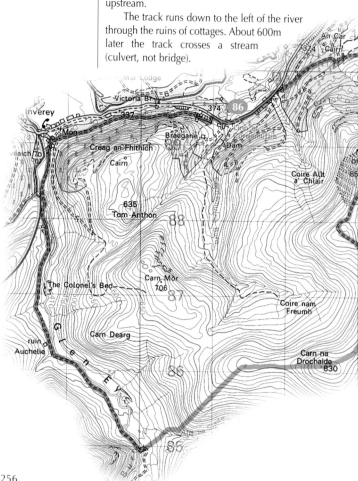

The track runs down-valley, with a short-cut path across its zigzag, to arrive at Knock Cottage above **Inverey**.

Here you can bear right through open pines to a little-used track through Knock Wood. RSPB and Mar Lodge ask you not to pass through during nesting of caper-caillie (March, April, May) and to keep to the path and not take a dog during the rest of the summer and early autumn.

(Alternatively, the Inverey road is just below.) The track passes through shady woodland. At the far end is a deer barrier that's chained loosely enough that you can step through between the gates.

Continue east along the road. Where it crosses the **Corriemulzie Burn** peer over the downstream side – there's a waterfall below. After another 800m there's a car park on the left. Opposite it, cross a stile onto a track leading up into forest.

Keep left at a junction just inside the trees. Ignore an old track on the left (on the map) and two newer ones (not on the map) to reach a small reservoir pond. Pass to the left of this, across its dam, into a narrow uphill track. Turn left at a T-junction, and in 50m keep ahead to a gate with a stile leading out of the trees (NO128902).

Here you enter the **Morrone Birkwood**. You can fork left on the Blue Trail and Route 85, but it's simpler to contour ahead on a narrow track through heather, juniper and scattered downy birches to revisit the view-point cairn at **Tomintoul**.

87 Creag nan Gabhar

Length

Difficulty

Start/finish	Auchallater NO155882
Distance	13km/8 miles
Ascent	470m/1600ft
Approx time	4.5hr
Max altitude	834m
Terrain	Tracks, and a heather path

Here's an easy half-day, on Landrover tracks, that bags you a Corbett and some fine views of Lochnagar, Glen Callater and Deeside. Sandals are helpful for the river crossing near the end of the walk. The following Route 88 extends this one into a jolly long day that also gathers three Munros.

Start from the roadside pull-off beside the A93 at **Auchallater**.

From the parking place, a track runs up through a locked gate with a small gate alongside, into Glen Callater. It runs to the right of the **Callater Burn** in its small gorge. After 2km, the track and river bend left, and here a smaller track doubles back right to zigzag uphill. Where it contours northwards stay with it – there's a great view of Braemar just ahead, and the track then doubles back to run along the crest over **Sron nan Gabhar** (Gahwar: literally, nose of the goat).

Over 3km the track gradually shrinks to become a small path onto the east end of Creag nan Gabhar. Surprisingly, beneath the heather this hill is composed of

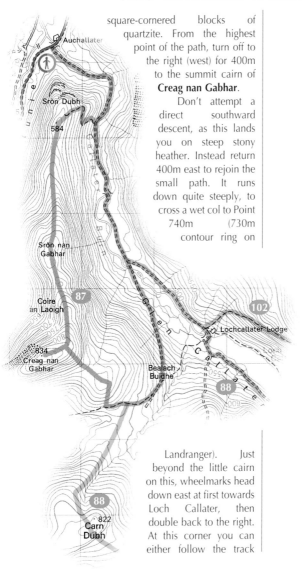

square-cornered blocks of quartzite. From the highest point of the path, turn off to the right (west) for 400m to the summit cairn of **Creag nan Gabhar**.

Don't attempt a direct southward descent, as this lands you on steep stony heather. Instead return 400m east to rejoin the small path. It runs down quite steeply, to cross a wet col to Point 740m (730m contour ring on

Landranger). Just beyond the little cairn on this, wheelmarks head down east at first towards Loch Callater, then double back to the right. At this corner you can either follow the track

*The longer **Route 88**
now continues
southwards across
the col.*

down to the right, ◀ or head more directly downwards on short heather, either way joining a Landrover track below.

The track slants left, down the side of Glen Callater, then crossing the Callater Burn by a wide, shallow, stony ford. Sandals make for the most comfortable crossing; if the burn is full, turn down the bank for a rough 1km to rejoin the track after its bridge. Having crossed the ford, the track joins a larger one where you keep ahead, down the valley, to cross the bridge. The track continues to the left of the Callater Burn, after 1km rejoining the outward route.

88 White Mounth and Jock's Road

Length

Difficulty

Start/finish	Auchallater NO155882
Distance	27.5km/17.25 miles
Ascent	1100m/3600ft
Approx time	9.5hr
Max altitude	1064m
Terrain	Tracks, dampish grassland, small peaty path
Maps	Harveys Lochnagar; OS Landrangers 43 Braemar and 44 Ballater; OS Explorers 387 and 388 (or Route 87's map and Explorer 388)

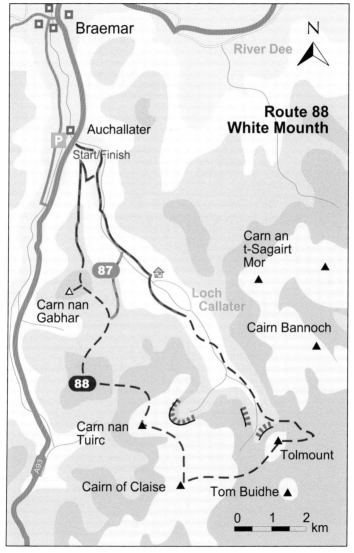

N

Braemar

River Dee

Route 88
White Mounth

P
Auchallater
Start/Finish

87

Carn nan
Gabhar

Loch
Callater

Carn an
t-Sagairt
Mor
▲

Cairn Bannoch
▲

88

Carn nan
Tuirc ▲

Tolmount ▲

Cairn of Claise ▲

Tom Buidhe ▲

A93

0   1   2
km

This Callater circuit starts on heathery crests with wide views, continues on bleak almost-arctic grassland, and finishes down a beautiful glen. By their normal route, from the Glenshee ski area, the three Munros are often found dull. This way they make a rich and varied walk that's interestingly different from the granite plateaux of the main Cairngorms.

Start as Route 87 (Creag nan Gabhar), to reach the track above Glen Callater. From the top end of the track (NO164834) above Moine Bhealaich Bhuidhe, peaty wheelmarks continue down southwest across the wet col and up the slope of Carn Dubh. Just below the crest the wheelmarks turn left, southeast, to pass across **Carn Dubh**'s small plateau 200m south of the quartzite cairn at 822m. (The opposite, southwest, corner of the plateau appears to be the actual summit.)

The rough track drops east into the next, boggy col, aiming for a line of newly excavated grouse butts. Head up past these, then follow a stream on the right, up onto the stony plateau. As the slope levels off keep right, to reach the large summit cairn of **Carn an Tuirc** (stonepile of the wild boar).

Head east across a stonefield to Carn an Tuirc's smaller east top, then down southeast. Once below the summit stonefield a clear path forms. Follow it southeast to join a wide path across the grassy meadow, rising onto the slopes of Cairn of Claise. When the track reaches a

On the White Mounth, looking for the little cairns that mark the top of Jock's Road. Broad Cairn above

wall end, follow this wall to **Cairn of Claise**'s summit (Cairn o' Clasha: stonepile of the hollow).

Head just north of east on a small path into a broad moorland col. Head northeast, passing to the left of a small rainwater peat pool with the path now clear, climbing gently onto **Tolmount**.

From this summit descend northeast, on no particular path. Just past the lowest point of the col, a few iron fence posts are scattered about, and among them you may notice the small cairns of the Jock's Road path, now less used than at any time since prehistory. (Meanwhile, car-park-to-Munro paths spread like a rash.)

Turn left, following cairns if you can find them, down the steep grassy headwall of **Glen Callater**. The small path is marked by occasional iron fence posts carried down from the fallen fencing above. The opposite side of the valley shows a large waterfall.

At the valley floor, head down to the right of a stream, with the path now fairly clear, sometimes on the grassy stream bank, sometimes keeping further to the right just above the swamps of the valley floor. Pass below the lovely side-cwm of Loch Kander; sadly the loch itself is invisible, as it is also from the plateau above. But you do get to look at another waterfall high on the left of the cwm.

The path continues down-valley to the right of the stream. As the valley widens to grassy flats, cross the **Allt an Loch** at a river island (NO195825). A grassy track starts on the other side. However, this track uses the stream bed for gravelly driving at various places, so just walk the grassy flats of the valley floor. At the loch head, the track runs up to the left, now stony, to pass along to the left of **Loch Callater**.

Near the loch head, where the track turns up left, follow wheelmarks ahead, rejoining the track to cross the loch outflow river to Lochcallater Lodge and bothy. At the bothy turn left on a track, to exit through a gate. Here bikes are chained by people using the path that heads up right towards Carn an t-Sagairt Mor.

The good track runs down the valley, after 2.5km crossing the **Callater Burn** by bridge and 1km later rejoining the outward route for the last 2km to the car park.

PART 7

BALMORAL AND LOCHNAGAR

Lochnagar is on the wrong side of the Dee – but right in every other respect. It's correctly Cairngorm in the way it rises from its river first in forest, then in heather, then finally in granite crag. Southwards, its high-level yellow grasslands stretch into Angus: it's the Great Moss, only slightly smaller. Golfers could treat the place as a giant fairway, tee-ing off on the Tolmount for a 5-mile drive down to the Driesh. More predictably, Munro-baggers can gather seven summits or more in one long upland romp.

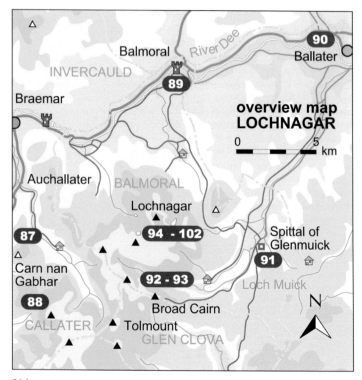

Lochnagar, seen on Route 89 from above Balmoral Castle

The Scottish Parliament, when drawing the boundaries of the National Park, decided that Lochnagar was Cairngorms even though it wasn't. And I agree with them. And so, presumably, did the 'Queen Dee', Victoria herself, who built a holiday castle at Balmoral and bought the forest of Ballochbuie to stop it being chopped down.

But bear in mind that 'Lochnagar' names not rock or moorland but a body of water. The hill is fine, but the wet bits are even better. On the mountain's dark side, the Corrie of Lochnagar, the blue pool below and craggy grey above are not just for the climbers of granite or ice. Below the eastern slopes, the loveliness of Loch Muick is circled by a wide and tempting path. While those who like their granite truly grim will stride up below the waterfalls to the Dubh Loch.

Underneath all that, the River Dee winds down from Balmoral to Ballater. Before the final section takes us onto dark Lochnagar itself, here are the last two of the eight walks in this book to feature the silvery river.

BALMORAL

89 Balmoral Castle

Length

■□□□□

Difficulty

■□□□□

Start/finish	Crathie NO265949
Distance	8km/5 miles
Ascent	240m/800ft
Approx time	2.5hr
Max altitude	442m
Terrain	Good paths
Food on route	Cafe at Balmoral Castle

This walk is on paths created, laid out and decorated with monster cairns by Queen Victoria. Royal walks don't come cheap and there's an entry charge to this one. For your £5 (adult) you get five of the monster cairns, a stretch of the River Dee, a glimpse under John Brown's kilt and a tour of a stonepile even more monster-massive than Prince Albert's Cairn.

The walk uses parts of three of the Balmoral Trails, but in the opposite direction to the waymarking (so as to get the initial riverside, climax at the Albert memorial, and end up at the castle and cafe). If you want easier path-finding, do it in reverse, using the Balmoral booklet – which will be another £5 of fealty transferred to Her Majesty by you the humble subject.

Castle and grounds open early April to end July. Attempt this walk in August and you'll be escorted out of the grounds by gentlemen in camouflage clothing (or even possibly shot).

Start at the large pay-and-display car park on the A93 opposite Crathie Church. Cross the River Dee to the lodge gateway into Balmoral Castle. Here you must pay to enter the grounds, and can also buy a booklet with a map of the marked walks. After 50m turn right off the tarred driveway, onto an unsurfaced track that bends to the left as it reaches the river. After 200m bear right on a wide path that continues along the riverbank.

At a junction after 300m, the path to the left would take you to the cafe and the castle. This walk keeps ahead, along the Riverside Path, screened from the river

Balmoral Castle

(and from paparazzi photographers on the A93 opposite) by a line of alder trees. After 800m it runs up to join a tarred driveway, with a dry drinking trough opposite. Follow the driveway ahead for 50m to a path rising on the left. At another driveway just above turn right for a few steps then left up an earth track under pine trees.

After 400m this reaches a junction with a map of estate paths. Keep ahead on the track. As the slope eases it bends left (east), passing through clearings to a T-junction with a view to Lochnagar.

Turn left, away from Lochnagar, on a wide grassy path. After 200m the path bends left: here an unused grassy path on the left leads up a slight rise and down to Prince Arthur's Cairn standing in a small clearing. Admire the stonework and a glimpse between tree trunks to Ben Avon, then return and continue along the main path to a junction with waymarks in blue and red.

Head up to the right to visit the large Purchase Cairn, with a wide view over Queen Victoria's holiday home and its patch of ground. The path passes to the right of the cairn: it's the Blue Trail backwards. It runs gently downhill and south, with a short side-path on the right to the cairn commemorating the marriage of Princess Louise. In another 500m, ignore the Blue Trail arriving from the left, and keep ahead, through a gate in a deer fence, to a junction of forest roads.

Take the unsurfaced road opposite, southwards. After 300m, with the forest edge visible ahead, a wide path turns up to the left, and leads up to the huge pyramidal cairn raised 'to the beloved memory of **Albert** the great and good; prince consort'.

The path continues on the right, away from the south wall of the cairn. It drops past a corner where trees have been felled to provide a view of the Lochnagar Distillery, and past a final cairn, massive and conical, that celebrates the marriage of **Princess Beatrice** to Prince Henry of Battenberg. The path descends through the deer fence to a tarred estate road.

Turn left, uphill, for 200m to a gate. Through this, turn immediately right through another gate, and go down a dirt track next to a paddock to join a wide path. Turn right, downhill under beautiful birches, ignoring one path back right and another back left. At a fork with a waymark pole, bear left, to reach after 50m John Brown's statue. The Queen's faithful servant has been done in bronze with such authenticity that you can, if interested, inspect what he wore under his kilt. Though it doesn't show on the statue, the undergarment must be imagined in matching tartan.

Prince Albert's memorial cairn

Continue slightly uphill to a path junction with blue and red waymarks. Here turn downhill, with a blue arrow pointing the way, to a junction of estate roads. Cross and bear left, with a yellow arrow, soon bearing right to a large stone waymarker with a yellow flag on top: it's **Balmoral Castle** at last.

The quick way out of the estate is to turn right, across the south front of the castle, and bear right on a tarred driveway. You can exit through a side door even after the main gates have closed at 5pm.

BALLATER

90 Craigendarroch and the Dee

Length
■ □ □ □ □

Difficulty
■ ■ □ □ □

Start/finish	Old Royal Station, Ballater NO369958
Distance	7km/4.5 miles
Ascent	260m/700ft
Approx time	2.5hr
Max altitude	402m
Terrain	Paths

This rather contorted route bends back on itself to take in three fine features: the rocky cleft of the Pass of Ballater, Craigendarroch summit, and the River Dee. So it's the eighth walk to do a bit of Dee. Actually, Dee you can't overdo.

Ballater from Craigendarroch

Start at the Old Royal Station information centre and car park.

Turn right out of the car park to cross the former railway bridge on the A93. After 400m, a street on the right is Craigendarroch Walk. After 75m, a waymarked path on the left leads up onto the hill. Craigendarroch appropriately means 'crag of the oak trees'.

After 50m a path on the left is waymarked, and signed 'To Top', but keep ahead on a smaller path that contours around the hill. After 100m it drops to join a wider path slanting up from the right. Keep ahead on this, gradually rising around the base of the hill and then rising more steeply in a zigzag. The path passes below the foot of crags to a junction with a bench.

Take the main path ahead. It runs around the hill, gently downhill, and at a waymark post zigzags down right and back left below. Now it crosses a steep slope, with views across the **Pass of Ballater** on the right. As the path passes round onto the western side of the hill, the slope eases, and a wall joins from below. In another 200m you reach a junction with waymarks, and the path up left signed 'To Top' high in a tree.

Turn up this rather steep path, with some stone steps and bare granite slabs, to emerge at **Craigendarroch** summit. Here there's an impressive view straight down onto Ballater, and a large cairn.

Just above the cairn, a bench marks the true summit. Behind it, a small path runs northeast, with a waymark after 50m. It runs under birches, dropping to the path junction with a bench on the east side of the hill. Turn right, down the outward route, to the street called Craigendarroch Walk and the main A93.

Turn right for 200m, then left into Braemar Place. After 75m turn right into Old Line Road, with a footpath on its right. This ends after 150m; ignore the Blue Trail forking right, but keep ahead to the **River Dee**.

Turn left, on a well-surfaced path alongside the river. After 600m, the golf clubhouse is in sight ahead; here the path forks slightly left, away from the river, under

low-voltage power lines. It soon rejoins the Dee, to reach
the corner of Ballater Caravan Site. Here turn left on a
fenced path between golf and caravans, then right into
Anderson Road. At the end of a cypress hedge, turn right
into the caravan site, and left through a children's play
area to the riverside. A small gate ahead is signed
'walkers welcome', and leads along the riverside to
Ballater Bridge.

Turn left up steps to join the main road ahead,
and follow it through Ballater's main square to the
Old Station.

LOCH MUICK

91 Around Loch Muick

Length

⬛☐☐☐☐

Difficulty

⬛☐☐☐☐

Start/finish	Spittal of Glenmuick NO310851
Distance	12km/7.5 miles
Ascent	90m/300ft
Approx time	3hr
Max altitude	430m
Terrain	Tracks and path

The walk round Loch Muick was loved by Queen Victoria and is very popular today. Very early or late in the day you'll find it unpeopled, but then
liable to get crowded out by large herds of deer on the flats at the loch foot.
For an extended walk that's more rugged underfoot and very much more so
overhead, take a side trip up to the grim Dubh Loch (see Route 92), and
even walk around it (see Route 93, Creag an Dubh-loch).

Start along a track that leads across a bridge and down
to pass a toilet block in a small pinewood, and then the
little nature and information hut with its coffee machine,

Loch Muick from its foot

Spittal of Glenmuick's £2 pay-and-display is large, but still full up on sunny weekends.

Loch Muick (Mick): Lake of pigs – as Queen Victoria commented, not a very pretty name.

standing in a slightly larger wood. Immediately past this, keep ahead on a track signed 'Loch Muick'. After 400m ignore a side-track forking up left (the Capel Mount), and then a path turning off right, and keep ahead on the track to reach the lochside.

The track continues alongside Loch Muick for 2km, then crosses the **Black Burn**. At once turn down right on a path signed 'Lochmuick Circuit' to return to the loch side. The path is rather narrow, and crosses a fairly steep slope. After 1.5km it reaches the loch head – ignore a path forking off uphill on the left just before this point. Instead follow the path to the right across two small

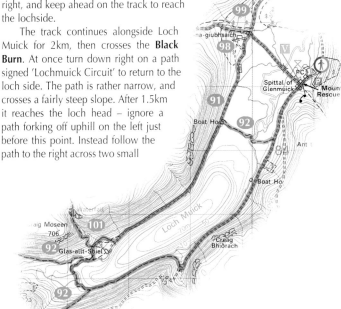

footbridges and past a beach, to round the loch's north-west corner.

The path continues along the loch side towards the plantation around **Glas-allt Shiel**. 100m before the plantation, ignore a path turning sharply back left; that one is heading for the Dubh Loch. ◀ Immediately before the plantation, fork left up rather slippery wooden sleepers through a wall gap, and go uphill just inside the plantation with the wall on your left. The path bends right to follow the top of the trees, and crosses a footbridge of the **Glas Allt** stream. It then descends gently through the trees, to meet a track at the lochside.

Turn left along the track, at once leaving the trees, and then following the loch side. At the loch's north corner keep ahead for another 1km, to the buildings at **Allt-na-giubhsaich**. Here turn right on a broad path, which soon joins a track to cross the valley floor to the information hut close to the walk start.

The diversion to visit the foot of the Dubh Loch adds about 6km, 250m of ascent and 2hr to the walk.

92 Dubh Loch and Broad Cairn

Length

Difficulty

Start/finish	Spittal of Glenmuick NO310851
Distance	27km/17 miles
Ascent	850m/2800ft
Approx time	9hr
Bike approach	To Loch Muick head (saves 2hr)
Max altitude	1047m
Terrain	Tracks, a rough little path above Dubh Loch, grassy plateau with a couple of boulderfields
Map	Harveys Lochnagar; OS Explorer 388 Lochnagar; OS Landranger 44 Ballater

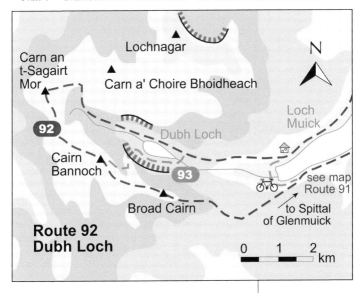

Route 92
Dubh Loch

You can bag seven Munros at once, or even nine, criss-crossing the White Mounth plateau on grassy paths. But you're missing the point if you do. Down below the plateau is one of Scotland's grimmest lochs. Grey granite overhangs it, boulders obstruct the path, and waterfalls splash in from either side. This is Dubh Loch, the Black Lake. It's dark because shaded by the area's highest crag, and in Route 93 we'll take a challenging line through the middle of that. On this walk we take it slightly easier beside the stream, then get three of those Munros anyway on a high-level return route around the top rim of Loch Muick.

Start at Spittal of Glenmuick's large car park. Follow the track down to pass the information hut. At the junction just beyond, keep ahead, signed for Loch Muick. In 1km, before the next pinewood, a path turns off right to cross a nice little footbridge at Muick's outflow. At a boathouse climb onto a smooth track and turn left along the loch side.

In 2.5km the track enters a pinewood and passes **Glas-allt Shiel**. The bothy is in a smaller building behind. The wide path continues, leaving the pinewood. Here ignore a path turning back sharp right, but after 100m bear right on a well-made path that passes below Stulan waterfall. On either side are scattered birches, very attractive in silver-and-gold autumn colouring – the area around Loch Muick is a nature reserve. The path rises gradually to a sudden view of the **Dubh Loch** ◄ in its valley of boulders and black peat, hemmed in by crags.

Here **Route 93** *(Creag an Dubh-loch) forks off left.*

The path passes to right of the loch, with fine views of the crags opposite. Above on the right are gentler slabs of Eagles Rock with a long waterfall. Once past the head of the loch the path deteriorates into a narrow trod. Follow it up, quite steep and rough, to the right of the long waterslide of the **Allt an Dubh-loch**.

On Cairn Bannoch, looking across the hollow of the Dubh Loch to Lochnagar

At the top of the stream, the path ends at a cairn (NO228833). The valley levels off now, becoming wide and boggy. Stay on grassy slopes to the right of the valley floor, passing across the broken slope of Carn a' Choire Bhoidheach then slanting up to a path/stream junction at NO218844.

Turn left along the path, contouring round the slope of Carn an t-Sagairt Beag for 200m or so, then slanting up right into the col between it and Carn an t-Sagairt Mor. Head southwest, up the line of a former fence, crossing a small boulderfield and passing the fuselage of a crashed plane to a cairn decorated with old iron fence posts. Turn left, south, to **Carn an t-Sagairt Mor**'s true summit cairn 200m away (Carn an Taggart Mor: big stonepile of the priest).

Head southeast, on a fairly clear path, across a wide col to reach the rocky top knoll of Cairn Bannoch (bannoch: a bun or bannock; like corrie, cairn, ceilidh, whisky, gob and ptarmigan, a Gaelic word taken into English or Scots). The descent from this is initially unclear over the rocks; head south along the rock spine for 20m to a lower cairn, and continue south over stones for another 150m. Then bend southeast on a path now clear, to cross to the right of the tiny cairn on Craig of Gowal (another Munro top, with Cairn of Gowal also a necessary visit for top-baggers). The path is again unclear across boulderfield to the summit tor of **Broad Cairn**.

Once again the descent line is unclear, with fragments of path appearing on various grassy islands among the boulders. Head down to the levelling at 850m, where an ugly sunken track begins. Paths run along its rim and short-cut its zigzags, down to a hut in a slight col. This is a stable for stalkers' ponies, and doesn't offer shelter to walkers apart from the bench on its gable end.

Pass to the left of the hut, and after another 150m slightly uphill, take a resurfaced path forking off left. ▶ It slants down the steep flank of **Corrie Chash** to the corner of Loch Muick. Keep ahead along the lochside path, and its continuation track, to rejoin the outward route for the last 1km back to Spittal.

Alternative If you prefer the heights to the lochside, stay on the track ahead; after 3km it too drops to the loch.

93 Creag an Dubh-loch

Start/finish	Spittal of Glenmuick NO310851
Distance	21km/13 miles
Ascent	800m/2700ft
Approx time	7.5hr
Bike approach	To head of Loch Muick (saves 2hr)
Max altitude	1012m
Terrain	Gully with boulders, stones and a little path
Map	Harveys Lochnagar; OS Explorer 388 Lochnagar; OS Landranger 44 Ballater

This route embellishes Route 92 by going up through the middle of the area's highest crag, Creag an Dubh-loch. **Central Gully** is described as a 'scramble' in Hamish MacInnes' *Highland Walks* and in the SMC *Climbers' Guide*. MacInnes in particular should know better. It is a steep walk, sometimes on ground reminiscent of the Chalamain Gap, sometimes on a little ferny path. As a walk, it's an imposing one, and makes a challenging route onto the two Munros above Loch Muick.

Start as on the previous Route 92 (Dubh Loch to Broad Cairn) and follow it to the Dubh Loch. Stop where the loch first comes into sight, with the huge **Craig an Dubh-loch** rising behind it. You can see, near the right-hand end of the crags, the large and obvious scree fan that emerges from **Central Gully** down to the head of the loch.

Just before the foot of the Dubh Loch a small path forks off left, crossing the outflow on boulders and then working through boulders and heather around the loch. It peters out as the climbers who formed it head for

A walker among climbs: in the Central Gully of Creag an Dubh-loch

different climbs across the crag. Go up through heathery boulders to the lowest point of the crag (Central Gully Buttress). Pass to the right, along grass below the crags, and up a small grassy path to the left of the scree-and-boulder fan that emerges out of **Central Gully** (NO233826).

As the grass strip peters out, move onto the awkward steep scree and stones of the gully fan. At the top of the scree fan, bear left into the gully, with the going now less steep. Scree and boulders form the first section, with some scrambling if you choose the largest possible boulders. Above that is a section with grass and fern, before a final bouldery section finishes abruptly on the plateau.

From the gully top, it's easy to rejoin Route 92 at either of its Munro summits. On the left, the hummock above **Creag an Dubh-loch** is a Munro top leading naturally to Broad Cairn. But if you want both the Munros, turn right and head west across the damp, shallow valley of the Allt Coire Uilleim Mhoir and up grassy slopes to the rocky top knoll of **Cairn Bannoch**. Either way, continue as on Route 92.

SUMMIT SUMMARY

LOCHNAGAR

Gaelic	From Loch na Gaire (the loch in its northeast corrie): loch of the raucous noise (or just possibly, loch of the laughter); its earlier name was Bincichins, from Beinn Ciochan, hill of the breasts, referring to Meikle and Little Paps.
Altitude	1155m/3790ft, Scotland's 20th highest
First recorded ascent	Lord Byron in 1803; Queen Victoria went up in 1848
Maps	OS Landranger 44 Ballater; OS Explorer 388 Lochnagar; Harveys Lochnagar (see also individual route headings)

Lochnagar from Inver, above the Dee

The standard route up Lochnagar is from Spittal of Glenmuick. It's a good one. For the ascent, Route 97 gives a clear, well-made path. At the Meikle Pap col there's a glimpse into the Corrie of Lochnagar, and then a stroll around its rim looking at the tops of all the rock towers. Then the descent, by Route 101, turns into a zigzag path alongside a waterfall that's almost alpine in feel. To end it all there's a stroll home along the loch side.

But Lochnagar demands to be walked up more than once. First of all, why be content with a glimpse into the Corrie of Lochnagar, when a small climbers' path (Route 100) takes you right in below those great granite faces? Then there's Queen Victoria's Route 94 from the north, with its forest waterfall for first course; and Byron's Route 95, which adds a rocky ridge-scramble.

For Corbett-baggers, or simple lovers of uncrowded mountains, Route 99 takes in the little granite-and-heather top of Conachcraig; while Route 102 from Loch Callater allows a grand traverse of the mountain, Braemar to Balmoral, with the Deeside bus to link the two ends of it. If all that's not enough – and on this hill, you do keep coming back for more – then Routes 92 and 93 in the previous section link in for a five-Munro circuit, or the dark delights of the Dubh Loch.

LOCHNAGAR ROUTES

94 Queen Victoria's Ballochbuie Route

95 Byron's Scramble by the Stuic (scramble) Grade 1

96 Tracks from Balmoral

97 Meall Coire na Saobhaidhe

98 Tourist Path from Spittal of Glenmuick

99 Conachcraig

100 Loch na Gaire

101 Falls of Glas Allt (descent)

102 From Loch Callater

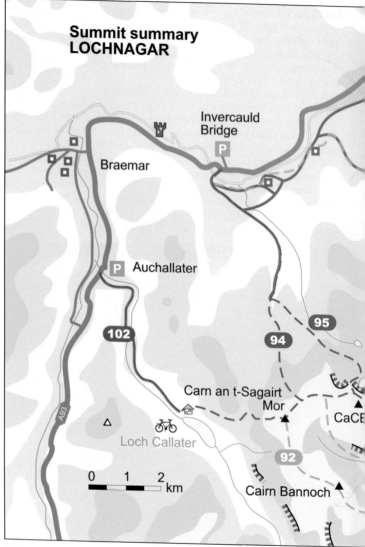

Summit summary LOCHNAGAR

Invercauld Bridge

Braemar

Auchallater

102

95

94

Carn an t-Sagairt Mor

CaCE

Loch Callater

92

Cairn Bannoch

0 1 2 km

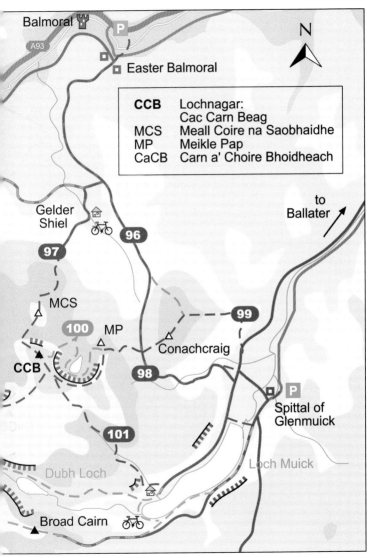

Balmoral
A93
Easter Balmoral

CCB	Lochnagar:
	Cac Carn Beag
MCS	Meall Coire na Saobhaidhe
MP	Meikle Pap
CaCB	Carn a' Choire Bhoidheach

N

to
Ballater

Gelder
Shiel
97
96

MCS
100
MP
CCB
Conachcraig
99
98

Spittal of
Glenmuick

101

Dubh Loch
Loch Muick

Broad Cairn

94 Queen Victoria's Ballochbuie Route

Start	Keiloch NO187913
Distance	12km/7.5 miles
Ascent	950m/3100ft
Approx time up	5hr
Terrain	Track, path, and smooth plateau – Queen Victoria did it on a pony
Map	OS Landranger 43 as well as 44; OS Explorer 388; Harveys doesn't cover this approach

A route that's rather easy but also rather long, with forest, a fine waterfall, and a wander along the high plateau.

About 200m east of Invercauld Bridge, a signed turning north off A93 leads to the walkers' pay-and-display car park.

Start back down the lane to cross the A93 onto a path to the River Dee. Turn right, upstream, to the old **Bridge of Dee**, and cross it. Through a deer gate, turn left on a track running southeast. After 400m – and having ignored one small track sharply back right – fork right into a lesser track. Follow this gently uphill, still southeast, straight across one junction, and over Glenbeg Burn.

In 300m ignore a side-track on the left and keep ahead towards the **Falls of Garbh-allt** (Garve Alt: rough stream) ahead on the left. A path forks off the track to visit them. Don't cross the elegant iron footbridge, but take a small path on uphill, winding away from the river and back, to reach a track above. Turn right on this for 20m, to rejoin the main uphill track. It emerges from forest at a gate, ◀ then rises alongside the river to end at a shelter hut for ponies.

Route 95 (the Stuic) turns off just above this point.

A good path continues to the right of **Feindallacher Burn**. After 500m, watch out for the crossing point, at the grassy abutments of a former footbridge (now washed away and lying 100m downstream). A good gravelly path runs roughly south up the spur crest, past cairns, petering out as it passes to the left of the tiny pool marked on Harveys. Continue straight uphill to **Carn an t-Sagairt Beag**, ▶ crossing stonefield, to its metre-high summit tor.

Head east into a wide grassy col. Now a former pony path runs ahead, but there's a Munro summit on the right, while on the left is an ideal sandwich stop at the sudden crag top of the Stuic. Best is to head first southeast to Carn a' Choire Bhoidheach (1110m, unnamed on Landranger); then head north, crossing the pony path, to **the Stuic** top for sandwiches and the view.

Follow the exciting crag rim east, with the pony path soon arriving from the right to join you. This well-trodden path leads up to the rock tor **Cac Carn Mor**. An even wider path now runs northwards; keep to the right of it for glimpses down into the Corrie of Lochnagar, before scrambling the summit rockpile **Cac Carn Beag** (Carn Cac Mor/Beag: large/small pile of excrement!).

To preserve its trees, Queen Victoria bought Ballochbuie Forest at the foot of her route up Lochnagar

Route 101 (from Callater) joins in here.

95 Byron's Scramble by the Stuic

Difficulty	Scramble Grade 1
Start	Keiloch NO187913
Distance	11km/7 miles
Ascent	900m/3000ft
Approx time up	5.5hr
Terrain	Track, rough hillside, rocky ridge
Map	OS Landranger 43 as well as 44; OS Explorer 388; Harveys doesn't cover this approach
Scrambling	100m

This fine scramble was used by Byron on the first recorded ascent of Lochnagar. Byron had a club foot; so you can be assured that the scramble is not just historic but also reasonably easy.

Start as Route 94, and follow it to the exit gate from the forest at 550m altitude.

Continue briefly up the track to choose a good line over the rough moorland to the left. Cross the stream, then head southeast up and across a moorland spur to a second stream (**Allt Lochan nan Eun**). Keep uphill beside this, to the **Sandy Loch**. At the lochan's outflow turn right. The Stuic is now directly above, looking intimidating. Pick a path through rocky ground to the base of the steep sharp spur.

The ascent is an easy scramble on piled granite blocks. There is a small path to show the way: the easiest line is a few feet left of the crest.

The ridge steepens to a final tower. The last step of this is steep and exposed, but can be

avoided by walking 5m to the left then slanting back up right on a ledge.

At the top, find a sheltered corner for sandwiches overlooking Loch nan Eun; both Byron and Queen Victoria paused here. Head south across the plateau, crossing the wide Pony Path, to the slight rise of Carn a' Choire Bhoidheach (1110m – Voyach: stony hill of the beautiful corrie). Head back northeast to join the Pony Path. It leads easily to **Carn Cac Beag** then north to the summit.

Scrambling the Stuic. The poet Byron, who suffered from a club foot, made Lochnagar's first recorded ascent this way (photo Tom Turnbull)

96 Tracks from Balmoral

Difficulty

| | | |

Start	Crathie (NS264949)
Distance	14.5km/9 miles
Ascent	900m/3000ft
Approx time up	5hr
Terrain	Track and wide path
Map	Harveys does not cover this approach

Unexciting but easy, so a useful descent route.

Balmoral Castle has a large car park on on the A93. **Start** from the information centre at the car park corner. Return briefly to the A93, then turn right into a lane that passes Crathie graveyard, where Queen Victoria's hillwalking leader John Brown is buried. Turn right to cross a splendid footbridge over the **River Dee**.

Option After 3km, strike up left onto Caisteal na Caillich, 'Witch's Castle'. Continue on a very small path over Point 850m to switch into Route 99 and bag the Corbett Conachcraig.

Turn right for 50m, up left, and then right again to the grocer's shop in **Easter Balmoral**. Before the shop, turn up left on an estate road marked 'Private' – it's a right of way for walkers. It leads up southwest through forest, becoming unsurfaced after a gate. In 600m turn left onto another track, southwards. About 2km after leaving the forest it reaches a junction.

Follow the main track ahead, uphill ◀ into the broad col between Conachcraig and Meikle Pap. At the highest point of the track, turn off right onto the broad, restored Tourist Path up Lochnagar (Route 98).

You may be aiming for Keiloch rather than Balmoral. Attractive tracks run south of Ripe Hill, to **Connachat Cottage**. After another 1km fork right to pass north of **Garbh Allt Shiel** and along by the Dee to the old bridge.

97 Meall Coire na Saobhaidhe

Difficulty

Start	Crathie NS264949
Distance	11km/7 miles
Ascent	950m/3100ft
Approx time up	5hr
Terrain	Tracks, small path, stony heather slope
Bike	To Gelder Shiel (saves 1hr each way)
Map	Harveys doesn't cover this approach

This subsidiary top gives a view from a remote and rocky perch onward to a whole lot more rock on the main mountain.

Start by following Route 96 to the track junction 3km above the top of the forest.

Turn right, slightly downhill, and in 300m left onto the track leading up to **Gelder Shiel**, where you pass between the Queen Mother's cottage (right) and a bothy. The track crosses the stream and continues up the moor. From its end a small path continues southwards, up the base of Creag Liath and then spiralling left, around its side. It's aiming for the Liath/Saobhaidhe col but peters

*Track to Lochnagar
from Gelder Shiel*

out well before it gets there. Head up into the col, and turn up left onto **Meall Coire na Saobhaidhe**.

Head south along the rocky crest (or avoid the rocks by keeping just down left), then drop into the col beyond. Now ascend quite steeply, keeping right of a fearsome little rockface of overlapping slabs, to reach the rock tor at the tip of Lochnagar's broad, gentle northwest ridge. Follow this ridge up southeast to the summit.

DESCENT

Because of the slabby crag, it's essential to follow the ridge northwest from the summit all the way down to the slight rise and rock tor (NO240863) at its tip. Then descend quite steeply north to find **Meall Coire na Saobhaidhe**.

98 Tourist path
from Spittal of Glenmuick

Start	Spittal of Glenmuick NO310851
Distance	8km/5 miles
Ascent	800m/1400ft
Approx time up	4hr
Terrain	Tracks and wide engineered paths

The standard route: big path, even bigger scenery.

Starting from the car park, the track runs gently downhill past a toilet block. Just past the small information office, turn right on the broad path signed 'Lochnagar path' to cross the valley floor. Just before **Allt-na-giubhsaich**

The Corrie of Lochnagar, from the Meikle Pap col

house, a path forks off slightly left to a small lodge building. Cross a track and take the path to the left of the building, again signed 'Lochnagar path'.

The path runs up to left of the Allt-na-giubhhsaich stream, joining a narrow track that arrives from the left. This track leads up into the broad pass behind Conachcraig. Some 50m before the high point of the track, fork off left onto the large well-built path ◀ climbing west towards the col between Meikle Pap and the main mountain. On the way up, a memorial stone on the left marks Fox Cairn Well, a good water supply. Another 10min sees you in the **Meikle Pap** col. You can make a quick up-and-down to Meikle Pap on the right for an even finer view and lunch spot.

Routes 99
(Conachcraig) and
96 (from Balmoral)
join here.

If you didn't visit Meikle Pap, then do take a few steps northwest through the Meikle Pap col for the view down to Lochnagar (the loch). ◀ Then turn up left, south, on a steep path, to arrive at the corrie rim. Follow this round to the right, with frequent glances into the fearful abyss alongside. The crag rim runs level at first and then climbs to reach the preliminary rockpile and cairn at **Cac Carn Mor**.

Route 100 continues
down ahead towards
the loch.

Head north for 400m, keeping to the right of the path for more corrie views, to reach the slightly higher rockpile of **Cac Carn Beag**, which forms the summit of Lochnagar.

99 Conachcraig

Difficulty
■ ■ ■ ■

Start	Spittal of Glenmuick NO310851
Distance	9.5km/6 miles
Ascent	1000m/3300ft
Approx time up	5hr
Terrain	Pathless hillside, only moderately rough, and summit of boulders, tors and heather

This route avoids the tourist path and bags a Corbett.

Start as Route 98, down the track to the information office and turning right on the 'Lochnagar Path' track across the valley floor. Approaching Allt-na-giubhhsaich keep on the main track, ignoring the Lochnagar path forking off slightly left. At **Allt-na-giubhsiach** turn right on a cross-track across a bridge. After 400m the track bends right; here keep ahead through open pines to slant up to a fallen wall. Head up **Carn an Daimh** by wherever the heather's been recently burnt.

There's a path across Carn an Daimh (Diyve: stony hill of the deer – and deer may well be seen on it), but it disappears for the next steep rise. Above that is easier going on short heather up to the rock tor Point 850m. This tor is not the final summit of Conachcraig, but it has fine Lochnagar views. Cross short heather on a small path along a wide ridge, with boulderpiles and more small tors, to **Conachcraig**'s summit rockpile.

A clear path runs down southwest to the col at head of Coire na Ciche (Kichah: Corrie of the Breast, that is to say of Meikle Pap). Keep straight across the track at the col, to join the Tourist Path at its bend just beyond, and continue on Route 98.

100 Loch na Gaire

Start	Spittal of Glenmuick NO310851
Distance	7km/4 miles
Ascent	950m/3100ft
Approx time up	4.25hr
Terrain	Small path, rough heather, bouldery ridge

Byron referred to the glories of dark Lochnagar, compared to which any-thing in England is tame and domestic. This route is what he was on about.

Start as Route 98 Tourist Path, and follow it (or Route 99 Conachcraig) to the Meikle Pap col.

Through the col, a small path slants down left into the Corrie of Lochnagar. It almost reaches the southeast corner of **Lochnagar** (the loch), but rock slabs block the way ahead, and anyway the people using the path are aiming for the crags above. So the path climbs to the stretcher box (NO251857). ◀ From the stretcher box slant down directly towards the southwest corner of the loch, passing through a cragband at a small mossy water-fall on the way down to the loch side. A small path runs alongside the loch to its foot.

Head up left, on heather, peat and boulders, to the northeast ridge. Going is easier once on the ridge as the boulders now have grass between them. Keep to the left for views into the corrie. Follow the main ridgeline to its top, then turn right, across the plateau, to nearby **Cac Carn Beag** with its trig point and viewpoint cairn.

*Directly ahead and above, at the corrie's back right corner, wide **Black Spout Gully** is a Grade 1 winter climb and will be my next walk up Lochnagar.*

101 Falls of Glas Allt (descent)

Finish	Spittal of Glenmuick NO310851
Distance	10km/6 miles
Descent	750m/2500ft
Approx time down	2.5hr (4hr in ascent)
Terrain	Good path and track

From the summit **start** south for 700m on the wide path to Cac Carn Mor. Follow the main path southeast down

The waterfalls and the zigzag path high above Loch Muick give this route an almost alpine feel. Its shelter and good path make this an apt route for descent, as do the views downwards to the loch.

the following slope for 800m. Look out for the point where the main path bends left, east; for here you must take the smaller path continuing ahead, and it can be missed due to the convexity of the slope.

Follow the path down into the wide shallow valley of the **Glas Allt**. The path stays to the left of the stream, keeping well above it as it descends in waterslides, then slants down to join it. A footbridge is signed 'Loch Muick'. Beyond, the path zigzags down into a steep valley, rejoining the stream at the foot of its waterfall, then slanting out across the right-hand (southern) valley wall to descend to the top of woods at **Glas-allt Shiel**.

Turn left, across a footbridge, to slant down through the pinewoods to join a wider path at the loch side. Follow the track left for 4km to Allt-na-giubhsaich, and turn right, across the valley floor, to Spittal of Glenmuick.

Best descent: by the Glas Allt to Loch Muick

102 From Loch Callater

Start/finish	Auchallater NO157882
Distance	14km/9 miles
Ascent	1000m/3300ft
Approx time up	6hr
Terrain	Track and path
Bike approach	To Lochcallater Lodge (saves 45min each way)
Map	Harveys covers this, but you'll need to supplement OS Landranger 44 with 43 Braemar, or OS Explorer 388 with the map for Route 87

This long-range route makes the most of the easy plateau rim. It's popular with east-bound backpackers, especially because of the bothies at either end. The less-laden walker can make a long day of it, from Braemar to Balmoral, with a return by bus. If starting from Braemar, use the minor road west of Clunie Water and a footbridge at NO154882 (1hr).

Start along the stony track up Glen Callater, a place of many boulders. At a gate just before **Lochcallater Lodge** and bothy, a rough path climbs steeply to the left, then slants up the flank of **Creag an Loch** above Loch Callater. It turns northeast and climbs towards a col (NO195845).

This point, at the Landranger map junction, is potentially confusing. Do not take the small path ahead through this col, as it will lead you through – after some serious bog-tramping – to Balmoral. Watch out for a small pool on the right as the path levels and starts to descend. This pool indicates that you're on the wrong path!

The correct path turns right before the little pool and climbs, northeast, over slabby ground beside the metal posts of a former fence. At a remaining gate in the absent fence the path heads off right, slanting up around the side of Carn an t-Sagairt Mor; most walkers prefer to head straight uphill, alongside the occasional fence posts, to the cairn at the north summit of Carn an t-Sagairt Mor.

Aeroplane wing on Carn an t-Sagairt Mor, with Lochnagar's summit tor still a long walk away

Turn right, southeast, for 150m to the true summit of **Carn an t-Sagairt Mor** (the true summit cairn does not have old fence posts in it).

In clear weather simply slant down northeast, passing some fuselage of a fallen aeroplane; in mist, it's easier to return to the north cairn and turn down to the right following the fence posts and passing a wing of the same plane. Either way, cross a wide col and climb gently to cross boulderfield to the tiny summit tor of **Carn an t-Sagairt Beag**. Here you join with Route 94.

THE LONG ROUTES

Two walks in the Cairngorms are celebrated as particularly demanding, and particularly rewarding.

The Cairngorms 4000s

With four of the UK's five highest hills so conveniently grouped, the circuit of the 4000ft Cairngorms has been an attractive challenge for a century at least. The first recorded circuit of Cairn Gorm, Macdui, Cairn Toul and Braeriach was in 1912, by Mr John Clarke (president of the Cairngorm Club) and Mr Ian Clarke. After cycling from Boat of Garten to Loch Morlich for warm-up, they took 10hr and 45min. However, a previous party in 1909 had crossed the same summits, preceded by Ben Avon and Beinn a' Bhuird, in a 19hr cross-country trip from Loch Builg to Gleann Einich.

Since then the circuit has been completed in winter, with and without skis, and been extended by hillrunner Mark Rigby into a full crossing of every Cairngorm Munro within 24 hours. The record for the circuit of the four summits was set by famous runner Eric Beard in the 1960s, and shortened by Dan Whitehead to 4hr 31min in 2001. He took just 62min between the summits of Cairn Toul and Macdui, disappointed by the lack of snow: on an earlier recce he'd bounded down snowfields from plateau to the Lairig Ghru in just 6min. The route used by runners excludes Angel's Peak, which wasn't a Munro in Beard's day. On the other hand it starts and ends down at Glenmore Lodge.

These short times don't make the 4000s into a short walk. It is a convenient mid-distance between easy and impossible; within the physical capacity of most strong hillwalkers, but above the 1200m contour for many miles, and seriously remote in its central section. Given good legs, and good weather, it's a magnificent outing: one of the finest on UK hills.

The convenient start-point is the Sugar Bowl car park: starting in Glenmore village adds 6km and 100m of ascent, and takes at least an hour longer. (That said, it does eliminate the Chalamain Gap at the end of the day, substituting a forest finish.) The walk up alongside the funicular should be before it starts running, and Cairn Gorm at dawn will be the first reward for the special endeavour.

After the easy stroll to Macdui, the descent to the Lairig Ghru is the first real challenge. You should certainly be fit and fresh enough to get down the boulders without any real strain. The route to south of the Tailor Burn (Route 35) is the least uncomfortable. In the Lairig Ghru you look at the schedule and determine whether there's enough time for the eastern half, as out through the Ghru is the last convenient escape.

The East Ridge of Cairn Toul (Route 61) looks like a short cut. In fact its rough grass and boulders will only save time – as against the good path in Coire Odhar – in the early season when vegetation is low. The River Dee will have to be reasonably low as well. However, the North Ridge probably won't actually lose much time either, and the odd scrambly bit does divert the mind from the grim necessity of the 600m of ascent.

After Angel's Peak, be aware of the possible escape by Route 63. There is a later and less comfortable escape by the east spur of Carn na Criche, the one that divides the two lobes of the Garbh Choire. But if you've time in hand, simply enjoy the wonderful circuit around the corrie and the gentle, but rather long descent over Sron na Lairige.

By a trick of perspective, the path out of the Lairig Ghru appears more uphill than it is. It's mostly almost level. However, nothing can remedy the Chalamain Gap.

By the reckonings used in this book, the walk would take 15hr (excluding rests). However, anyone undertaking it will be somewhat fitter than the 'moderately paced walker' assumed elsewhere. The schedule below also builds in some slowing down as the day goes on. It is not intended as a target, but as an aid to starting slow enough, and to working out how late you're going to be at the Chalamain Gap.

Finishing the 4000s: descending over Sron na Lairige on a summer evening

CAIRNGORMS 4000s						
	km	ml	m	ft	hr/min	cum hr/min
Start Sugar Bowl [P]						0:00
Cairn Gorm	4.5	2.8	780	2600	2:15	2:15
Ben Macdui	6.4	4.0	340	1100	1:50	4:05
Lairig Ghru (Corrour Bridge)	4.5	2.8	—	—	1:30	5:35
Cairn Toul	6.9	4.3	660	2200	3:00	8:35
Braeriach	5.4	3.4	350	1200	1:50	10:25
Sugar Bowl [P]	9.8	6.1	100	300	2:35	13:00
Totals	37.5	23.5	2200	7400	—	13hr

(km/ml:distance covered over each section; m/ft = height gain for each section; hr/min = time for each section; cum hr/min = total time from start)

The Lairig Ghru

'Lairig' is a long pass of the through-route sort; 'Ghru' is obscure. The walk through the high pass of the Lairig Ghru has been a serious long-distance challenge for much longer than a mere century. It's one of the old drove roads of Scotland, used every autumn for driving black cattle to the markets of Crieff and Falkirk. In the 1820s the athletic Lord Kennedy, for a wager of £2500, walked from Banchory to Inverness in 35hr, through two nights. His route through the Grampians was almost certainly the Lairig Ghru; it proved 4hr quicker than the road.

The farmwives of Rothiemurchus used to walk to market through the pass carrying baskets of eggs on their heads. Three tailors wagered to dance a reel on New Year's Night at the Dells of Abernethy and Rothiemurchus and at Dalmore near Braemar. They danced the first two: the Clach nan Taillear marks the spot where they perished in the pass on their way to the third.

It's the grandest of through routes, a low-level line that at the Pools of Dee rises to over 800m. The central section is remote and often windswept. The traditional full route, from Braemar to Aviemore, was covered in the annual hill race in 3hr 11min by D. Brown in 1984. If that's too quick, you could aim for the ladies' time of 3hr 45min set by Helen Diamantides in 1992 ...

While the walk through the pass is long and tiring, it's not as tiring as it used to be before Mar Lodge Estate smoothed out most of the rugged and stony path. Today, the problem even more serious than making it through the pass could be the getting back again afterwards. A return by public transport involves a bus or hitch to Aviemore, two trains, and the single daily bus between Braemar and Aberdeen. Even an ever-loving spouse in a car will have a 2hr drive round by Corgarff and Tomintoul. The radical step of turning round after a night at Glenmore village and coming south through the Lairig an Lui is

Heading north through the Lairig Ghru, below Coire Bhrochain

more sensible than it sounds; for you can then shorten both walks by a bike left at Derry Lodge.

The traditional full route still has a lot to be said for it. The gentle descent under the pines past Loch an Eilein is an excellent end to the day. Deeside at dawn is almost as good. And it's easier to get yourself dropped off at Braemar youth hostel the night before, than at Linn of Dee at five in the morning.

If you really want to avoid road, you can use Route 86 in reverse to set off through the Morrone Birkwood. But in the dark you'll appreciate the easy 5km along the empty road to Victoria Bridge. Because of its better path, the route into the Lairig by Derry Lodge is 30min quicker than by White Bridge and Glen Dee; and you can shave off a few more minutes, as well as eliminating tarmac, by crossing Victoria Bridge to Claybokie and the Doire Bhragad (Route 76 in reverse).

Corrour bothy is often used as a halfway stop; on Saturday nights it may well be uncomfortably crowded. The clear path through the pass means that only a combination of mist and fresh snow will make navigation any problem. It's 40 years ago that a Lairig Ghru walker accidentally turned left into the Garbh Choire and spent several days wandering on the Great Moss.

At the top of the pass, the Sinclair Memorial Hut, marked on old maps, was removed in the 1990s. That's where you bear right through the Chalamain Gap for the high car park under the ski slopes; for Glenmore village, it's more comfortable to take the path 2km further down by Rothiemurchus Lodge. Aviemore walkers head down to Piccadilly (NH937075). Here the path ahead is small and little used, but the path to the left, for the Cairngorm Club footbridge, is wide and smooth and can be walked by moonlight or torch.

The next path north is also quite small and rough, but from Lochan Deo (NH917079) there's a smooth track to Coylumbridge. The extra kilometre to pass lovely Loch an Eilein may be a step too far for sore feet, though. As on Route 10, after Inverdruie bear right to the older bridge to save a few of the final footsteps.

The schedule below is calculated on the same basis as those in the rest of the book; even the moderate walker will only take 12hr!

	km	ml	m	ft	hr/min	cum hr/min
Start Braemar (Clunie Br)						0:00
Victoria Bridge	5.7	3.6	80	250	1:40	1:40
Derry Lodge	7.8	4.9	100	350	2:15	3:55
Corrour (opposite)	7	4.4	200	600	2:15	6:10
Pools of Dee	5.4	3.4	250	900	2:00	8:10
Piccadilly	7.7	4.8	20	70	2:00	10:10
Aviemore (station)	7.8	4.9	—	—	2:00	12:10
Totals	42	26	660	2200	12hr	10min

(km/ml:distance covered over each section; m/ft = height gain for each section; hr/min = time for each section; cum hr/min = total time from start)

Alternative starts, to Derry Lodge					
From Linn of Dee	4.8	3	60	200	1:10
Or from Inverey YH	6.9	4.3	70	200	2:00

Alternative ends, from Pools of Dee					
To Sugar Bowl [P]	8.1	5	120	400	2:20
Or to Glenmore YH	12.7	7.9	60	200	3:20

Thus the shortest version, Linn of Dee to Sugar Bowl, comes out at 25km and 8hr! The return to Inverey by bus, two trains, another bus and postbus, takes just under 20hr!

APPENDIX I

ROUTE SUMMARY

Part 1 Aviemore and the Spey

1 Grantown and Spey
12km/7 miles; 70m/200ft ascent; max altitude 210m; low

2 Spey at Boat of Garten
10km/6 miles; 100m/300ft ascent; max altitude 265m; 2.5hr; low

3 Craigellachie Birches
5km/3 miles; 280m/900ft ascent; max altitude 490m; 2hr; low

4 Geal-charn Mor
18km/11.5 miles; 700m/2400ft ascent; max altitude 824m; 6.25hr; Corbett

5 Around Loch an Eilein
5km/3 miles; no ascent; max altitude 270m; 1.15hr; low

6 Ord Ban
7km/4 miles; 180m/600ft ascent; max altitude 428m; 2hr; low

7 Argyll Stone
15.5km/9.5 miles; 600m/2000ft ascent; max altitude 848m; 5.5hr; medium

Part 2 Glen More

8 Gleann Einich and the Sgorans
27km/17 miles; 1000m/3400ft ascent; max altitude 1118m; 9.25hr; Munros

9 Creag a' Chalamain and the Cat Notch
16km/10 miles; 550m/1800ft ascent; max altitude 787m; 5.25hr; medium

10 Down Cairn Gorm
20km/112.5 miles; no ascent; max altitude 620m; 5hr; low

11 Lochan Uaine
8km/5 miles; 130m/450ft ascent; max altitude 420m; 2hr; low

12 Meall a' Bhuachaille
19km/12 miles; 750m/2500ft ascent; max altitude 810m; 6.5hr; Corbett

13 Creag Mhor and Bynack More
31km/19 miles; 1200m/4000ft ascent; max altitude 1090m; 11hr; Munro + Corbett

14 Beinn Mheadhoin
36km/22.5 miles; 1000m/3400ft ascent; max altitude 1182m; 11.5hr; Munro

Summit Summary: Cairn Gorm

15 Bynack More and the Saddle
16.5km/10 miles; 1300m/4300ft ascent; 7.25hr

16 Strath Nethy and the Saddle
14.5km/9 miles; 900m/3000ft ascent; 6hr

17 Lairig an Lui, Loch Avon, Coire Raibert
20.5km/13 miles; 1100m/3600ft ascent; 7.75hr

18 Lochan na Beinne and Cnap Coire na Spreidhe
7.5km/4.75 miles; 800m/2600ft ascent; 3.75hr

19 Coire Cas (descent)
3km/2 miles; 600m/2000ft descent; 1.25hr

20 Coire an t-Sneachda: Headwall
5.5km/3.5 miles; 700m/2300ft ascent; 3hr; scramble Grade 1

21 Coire an t-Sneachda: Pygmy Ridge
5km/3 miles; 4hr; scramble Grade 3

22 Coire an t-Sneachda: Goat Path
5.5km/3.5 miles; 700m/2300ft ascent; 3hr

23 Fiacaill Ridge of Coire an t-Sneachda
6.5km/4 miles; 800m/2600ft ascent; 4hr; scramble Grade 1

24 Lurcher's Crag
9.5km/6 miles; 900m/2900ft ascent; 4hr

25 Plateau route from Macdui
6.5km/4 miles; 200m/700ft ascent; 2hr (+ getting up Macdui)

Shelter Stone Summary

26 Strath Nethy and the Saddle
15.5km/9.5 miles; 500m/1700ft ascent; 5hr

27 Lairig an Lui, Loch Avon
19km/12 miles; 600m/2000ft ascent; 6.25hr

28 To Coire Cas or Cairn Gorm by Coire Raibert
5.5km/3.5 miles (to Coire Cas); 400m/1500ft ascent, 500m/1700ft descent; 2.5hr

29 From Coire Cas by Coire Domhain
5.5km/3.5 miles; 500m/1700ft ascent; 2.75hr

30 From Linn of Dee by Loch Etchachan
15.5km/9.5 miles; 550m/1900ft ascent; 5hr

31 To Ben Macdui by Loch Etchachan
5km/3 miles; 550m/1900ft ascent; 2.75hr

32 To Carn Etchachan by Pinnacle Gully
1km/0.75 miles; 400m/1200ft ascent; 1.5hr; scramble Grade 1

33 Forefinger Pinnacle
20m/65.5ft; scramble Grade 3

34 To Ben Macdui by Avon Slabs
3km/1.5 miles; 600m/2000ft ascent; scramble Grade 1 or 2

Summary: Ben Macdui

35 From Lairig Ghru by Tailor Burn
16km/10 miles; 1000m/3300ft ascent; 6.5hr
36 From Derry Lodge by Carn a' Mhaim
15km/9.25 miles; 1200m/4000ft ascent; 6.5hr
37 Sron Riach
13.5km/8.5 miles; 900m/3000ft ascent; 5.75hr
38 Via Derry Cairngorm
15km/9.25 miles; 1100m/3700ft ascent; 6.5hr
39 Coire Etchachan
16km/10 miles; 900m/3000ft ascent; 6.5hr
40 From Coire Cas
8km/5 miles; 700m/2300ft ascent; 3.5hr
41 Plateau route from Cairn Gorm
6.5km/4 miles; 250m/750ft ascent; 2.25hr (+ getting up Cairn Gorm)

Part 3 Badenoch

42 Badenoch Way
18.5km/11.5 miles; 230m/750ft ascent; max altitude 330m; 5hr; low, linear
43 Insh to Aviemore
28km/17.5 miles; 270m/900ft ascent; max altitude 330m; 7.5hr; low, linear
44 Druid Circle at Dalraddy
10.5km/6.5 miles; 40m/120ft ascent; max altitude 250m; 2.5hr; low
45 Take an Insh
11.5km/7 miles; 170m/600ft ascent; max altitude 340m; 3hr; low
46 Carn Dearg Mor
20km/12.5 miles; 600m/2000ft ascent; max altitude 857m; 6.5hr; Corbett
47 Mullach Clach a' Bhlair by Coire Garbhlach
19.5km/12 miles; 750m/2600ft ascent; max altitude 1019m; 6.75hr; Munro
48 Badan Mosach waterfall
4km/2.5 miles; 80m/250ft ascent; max altitude 400m; 1.5hr; low
49 Summer Road to Ruthven
9km/5.5 miles; 200m/600ft ascent; max altitude 400m; 3hr; low
50 Glen Tromie: Croidh-la
16.5km/10 miles; 550m/1800ft ascent; max altitude 640m; 5.5hr; medium
51 Creag Bheag
7km/4.5 miles; 260m/900ft ascent; max altitude 486m; 2.5hr; medium

Summary: Braeriach

52 From Glenmore by Chalamain Gap and Sron na Lairige
12km/7.5hr; 1100m/3700ft ascent; 5.75hr

53 From Rothiemurchus by Sron na Lairige
12km/7.5 miles; 1000m/3400ft ascent; 5.5hr
54 Gleann Einich and Coire Ruadh
12km/7.5 miles; 1000m/3400ft ascent; 5.5hr
55 Gleann Einich and Coire Dhondail
16km/10 miles; 1000m/3400ft ascent; 6.5hr
56 Coire Dhondail scramble
100m/328ft; scramble Grade 1
57 South Ridge of Coire Bhrochain
12.5km/8 miles; 950m/3200ft ascent; 6hr
58 Ridge route from Cairn Toul
5.5km/3.5 miles (+getting up Cairn Toul); 350m/1200ft ascent; 2hr

Summary: Cairn Toul

59 Coire Odhar
3.5km/2 miles; 750m/2500ft ascent; 2.5hr
60 Great Moss
13km/8 miles; 1150m/3800ft ascent; 6hr
61 East Ridge
2km/1.5 miles; 750m/2500ft ascent; 2.5hr; scramble Grade 1
62 North East Ridge of Angel's Peak
2.5km/1.5 miles; 500m/1800ft ascent; 3hr; scramble Grade 1
63 Corrie of the Chokestone Gully
4km/2.5 miles; 500m/1800ft ascent; 3hr
64 Ridge route from Braeriach
5.5km/3.5 miles (+ ascent of Braeriach); 350m/1200ft ascent; 2.25hr

Part 4 Glenlivet and Tomintoul

65 Hills of Cromdale
19km/12 miles; 900m/3000ft ascent; max altitude 722m; 7hr; medium
66 Carn Daimh
10.5km/6.5 miles; 350m/1200ft ascent; max altitude 570m; 3.5hr; medium
67 Around the Brown
13km/8 miles; 300m/1000ft ascent; max altitude 400m; 4hr; low
68 Glen Brown and Ailnack Ravine
19.5km/12.25 miles; 450m/1500ft ascent; max altitude 530m; 6hr; low
69 Ben Avon by its River
40km/24 miles; 1000m/3300ft; max altitude 1171m; 12.5hr; Munro
70 Tors of Ben Avon
80m+/260ft+; scramble Grade 1–2
71 Cnap Chaochan Aitinn
29km/19miles; 500m/1700ft ascent; max altitude 714m; 8.5hr; medium
72 Ailnack Upper Ravine
21.5km/13.5 miles; 400m/1300ft ascent; max altitude 650m; 7hr; scramble Grade 1

Part 5 Donside
73 Carn Ealasaid
16.5km/10.25 miles; 550m/1900ft ascent; max altitude 792m; 6hr; Corbett
74 Brown Cow Hill
19km/11.5 miles; 500m/1700ft ascent; max altitude 829m; 6.25hr; Corbett
75 Don to Ben Avon
32.5km/20 miles; 750m/2500ft ascent; max altitude 1171m; 10hr; Munro

Part 6 Deeside Braemar
76 Clais Fhearnaig
16m/10 miles; 250m/800ft ascent; max altitude 520m; 4.5hr; low
77 Derry Cairngorm by Lochan Uaine
23km/14.5 miles; 900m/2900ft ascent; max altitude 1156m; 8hr; Munro
78 The Happy Face of Beinn a' Chaorainn
29.5km/18.5 miles; 1000m/3300ft ascent; max altitude 1082m; 9.75hr; Munros
79 Dee and Derry
25km/15.5 miles; 250m/800ft ascent; max altitude 610m; 6.5hr; medium
80 Around Glen Geusachan
19km/12 miles; 1400m/4700ft ascent; max altitude 1293m; 8.75hr; Munros
81 The Devil's Back Side
6km/4 miles; 500m/1600ft ascent; max altitude 1003m; 3.25hr; Munro
82 Glen Quoich
13.5km/8.5 miles; 200m/700ft ascent; max altitude 500m; 4hr; low
83 Beinn a' Bhuird
28.5km/18 miles; 950m/3200ft ascent; max altitude 1197m; 9.5hr; Munro
84 Carn na Drochaide and the Fairy Glen
15km/9.25 miles; 500m/1700ft ascent; max altitude 818m; 5hr; Corbett
85 Morrone Birkwood and the Dee
9km/5.5 miles; 150m/500ft ascent; max altitude 450m; 2.75hr; low
86 Morrone and Glen Ey
20km/12.5 miles; 700m/1700ft ascent; max altitude 859m; 6.75hr; Corbett
87 Creag nan Gabhar
13km/8 miles; 470m/1600ft ascent; max altitude 8334m; 4.5hr; Corbett
88 White Mounth and Jock's Road
27.5km/17.25 miles; 1100m/3600ft ascent; max altitude 1064km; 9.5hr; Munros

Part 7 Balmoral and Lochnagar
89 Balmoral Castle
8km/5 miles; 240m/800ft ascent; max altitude 442m; 2.5hr; low
90 Craigendarroch and the Dee
7km/4.5 miles; 260m/700ft ascent; max altitude 402m; 2.5hr; low
91 Around Loch Muick
12km/7.5 miles; 90m/300ft ascent; max altitude 430m; 3hr; low
92 Dubh Loch and Broad Cairn
27km/17 miles; 850m/2800ft ascent; max altitude 1047m; 9hr; Munros
93 Creag an Dubh-loch
21km/13 miles; 800m/2700ft ascent; max altitude 1012m; 7.5hr; Munros

Summit Summary: Lochnagar
94 Queen Victoria's Ballochbuie Route
12km/7.5 miles; 950m/3100ft ascent; 5hr
95 Byron's scramble by the Stuic
11km/7 miles; 900m/3000ft ascent; 5.5hr; scramble Grade 1
96 Tracks from Balmoral
14.5km/9 miles; 900m/3000ft ascent; 5hr
97 Meall Coire na Saobhaidhe
11km/7 miles; 950m/3100ft ascent; 5hr
98 Tourist path from Spittal of Glenmuick
8km/5 miles; 800m/1400ft ascent; 4hr
99 Conachcraig
9.5km/6 miles; 1000m/3300ft ascent; 5hr
100 Loch na Gaire
7km/4 miles; 950m/3100ft ascent; 4.25hr
101 Falls of Glas Allt (descent)
10km/6 miles; 750m/2500ft descent; 2.5hr (4hr in ascent)
102 From Loch Callater
14km/9 miles; 1000m/3300ft ascent; 6hr

The Long Routes
The Cairngorms 4000s
37.5km/23.5 miles; 2200m/7400ft ascent; 13hr
The Lairig Ghru
42km/26 miles; 660m/2200ft ascent; 12hr

APPENDIX II

ACCESS
(in particular during the deer-stalking season)

The Access Law passed by the Scottish Parliament in 2003 (which came into force 2005) gives access on foot to virtually all land apart from growing crops and private gardens. However, access must be taken 'responsibly'. What counts as responsible access is detailed in the Access Code (**www.outdooraccess-scotland.com**); it involves obvious measures like not leaving litter or interfering with livestock, and may be summarised as:

causing no damage to the countryside

not interfering with land managers in their daily work

taking responsibility for your own safety.

Tent near the Shelter Stone. Unobtrusive and traceless wild camping is now a legal right in Scotland

The access rights explicitly include wild camping (though that doesn't mean roadside camping), access at night, and rock-climbing. They also include cycling, but as responsible cycling is defined as not damaging paths, the cyclist is still in effect restricted to estate tracks.

'Responsible Access' also includes taking steps not to interfere with stag stalking, which takes place between mid-August and 20 October. While this provides sporting excitement for a certain sort of person, it is also a necessary and humane way of checking deer numbers, and provides local employment.

During stag stalking, some of the estates (such as NTS and the Forestry Commission) do not seek to restrict access at all. Others subscribe to the hillphone system with daily advice

Red deer on Carn an Daimh (Route 99)

of the particular glen or corrie where stalking is taking place. Estate boundaries are marked on the overview maps at the beginning of the book and at the start of Part 7.

On the whole, forest paths and standard Munro routes will remain walkable. There is no stalking on Sundays.

Roe-deer culling happens in woodlands, dawn and evening, in May, June and July. Daytime walkers on recognised paths shouldn't have any impact on it.

Hillphones: **www.snh.org.uk/hillphones**, **www.walkingwild.com/stalking**

Rothiemurchus
Stag stalking: September and October Walkers asked to keep to forest paths, Lairig Ghru, and the two routes to Braeriach via Gleann Einich/Coire Dhondail and via Chalamain Gap/Sron na Lairige.
Rangers at Rothiemurchus Visitor Centre, Inverdruie tel: 01479 812345; map on **www.rothiemurchus.net**

Cairngorm (CG on map pp10–11) (Highland & Island Enterprise)
No restrictions. Cairngorm rangers tel: 01479 861703 **www.cairngorm-mountain.com**

Forestry Commission: Glenmore and Inshriach (FC on map pp10–11)
No restrictions. In the forest April to end August please keep to paths, and keep dogs on leads, for capercaille recovery. Glenmore Visitor Centre tel: 01479 861220.

RSPB (Abernethy Reserve)
No restrictions.

SNH (Inshriach)
No restrictions. Walkers are asked not to light open fires in this combustible and precious habitat. The bothy does not have a fireplace.

Glenlivet Estate (Crown Estates)
Roe-deer culling in summer, see above. Limited red-deer stalking on the Ladder Hills in October and November. Grouse shooting on Hills of Cromdale, Ladder Hills 12 August to mid October, not Sundays. Estate ranger tel: 01807 580283; walking map available on **www.crownestate.co.uk/glenlivet**

Glenavon Estate (Cairngorm Strathspey Deer Management Group)
Head keeper Mr Gibson tel: 01807 580256

**Mar Lodge Estate
(National Trust for Scotland)**
This large estate, embracing most of the southern Cairngorms, does not seek to restrict walkers during the stag cull. However, if you plan to venture off the main ridge routes into remoter corries (such as the Dubh-Ghleann) on an autumn weekday, then you could help the rangers by phoning them first on Braemar (013397) 41669.

Invercauld
Stag stalking: 29 September–20 October
Hillphone Braemar (013397) 41911

Callater & Clunie
Stag stalking: 2 September–20 October
Hillphone Braemar (013397) 41997

Balmoral/Lochnagar
Stag stalking: 9 August–20 October
Hillphone Ballater (013397) 55532
Routes around Balmoral Castle closed from end July (royalty in residence).

APPENDIX III

MOUNTAIN BOTHIES

The bothies in the Cairngorms are maintained by the Mountain Bothies Association and other voluntary bodies 'for the benefit of all who love the wild and lonely places'. The word 'bothy' comes from the Gaelic 'bothan', a hut: 'bothan airigh' is the shieling shack whose remains are in Glen Quoich and elsewhere.

Faindouran bothy in Glen Avon

They are free, unlocked and unwardened. However, it is unwise to rely on them as your sole source of shelter as they may be full up (particularly Corrour), burnt down (as Bob Scott's at Derry Lodge was in December 2003) or demolished (as the Sinclair Hut was in 1991, and as Corrour may be). Corndavon Lodge south of Brown Cow Hill is no longer available as a bothy.

The MBA make various requests of users, summarised below (with the full version on **www.mountainbothies.org.uk**).

Fires should be small, and always watched over. Burning plastic waste can create toxic fumes.

Please leave the bothy clean, tidy, with dry kindling and with the door closed against sheep.

Toilet facilities consist of a spade. Please use it.

Don't leave perishable food for later visitors: it will actually feed mice.

There is no rubbish removal service. Leave no rubbish of your own. If there is rubbish in the bothy (as there usually is at Corrour) consider clearing loose litter in and around the bothy, and carrying out a little of the sordid heap. Don't leave empty plastic sacks or bags, as the simple-minded interpret them as being for their rubbish.

APPENDIX IV

GAELIC PLACE NAMES

The last native Gaelic speaker in the Cairngorms lived over 50 years ago. Today, the only Gaelic here is spoken by hill-goers naming their hills.

What ought to happen at this point is that the Gaelic names gradually get absorbed into the English or Scots actually spoken. 'Cairn Toul' and 'Braeriach' are better Gaelic than unsuccessful attempts to pronounce Carn an t-Sabhail or Braigh Riabhach. But because most of us get our hill names off the map, the opposite is actually happening. Creag Bheag retains its Gaelic spelling, but already the dog-walkers of Kingussie refer to it, not as 'Krek Vick' but as 'Craig Beg'. The ranger at Invercauld, on the stag-season phone line, mentions 'Carn Lee-ath'.

Fortunately, much Gaelic is unpronounceable in English as spelt. Nobody can be happy trying to say Beinn Mheadhoin as Ben MahDoin. Gaelic spelling is very different from English but, unlike English, it is straightforward and logical. For instance, a word beginning with C, such as Coire, when it follows a vowel will become Choire: the process is called Lenition. In the same way, Pris (price) becomes Phris (frice). In the same situations, the word Mor (large) changes its sound to Vore: and this is represented, logically but not altogether helpfully, by adding the same letter H.

Thus Mh and Bh are both pronounced as V; Dh and Fh are silent; and Beinn Mheadhoin (Middle Hill) is 'Ben Vane'.

Let's now go one step further. A consonant preceded or followed by a slender vowel (E or I) will have a different sound than when preceded or followed by a broad one (A, O or U). Thus Daimh 'Diyve' (stag) but Dearg 'Jerrack' (red). No consonant may be preceded by a broad and followed by a slender, or vice versa: and so some vowels are there for purely technical reasons.

Even those, slightly oversimplified, rules will let you get more than half your hill names close enough to be understood. Once you get an idea of how the Gaelic words in the text have the (approximate) English pronunciations, then you're most of the way to saying a new hill name straight off the map.

Even so, I hope never to be calling the Mountain Rescue into Coire an t-Sneachda. Will Grampian police know the mysterious changes to S and N after T, and where 'Corrie an Treyach' is at all? Or maybe they do, and won't ever recognise 'Corrie an Shnechter'? Safest just to break a leg on the Devil's Point.

APPENDIX V

LISTS OF HILLS

Of the hills of 3000ft (914.4m) listed by Sir Hugh Munro – and amended most recently in 1997 – there are 18 in Section 8 (the Cairngorms) and 8 in the northern part of Section 7 around Lochnagar. I have marked them as black triangles on route maps and the overview maps; this book has at least one route up each of them. However, I haven't bothered with former Munros Carn Cloich-mhuillin, Meal Dubhag, Carn Ban Mor and Geal Charn, all of which are on the corners of the Great Moss and were de-listed in 1984. The last of the deleted Munros, A'Choinneach, is on Route 15.

Munro also listed high points not important enough to be considered as separate hills, known confusingly as 'Munro Tops'. Few people today attempt to tick these off, and I have not tried to cover them here.

Grade 1 scrambling beside Garbh Uisge (Route 34)

J. Rooke Corbett listed the hills of 2500ft but under 3000ft (762–914m), having 500ft (152m) of clear drop on all sides. There are nine in the Cairngorms and two alongside Lochnagar. Routes in this book go up all except Sgor Mor, Carn Liath, Culardoch and Geal Charn. On the two overview maps I've reserved the white triangle for the Corbetts, just in case you want to track down the boring four.

The ultimate hill list is the Marilyns: all points, however high or low, that have 150m of clear drop round. This excludes both Cairngorm and Derry Cairngorm, with only 140m of drop each, but gathers such small delights as Ord Ban above Loch an Eilein (Route 6). Other small Marilyns included here are Creag Bheag (Route 51), the two Hills of Cromdale (Route 65), Carn Diamh (Route 66), Cnap Caochan Aitinn (Route 71), Creag Bhalg (Route 76) and Craigendarroch (Route 90).

APPENDIX VI

SCRAMBLES SUMMARY AND GRADING

The Cairngorms is the best area of Britain still without any scramblers' guidebook. I'm not intrepid enough to explore the crumbling granite buttresses, waterfalls, gorges and pinnacles. However, I have managed to haul my trembling limbs onto one or two interesting places. For those who seek out such stuff, I summarise the scrambles below. An asterisk (*) implies a quality route.

14 Beinn Mheadhoin NE Ridge – Grade 1, 30m
A bit of slab scrambling can be incorporated into this long walk.

20 Coire an t-Sneachda Headwall – Grade 1, 100m
Easy and scrappy scrambling, but serious situations.

21 *Pygmy Ridge – Grade 3(S), 100m
A lovely buttress and ridge climb, steep and exposed.

23 *Fiacaill Ridge (Fiacaill Coire an t-Sneachda) – Grade 1, 200m
A classic ridge scramble.

32 Pinnacle Gully – Grade 1, 200m
Mostly very scenic walking, with a 5m wall to finish.

33 *Forefinger Pinnacle – Grade 3(S), 20m
An exposed pinnacle, short but extremely intense, worth the long walk.

34 *Avon Slabs – Grade 1 or 2, 500m
A mountaineering scramble, excellent at either grade.

47 Coire Garbhlach – Grade 1, 50m
A short scrambling option at the corrie head.

56 *Coire Dhondail West Ridge – Grade 1, 100m
A short but otherwise enjoyable ridge scramble.

61 Cairn Toul East Ridge – Grade 1, 100m
Easy with one serious moment, a tough haul for a fairly small scramble.

62 *Angel's Peak Northeast Ridge – Grade 1, 100m
Rocky only at the very top, but a magnificent ridge.

70 Ben Avon Tors – Grade 1–3, 80m
Add extra interest to the long Avon walk.

72 *Ailnack Upper Ravine (the Castle) – Grade 1, 1.5km
Water levels must be low.

78 *Happy Face Scramble – Grade 1, 50m
Sweet but short, with a long, long walk in and off the top.

81 Devil's Point Burn – Grade 2, 20m
A nice walk with one nasty scramble on earth to avoid a waterfall.

83 *Beinn a' Bhuird: NE Ridge A'Chioch – Grade 1, 100m
Scrambling options add interest to a fine route.

95 *The Stuic – Grade 1, 150m
A bouldery ridge scramble.

Grade 1 Hands will have to be used, but difficulties can usually be bypassed, and there will not be appreciable exposure (empty air underneath you) unless you really seek it out. In good conditions, confident walkers could tackle Grade 1. Confident scramblers tackle Grade 1 in bad conditions or in descent.

Grade 2 may involve exposed situations, problems in route-finding, and judgement of loose rock. Less experienced scramblers would often carry a rope in the rucksack as a precaution.

Grade 3 Exposed scrambling in situations with route-finding difficulties in committing situations. Less experienced scramblers would usually treat it as a roped climb.

Grade 3(S) As Grade 3, but involving technical difficulties of rock-climbing grade Mod or Diff.

Clean granite grips well even when wet, but all scrambles get more serious in wind, and in winter become proper winter climbs. Unroped scrambling carries more risk than most mountain acts – it is riskier than roped rock-climbing. Part of the satisfaction of scrambling is in the judgement of its (fairly small) risks against its (quite considerable) rewards.

I've compiled a much longer list of potential scrambles, which I can pass to anyone interested.

APPENDIX VII

ACCOMMODATION AND INFORMATION

Tourist Boards
Highlands: www.visithighlands.com tel: 0845 2255121 or 0870 050 4000 (it's impossible to phone individual TI centres in Aviemore, Badenoch)
Aberdeenshire: www.aberdeen-grampian.com or phone TI centres below

Scottish Youth Hostels Association
www.syha.org.uk; Central Bookings tel: 0870 1 55 32 55

Independent Hostels
www.hostel-scotland.co.uk or get the 'Blue Guide' from TI centres

Campsites
www.UKCampsite.co.uk

Travel
Journey planner: www.travelinescotland.com tel: 0870 608 2608
Rail travel: www.firstscotrail.com tel: 08457 48 49 50
Coach travel: www.citylink.co.uk tel: 08705 505050
Buses: www.rapsons.co.uk tel: 01463 710555

Aviemore and the Spey
Public transport frequent trains to Aviemore and coaches from Glasgow, Edinburgh and Inverness. Low-cost airline Easyjet (www.easyjet.com, tel: 08717 500 100) flies daily to Inverness from London Stansted and Luton. Buses every couple of hours to Nethy Bridge, Grantown. Strathspey Steam Railway Aviemore – Nethybridge Easter – October (www.strathspeyrailway.co.uk 01479 810725).
Tourist information Grampian Rd, Aviemore PH22 1PP; 54 High St, Grantown-on-Spey PH26 3EH
Pubs and restaurants A wide selection, with nowhere outstanding; the Cairngorm Hotel has good basic pub food if you don't mind Sky Sports with your meal.
Supplies Supermarket, bank, outdoor shops
SYHA Aviemore 25 Grampian Road, Aviemore PH22 1PR; open all year; tel: 0870 004 1104
Independent hostels Carrbridge, Grantown on Spey, Aviemore, Boat of Garten, Nethybridge
Camping Aviemore, Boat of Garten, Grantown on Spey

Glen More
Public transport Cairngorm link bus, hourly, from Aviemore to Glenmore village and the high car parks. Funicular www.cairngormmountain.com, tel: 01479 861261; you cannot use the Cairngorm Mountain Railway to gain access to the plateau.
Tourist information Aviemore, as above; Glenmore Visitor Centre (Forestry Commission) tel: 01479 861220, www.forestry.gov.uk
Pubs and restaurants Cafes at Glenmore village (home baking) and at the FC information centre (quiche etc). Meals at Glenmore Lodge, served till 9pm, tasty but rather small.
Supplies Village shop, closes 5.30pm

SYHA Cairngorm Lodge (Loch Morlich) Glenmore, Aviemore, PH22 1QY; closed Nov–mid Dec; tel: 0870 004 1137
Camping Glenmore tel: 01479 861 271; Rothiemurchus tel: 01479 812800

Badenoch
Public transport Rail to Kingussie, coach to Kingussie and Newtonmore, see Aviemore above. Frequent bus links to Aviemore.
Tourist information Duke St, Kingussie PH21 1JG; The Wildcat Centre, Main St, Newtonmore PH20 1DD, tel: 01540 673131
Pubs and restaurants Kingussie (Tipsy Laird/Laird's Kitchen has excellent food till 9pm) and Newtonmore.
Supplies Small supermarkets in Kingussie and Newtonmore
Independent hostels Newtonmore (four), Laggan Bridge, Kingussie, Insh (Bothan Airigh, tel: 01540 661051), Glen Feshie (tel: 01540 651323, warm and friendly)
Camping Glentruim; Dalraddy Holiday Park, tel: 01479 810330 (at the end of the Badenoch Way)

Glenlivet Tomintoul
Public transport Infrequent and unhelpful bus service; it takes two separate buses to reach the rail network at Elgin.
Tourist information Tomintoul Visitor Centre, the Square, tel: 01309 673701
Pubs and restaurants Three hotels serve bar meals, my favourite being the Richmond Hotel which serves food till 9pm.
Supplies Ian Birnie Stores, closes 6pm. Also specialist whisky shopping.
SYHA Tomintoul Main Street, Tomintoul, Ballindalloch AB37 9EX; closed Oct–mid March; tel: 0870 004 1137
Camping Informal, free backpackers' site at the Crown Estates visitor centre, Tomintoul.

Donside
Public transport **None**
Tourist information Railway Museum, Station Yard, Alford AB33 8AD, tel: 019755 62052; 23 Union St, Aberdeen AB11 5BP, tel: 01224 288828
Pubs and restaurants Just one, the Allargue Arms at Cock Bridge (inexpensive B&B and a bunkhouse, tel: 019756 51410)
Supplies No shops in the upper valley
Independent hostel Jenny's Bothy Crofthouse Comfortable and friendly, but approach is 1.5km of rough track; open all year; tel: 01975 651449

Deeside Braemar
Public transport Fairly frequent buses to Ballater, with connecting buses to Aberdeen. No buses from the south. Cheap flights to Aberdeen from Dublin (Ryanair) and London Luton (Easyjet) – making Luton the slightly convenient start-point for attempts on the Lairig Ghru by public transport.
Tourist information The Mews, Mar Rd, Braemar, Ballater AB35 5YL, tel: 013397 41600
Pubs and restaurants Fife Arms, Braemar, serves hill-walker portions. There is also a useful take-away, open till 11pm in summer.
Supplies Useful village shop, plus abundant tartan souvenirs
SYHA Inverey By Braemar AB35 5YB; closed Oct–April: a hut in the woods, no hot water or showers; tel: 0870 004 1126
SYHA Braemar Corrie Feragie, 21 Glenshee Road, Braemar AB35 5YQ; closed Nov–mid Dec; tel: 0870 004 1105

Independent hostels Braemar Lodge, tel: 01339 741627; Rucksacks, Braemar, tel: 01339 741517
Camping Invercauld Caravan Club Site, Glenshee Road, Braemar (tel: 01339 741373, closed mid Oct–mid Dec); it's also acceptable to use informal sites alongside the River Clunie south of Braemar, though these lovely pitches are somewhat marred by litter.

Balmoral and Lochnagar
Public transport Buses to Aberdeen and up Deeside to Braemar
Tourist information Bamoral at the Car Park, Crathie, Ballater AB35 5UL, tel: 013397 42414; The Old Royal Station, Station Square, Ballater AB35 5QB, tel: 013397 55306
Pubs and restaurants A wide selection in Ballater, with good food in all price brackets. The Ballater Chip Shop is celebrated. Cafe Balmoral Castle.
Supplies Ballater has late-opening Co-op, grocers and banks; Prince Charles' outdoor shop is more geared to fishing and shooting. Small grocer at Easter Balmoral.
Camping Ballater Caravan & Camping Site, Anderson Road, tel: 01339 755727 on riverside.

APPENDIX VIII

FURTHER READING

The Cairngorms by Ronald Turnbull, p/b Pevensey Press ISBN 1 898630 50 X
(2002)

Natural history, local history, legends and lots of photos – and it's quite cheap
too.

Cairngorms: a Landscape Fashioned by Geology by British Geological Survey, p/b
SNH ISBN 1 85397 086 7 (1994)

Well illustrated and lucidly written.

Climbing Guide – The Cairngorms Vol 1 (including Cairn Gorm, Ben Macdui and
Braeriach) ISBN 0907521452; *The Cairngorms Vol 2* (including Lochnagar,
Creag an Dubh-loch, Glen Clova and Beinn a' Bhuird) ISBN 0907521460;
both by Allen Fyffe, Andrew Nisbet SMT (1995)

The definitive guides for rock- and ice-climbing, but with some routes that are
barely more than scrambling or advanced winter walking.

Winter Climbs – Ben Nevis and Glencoe by Alan Kimber, p/b Cicerone Press,
ISBN 1 85284 348 9 (2003)

The Speyside Way by Sandy Anton, p/b Cicerone Press, ISBN 1 85284 331 4
(2002)

LISTING OF CICERONE GUIDES

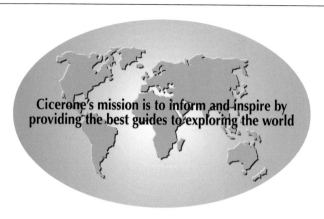

Cicerone's mission is to inform and inspire by providing the best guides to exploring the world

Since its foundation over 30 years ago, Cicerone has specialised in publishing guidebooks and has built a reputation for quality and reliability. It now publishes nearly 300 guides to the major destinations for outdoor enthusiasts, including Europe, UK and the rest of the world.

Written by leading and committed specialists, Cicerone guides are recognised as the most authoritative. They are full of information, maps and illustrations so that the user can plan and complete a successful and safe trip or expedition – be it a long face climb, a walk over Lakeland fells, an alpine traverse, a Himalayan trek or a ramble in the countryside.

With a thorough introduction to assist planning, clear diagrams, maps and colour photographs to illustrate the terrain and route, and accurate and detailed text, Cicerone guides are designed for ease of use and access to the information.

If the facts on the ground change, or there is any aspect of a guide that you think we can improve, we are always delighted to hear from you.

Cicerone Press
2 Police Square Milnthorpe Cumbria LA7 7PY
Tel:01539 562 069   Fax:01539 563 417
e-mail:info@cicerone.co.uk   web:www.cicerone.co.uk